HISTORY
of
RANDOLPH COUNTY
ARKANSAS

**Greenville
South Carolina**

This volume was reproduced from
A personal copy located in the
Publishers private Library

All rights reserved. No part of this publication may be reproduced,
stored in a retrieval system, transmitted in any form, posted
on to the web in any form or by any means without
the prior written permission of the publisher.

Please direct all correspondence and orders to:

www.southernhistoricalpress.com
or
SOUTHERN HISTORICAL PRESS, Inc.
PO BOX 1267
Greenville, SC   29601
southernhistoricalpress@gmail.com

Originally published: 1946
ISBN #978-1-63914-018-3
All rights Reserved.
Printed in the United States of America

DEDICATION

Dedicated to the men and women, hardy pioneers, who blazed a pathway and trail to the West, and settled in what is now Randolph County, Arkansas, more than one hundred years ago. Who cleared her forests, builded their homes, and started a civilization that has grown brighter through the years. It was upon the faith of these people that happy homes were built and our history made possible. It was the hope and wish of the writer to preserve for future generations the glory and history of our yesteryears as an inspiration for the days to come. The work necessary in the preparation of this book has been a labor of love, and I am dedicating it to their memory in the hope that it may inspire us to greater deeds and greater efforts.

Respectfully,

LAWRENCE DALTON
THE AUTHOR

PREFACE

In writing the history of any county, if written by one of its inhabitants, the job sums up to be the recording of the story of his neighbors and their foreparents, in as fair and impartial manner as possible.

With this idea before the reader, the author desires to make the following statements. This book is not a high-powered treatise on the subject of social science, or a deep and weighty text burdened down with the different angles which could be introduced here.

This is simply a story of the author's own county, told in plain everyday language, such as he has been using for a number of years in the writings which we have been doing for the local weekly, and a few special feature articles which we have furnished to a few city dailies.

The source of our information has been legal records of the state of Arkansas and also from Lawrence and Randolph counties, a sprinkling of material has been secured from papers and magazines and state histories.

Besides this, a lot has been secured from the lips of men and women whose parents or grandparents were here "when it happened." We gratefully acknowledge this help. The political data came from state records, but so far as we know this is the first time anyone has ever attempted to write a history of Randolph County.

To the critics who may peruse the pages of this book, we would say: Please remember that in so far as the historical material is concerned, in a general sense, we will defend its authenticity to the end, but if you desire to look at this work from a literary standpoint, please bear in mind that when we were pouring over the musty old records or searching the pages of some long forgotten historical work, we were looking for Randolph County history and not for points on rhetoric and composition.

There are errors, both grammatical and historical, for which we ask the readers kind indulgence. It is impossible to write a book of this kind and not include some misinformation, but we hope and believe the instances are few.

We sincerely thank everyone who has helped us, in any way, in getting this material together.

The author humbly presents this book, not in the hope of any great monetary reward, but with the desire to present and preserve for future generations interesting and valuable historic records of our county and our fine people, while we have the time and opportunity.

THE AUTHOR

THE AUTHOR'S FAMILY
Mr. and Mrs. Lawrence Dalton and Son, Herman

Table of Contents

GENERAL HISTORY—Part One.

	Page
Before History Began	1
First History of the County	5
First Inhabitants—Indians	7
Randolph County in 1800	8
First White Settler	9
First Court	13
Old Military Road	16
Other Early Roads	21
Early Lines of Transportation	23
Early Social and Religious Life	26
Early Watermills	29
Early Churches	33
Early Schools and Educators	43
Drew—Our Only Governor	47
Pocahontas' Three Courthouses	54
Randolph County Prior to Civil War	61
The Civil War	66
Streams of the County	72
Railroads of the County	77
Catholic Church in the County	81
Randolph County Newspapers	87
Randolph County's Part in War	90

MISCELLANEOUS—Part Two

List of All County Officials	97
Courthouse Gang in 1946	98
Odds and Ends of County History	102
Interesting Items	110
Where Our People Came From	113
Who Lives in Randolph County	114
Carry Me Back to Old Virginia	118
Oldtime Religion	120
Oldtime Country Store	126
Oldtime Singing	130
Ku Klux Klan	131
Slavery	133
Some of the County's Noted Men	136
Randolph County Politics	155
Historic Sites	158

COMMUNITIES—Part Three

Attica	161
Albertha	163
Biggers	164
Black River Bottoms	168
Dalton	172
Davidsonville	173
Fourche de Thomas	179
Glaze Creek Church	184
Gravesville	185
Hamil	187
Johnstontown	188
High Point School	190
Middlebrook	190
Maynard	194
Maynard's Schools	198
Noland	200
Water Valley	202
Oconee	203
Pitman	205
Palestine-Ingram	212
Pocahontas	215
Ravenden Springs	231
Reyno	235
Supply	238
Siloam Church	241
Union Township	243

FAMILY HISTORIES—Part Four

	Page
Elm Store	246
Warm Springs	247
D. T. Athy Family	254
Dr. John W. Bryan	257
The Campbells (T. W.)	261
Dalton Family (General History)	264
James L. Dalton—Inventor	268
Elijah F. Dalton Family	273
Joe S. Decker Family	283
Davis-Spikes Family	286
Hite Family	288
Dr. Martin Hogan Family	290
Prof. John Hogan and Wife	292
Ingram Family	293
Jarrett Family	297
Rev. S. L. Johnston Family	300
John A. Johnson Family	303
Landon Christopher Haynes	306
Holt Family	307
John Lamb Family	309
Charles Wiley McCarroll	314
W. L. (Fayette) Mock Family	316
Marlette Family	319
Maynard Family	322
Martin Family (L. R.)	324
A. F. Rickman Family	327
Dr. Horace E. Ruff Family	328
Shride Family	331
William T. Stubblefield	333
Eugene G. Schoonover	336
S. A. (Dore) Smith Family	340
Shaver Family	342
Spikes Family	347
Ben. F. Taylor Family	349
William Jefferson McColgan	351
Eugene Thompson	352
Lemmons Family	313
Oscar Prince Family	326
Wyatt Family	355
Solomon M. White	357

ILLUSTRATIONS

The Author's Family	Front
James G. Russell House	13
Some of the County's Teachers in the Eighties	42
Mrs. Eliza Hogan's School in Pocahontas About 1885	42
Thomas S. Drew	48
Governor Drew's Monument	50
Old Courthouse	56
New Courthouse	56
Hite Cemetery Building	166
Old Davidsonville	174
Old Columbia Church Site	181
Old Masonic Hall	191
Pitman Ferry Site	206
Pitman Cemetery	208
Bettis Bluff Today	215
Six Churches in Pocahontas	219
Southside Square in 1880	229
The Campbell Sisters	260
John Stone Campbell	260
Tom W. Campbell	261
Mrs. Tom W. Campbell	262
Mr. and Mrs. Elijah Dalton	274
Joe S. Decker	284
Elder John M. Lemmons	312
Mr. and Mrs. William H. Johnston	346

General History

Part One

"BEFORE HISTORY BEGAN"

The part played by those who have appeared on the stage of discovery, exploration, settlement and improvement of our native land goes into the making of the greatest human drama of all times.

From the day that Hernando de Soto and his followers crossed the hills and dales of Randolph County, unto the present day of atomic energy, penicillin and political purges, there has been unfolded, day by day, scenes which go into the making of one of the most colorful stories ever told.

To go farther back, we could picture the Redman, as he moved slowly but surely south from the Aleutian stepping stones. When the curtain rose and showed us the initial scene of the long forgotten ages, wherein the father and mother of the Indian, as yellow skinned Mongolians, whose fishing boat which had been blown far from its course, had been wrecked on Attu or Rat Island, instead of the long finger of continental Asia, as the story may have happened, we would, here and there, have been placed in the spot, in the story of Time, where we say, in modern movie language, "Here is where we came in."

The next scenes before us would show the fight for survival of those who were destined to "multiply and replenish the Earth," especially that part which we call the Americas. Some of the children of these ancient people moved south, far south, where the sun, the seasons and Father Time had changed that yellow to copper or brown and in the long trek from the Aleutians to Panama, by way of the Pueblos of New Mexico, had trained their hands to work in many ways foreign to the original fishermen.

Here we would see unfolded, century by century, the story of the Aztecs and their gold and tropical cities; the Eskimo who had retained his mother color; the Seminoles of the Florida Everglades, the Algonquins of New England and the Osages and Cherokees of our own Randolph County section.

Flash! And the flickering screen of time would throw before our eyes the landing of the Pinta, the Nina and the Santa Maria!

Along with the sound of splashing waves and flapping sails we would hear, on Time's sound track, that joyous shout of land! land! from the tongues of the Thirteenth Century Spaniards, whose leader was that illustrious "Dago" from Genoa, Christopher Columbus.

When those Redmen of San Salvador ran down to the seashore to look upon the "great white birds from the east," there was a reunion.

This reunion was that of fragments of the great human family which, spread from God's own Garden of Eden, around the world, by way of Greece, and Rome, the shores of the Mediterranean, Saxony, Gaul and ancient land north of Gibraltar, to cross the stormy Atlantic, to meet the other end of that human throng which had travelled across India, Thibet, Manchuria and Eastern Siberia to board the Behring Sea fishing boat in the early morning of time to be blown by the icy winds on to the shore of Attu, Rat Island or maybe the Pribilofs, here to bury their identity as Mongolians and to forever in the future be known as the Redman.

Though this act is back in that space of time which is four hundred and fifty-four years down the avenues of time behind us, yet we must record this event not only as the "Genesis" of our American history, but also classify it as the dawn of modern history in the Western Hemisphere.

The story of Columbus is known by all who have gone to school or who has delved into the musty recordings of the past.

Then came the Cabots, Champlain, Henry Hudson, Captain John Smith, Ponce de Leon and many others during the

GENERAL HISTORY

first two centuries following the Spanish landings in the West Indies, including Hernando De Soto, who we claim was the first white man to set foot on Randolph County soil.

In an unsuccessful and fatal search for gold which led De Soto to our part of the continent, in 1539 he sailed from Cuba and landed on the coast of Florida. For the next year and a half he and his men wandered around over what is now the southeastern part of the United States, looking for gold and fighting Indians. In 1541 they crossed the Mississippi River near the site of Memphis and then travelled around over Arkansas for several months, finally crossing into what is now Louisiana, where he died May 21, 1542. No one will ever know exactly where his trail ran. It is supposed to have ran up as far as New Madrid, Missouri, and then turning, came back across the hills by way of what is now Butler County and Ripley County, in Missouri and across Randolph, and other counties of Arkansas.

Just what month and time of year he came down the old Indian trail, which later became to be the old National road and still later the old Military road, is not known, but there is good evidence that he did come our way.

Time marches on. The scroll continues to roll, when down from the land of the Illinois and the headlands of the "Father of Waters" came La Salle and his noble band of Frenchmen, including De Tonti who was destined to carry on after La Salle quit the walks of men, in the state of Texas. This was in the year 1682 that La Salle came. Four years later De Tonti erected a cross at the site of the future town of Arkansas Post and claimed all this section for the king of France.

De Soto opened the door of Arkansas and our county to the world and modern history when he crossed the mighty river in 1541, but for the next one hundred and forty-one years the forests stood and the river rolled on unmolested by the hand of white men. De Tonti "started something" when he established Arkansas Post. These early Frenchmen fared far better in this new land than the Spanish. The Spanish came to rob and steal. The French came to open settlements and bring Christianity to the Indians. Marquette, who came this way, from the "cold and frozen north" in 1673, was also a man of God who saw in the Redman another human being, and recognized and acknowledged the brotherhood of man.

From 1686 until another century had rolled into the past and gone, we have no record of anyone coming Randolph County's way.

When the first rays of the dawning of the morning of the nineteenth century showed above the horizon, what is now Randolph County was yet an unbroken wilderness. Possibly old De Maux, for whom the river Fourche de Mas was named, was living here in the backwoods fastness of our county's verdant hills. Tradition tells us that he was a son or grandson of one of the men left at the Post of Arkansas by his ancestor countryman, De Tonti, many moons ago. Here his sire married an Indian girl, and for the first time in centuries beyond number the blood of the east was mixed with the blood of the west to produce the first man who called himself "white," who was a native of our local soil.

Such was the setting of the stage for the last act of our drama which we call "modern times," which has consumed a hundred and fifty years of God's great Eternity and goes on!

Such was the stage which was set for the appearance of John Janes, Matthias Mock, William Jarrett, William Hix, John Davidson, William O'Neal, John Shaver, Jerome Mattix, Obediah Hudson, Shadrach Nettles, the DeMunns, the Millers, the Pitmans, the Luttrells, the Bettis and the dozens and dozens of others who came here during the first days of the past century to take their places on that vast stage of human activities, joys and sorrows, success and failure which continues to play and which will continue to do until the curtain falls "and time shall be no more."

GENERAL HISTORY

This is the story of Randolph County, Arkansas, from the time "before the time we know about" until we come to the actual recorded part which is contained in this book, beginning around the year one thousand, eight hundred one, and continuing until the present, which we call 1946.

FIRST HISTORY OF RANDOLPH COUNTY

What is now Randolph County was originally a small part of that vast territory first known to us as the Louisiana Purchase. The first white man to set foot on its soil is supposed to have been the Spanish explorer, Hernando De Soto, and his men in the year 1541. Some historians deny this. Actually no one knows exactly the route these men travelled; but the first settlers in the vicinity of the present-day Pitman Ferry community found Spanish armor and Spanish coins of this date on the site of what was supposed to have been a camping ground of De Soto. Also a Spanish sword of the same design as carried by De Soto in his travels through the Mississippi Valley was unearthed near the site of the old town of Davidsonville a few years ago. Tradition tells us that this place was first known to the white man as an ancient Indian village and that De Soto and his men stopped here quite awhile in the cold winter of 1541.

The next white man to visit in this section was the Frenchman, Marquette, in the year 1673. He was followed by other Frenchmen, La Salle in 1682 and De Tonti in 1686. The latter established at Arkansas Post, in 1686, the first permanent settlement in the Mississippi Valley.

All the land west of the Mississippi was first claimed by the Spaniards because of their right of discovery. Just how and when it became the property of the French is not known, but the French ceded it to Spain in 1763. Spain again ceded it to France in 1800. France only owned it three years the last time, selling it to the United States in the year 1803.

This is known in history as the "Louisiana Purchase." The deal was made during the administration of Thomas Jefferson and is by far the most important land deal which our nation has ever made.

After the United States became owner of this vast land area, which was approximately the western half of the entire Mississippi Valley, it was cut up into various "districts" and "territories." What is now Randolph County was first a part of the District of Louisiana, being so designated in 1804. In 1805 it was made a part of the District of New Madrid, where it remained until 1813. From 1813 to 1815 it was a part of the County of New Madrid in the Territory of Missouri. It was a part of the County of Lawrence in the Territory of Missouri from January 15, 1815, to July 4, 1819. From July 4, 1819, until October 29, 1835, it was a part of Lawrence County, Arkansas Territory. On this latter date Randolph County came into existence as a separate county in the Arkansas Territory until the next year (1836) when the territory became one of the states of the Union.

Randolph County has been a part of four great countries (including the Confederacy), three territories, two states, four counties, and is older by one year than the state of Arkansas itself. Being located almost in the very "heart" of the original vast Louisiana Purchase, we who call Randolph County our home appreciate and respect the statement made by Robert Livingston who negotiated the deal with France whereby the United States became the owner of this vast domain, when he said on that memorable day of May 4, 1803, "We have lived long, but this is the noblest work of our entire lives. It will change vast solitudes into flourishing districts." Such was the opinion of the statesman who made the deal whereby our nation became owner of over 1,182,000 square miles of rich virgin territory for a sum of only about fifteen million dollars. Randolph County is a part of that purchase.

GENERAL HISTORY

FIRST INHABITANTS — THE INDIAN

There are many signs of work done by the so-called prehistoric Mound Builders in this section. These people were supposed to have been a people who inhabited much of the North American continent, and especially the Mississippi Valley. Just who these people were and from whence they came and where they went will probably never be known. They were different from the Indians who were here when the first white man came. Their name suggests one of their traits. They built huge mounds, usually in the valleys or lowlands. Excavations in these mounds reveal that they were used as burying grounds and other purposes. Some of these mounds are found in Randolph County but none with evidence such as has been found in other parts of the state.

This section was once the home of at least two distinct branches of the North American Indian, the Osages and the Cherokees. Both branches had lived here long before the coming of the first white settler and most of them had moved farther west even before permanent white settlements had made much headway. Cherokee Bay in eastern Randolph County was named for the Cherokees who resided along the ridges in that section and hunted and fished in the low bottoms and along the banks of Black and Current rivers. The Osages also lived in this section and there is evidence that the latter drove the Cherokees out sometime during the early Indian wars when the first settlers on the eastern shores of our nation were driving all the Redmen westward. Randolph County escaped the trouble with the Indian that many of the eastern pioneer communities had. So far as we are able to learn, no fight was ever made between the whites and Indians within the present borders of Randolph County.

RANDOLPH COUNTY IN 1800

We who now live, being used to the mars and scars made by human habitation upon the face of the land, can scarcely realize just how our country looked before the devastating hand of man started working. Where broad fields now spread, once stood giant hardwood trees, the age of which dated back to the Dark Ages. Where we now see old fields wounded by deep gullies and overgrown by sage grass, once stood walnut trees which would fit in with any cabinetmaker's wildest dream. The lowland sections of the county was a vast carpet of trees and vines divided here and there by sloughs and marshes. Black virgin soil, three feet deep, made up of the accumulation of decayed vegetation for centuries. Wild fruits and berries grew in abundance everywhere. On the uplands were found practically the same picture except that it was higher and not marshy. The streams like Fourche, Janes Creek and others were clear, deep mountain streams. Deep pools of water surrounded by large softwood trees and shoals lined with willows and other shrubs and trees whose roots sought the damp, rich banks of the creeks. No "washes" and wide gravel bars were to be found before men came and cut away the timber and plowed loose the soil to be washed down the creeks by every big rain which fell. Not a mark scarred the miles and miles of virgin forests except the narrow thread-like trails of the buffalo and Redman. Such was the setting of the stage upon which the first settlers moved onto to start that colossal drama of human activity of which we are now a part.

Wild game was present in abundance. Fish, fowls and fur-bearing animals found a veritable paradise. Buffalo, bear, wolves, panthers, deer and all the smaller animals were natives of this section. Wild turkeys, geese, ducks, and other fowl life was plentiful, and the streams abounded with fish. All this was the "Manna of Life" for the American Indian as well as the early pioneer. It is almost beyond our power of imagination to realize the immense contrast in what the traveller of 1800 saw in a trip from O'Kean to Elm Store or from Reyno to Ravenden, compared with the scene along the way in 1946! Blooded cattle graze along the slopes of the upland, set in Bermuda or lespedeza, where once grazed the buffalo, under the giant trees. Tractors hum across the alluvial fields where once the bear and deer made their way along the narrow paths through the cane and vine entanglements. Thus is a century and a quarter of transformation.

FIRST WHITE SETTLERS

Just who the first white man was who came into what is now Randolph County to make his permanent home will never be known. No record has ever been made of an early French settler in this county. The mother county of Lawrence, just to the south of us, knows and recognizes the fact that it was possibly the French who established the first permanent homes in that county. They probably did the same in this county in the vicinity of Davidsonville and along Fourche DuMas creek. De Tonti left ten Frenchmen in Arkansas when he was here in 1686. Whether any of these men reared families will never be known. The first name for this creek was of French origin. It was written "Fourche De Maux." Who can deny that away back in 1686 when De Tonti left these men here in this remote wilderness that one or more of these men did not come to Randolph County and marry a legendary Indian Princess and adopt the ways and life of the Redman, and though leaving a few French names scattered around, lived and died with the Indians to bury forever the story of the first white settler of Randolph County!

There is some evidence to support the claim that there was an active French trading post at Pocahontas before 1790.

But with all this, it remains for the historian to designate, so far as is possible, the name or names of the first families to make this their permanent home. Shinn's History of Arkansas says that John Janes, a Revolutionary soldier, settled on the creek which bears his name in the year 1809. Reynold's History of Arkansas, which was used as a text-book about 1910, states that Matthias Mock settled on Mud Creek in central Randolph County in 1815 to become the first settler. The Jarrett family has records that tend to prove that their ancestor, Dr. William Jarrett, settled at what is now known as the Foster ford on Fourche near 1800. William Jarrett, who died in Little Rock in 1944 at the age of ninety-five, stated years ago that the Dr. Jarrett named above came here from Lincoln County, N. C., in 1800 and that he bought land at "Columbia" at that early date from Richard Fletcher. This Richard Fletcher was the father of John Gould Fletcher, the sire of the noted Fletcher family of Arkansas. More will be related about this family in another chapter. C. L. Freeman, in his History of Northeast Arkansas, stated that William O'Neal, Obediah Hudson and Shadrack Nettles settled on the state line between Oregon County, Missouri, and Randolph County, Arkansas, in 1812. David Black settled on Elevenpoint at what is still known as Black's Ferry in 1815. Tom Holt settled near Warm Springs in 1821. George Mansker settled on the creek which bears his name just north of the city limits of Pocahontas in 1817. May 27, 1815, William Clark, Governor of Missouri Territory, appointed William Russell as Justice of the Peace "within and for the Settlement of Fourche de Thomas." Two days later he also appointed William Harris for the same place and position. On the first records of Lawrence County, Elijah Baker is recorded to have made a property transfer to Beverly Baker, June 8, 1815. These Bakers lived on Elevenpoint River, Randolph County. November 15, 1818, James Smith sold his improvement on "Glaze Kenon Creek" to William Linn. In his deed Smith stated that he had actually improved and cultivated this place before April 12, 1814, the date the settler's right to preemption claim on real estate came into effect. John Shaver settled on Mud Creek near the present-day Ingram about

1818 or earlier. Solomon Hewitt sold the farm on which the first court of Lawrence County was held to Benjamin Crowley, October 12, 1819. This property is described on the records as being "on the north bank of Spring River, two miles above the mouth of Elevenpoint." Crowley already lived here at this time. This Benjamin Crowley is the man who settled at Walcott, Greene County, and for whom Crowley's Ridge was named. Edward McDonald, who was Lawrence County's first Representative in the Territorial Legislature in 1820, lived near the present village of Supply prior to that time. Charles Hatcher lived in the south end of Davidson township before 1818. He was appointed Justice of the Peace in that year. Dr. Englemann, the noted German physician and scientist, travelled from St. Louis to Little Rock in 1837. He spent some time at the home of Dr. Peyton R. Pittman at Pittman's Ferry and stated that the latter had lived here over twenty-five years at that time. William Hix owned this ferry years before Dr. Pittman became owner. Evidently Hix's Ferry was in operation around 1800. The census for the year 1830 listed the following persons in Randolph County aged 60 to 70: William Hix, John Pierce, Isaac Flannery, William McKnight and James Davis; aged 70 to 80, Nathan Luttrell, James Boyd, Martin Vanzandt, and Mrs. Joe Kellett; over 80 years of age, John Shaver. The following names are listed as leading citizens of the Davidsonville community before 1815: Louis De Mun, William Robinson, William Hix (evidently Hix moved to Davidsonville when he sold out at Pittman), Solomon Hewitt, Andrew Criswell, James M. Kuykendall, Isaac Kelley, Charles Kelley, Morris Moore, James Campbell, Richard Searcy. On Elevenpoint River before 1815 were William Looney, William Meredith, Massach H. Jones, John Miller, James Hallock, and the McIlroy and Stubblefield families. On Janes Creek were John Janes, Lot Davis, and up near the state line William O'Neal, Obediah Hudson and Shadrach Nettles. Henry Schoolcraft passed through Randolph County in 1819 and stopped at the village of Fourche de Thomas and in his written report stated that he was amazed at the many improved farms in this section at that time. The early Luttrell, Duckworth, McElmurry, Winningham, Slavens, Shaver and other families were represented in Cherokee Bay before 1820. The Eldridge family, Ators, Cross, Grissom, Robinson, Dalton and others were living in what is now Siloam township near this period.

It is impossible to list all the very first families who settled in Randolph County, even if they were known. And it must be remembered by the reader and historian that in any section the great handicap in learning who were there early is the lack of written records, and also, even though records are in existence, many of the early settlers led a quiet life apart from their neighbors, and unless they made some sort of legal transaction or were identified with some of the early activities, their name may never appear in the annals of the first quarter of a century of settlement. In the family histories of this book and in the articles dealing with the different towns and settlements many of the above persons and others not named above will be listed. The aim of the writer, in this chapter, is to give the reader a brief but general list of the names appearing in the records for the first twenty-five years after the opening of the century (1800).

FIRST COURT IN RANDOLPH COUNTY

The first court held in Lawrence County, before the formation of Randolph, was held in what is now Randolph County. This court was held in April, 1815, at the home of Solomon Hewitt, on the east side of Spring River about two miles above the mouth of Elevenpoint. This land is now owned by Albert Davis and Eugene McCarroll. This is supposed to have been the first actual term of court convened in Arkansas.

This court was held in the house which has been pictured in one or two Arkansas histories and in numerous newspapers and called the "first courthouse at Davidsonville." This is an

"HOUSE OF JAMES C. RUSSELL"
First actual Randolph County court held here in 1837.

error. The courthouse at Davidsonville was a two-story brick. The first trial was between Thomas Graves and James Haddock over the ownership of some hogs. The grand jury was composed of Jess Jeffrey (foreman), George Grant, William

Compton, Sam Russell, John Bollinger, Thomas Morris, Asa Lausacum, Culbert Hudson, Sam Wilson, John Walker, John Lafferty, Nat Robbins, William Caraway, Robert Cravens, William Stubblefield, William Webb, Edward McDonald and William Hix.

The petit jury was made up of the following: Joseph Hardin, James Kuykendall, Robert Rollins, William D. Holt, William Cravens, Sol Carter, Frederick Keel, Richard Murphy and William Robertson.

Richard Thomas, who was the presiding judge for the southern district of Missouri, was the judge. James Campbell was sheriff, Lewis DeMunn was clerk (DeMunn resigned in 1816 and Richard Searcy was appointed). John Rodney was surveyor and G. W. Wright was assessor. The sheriff was required to give bond (as collector) for an amount twice the anticipated revenue for the year. The bond was for $150.00 and is still in existence in the vault at Powhatan. This was the only term of court held at the home of Solomon Hewitt. The next was held at "the new house of Richard Murphy." After this the county seat had been located at Davidsonville. For an account of the establishing of the county seat at Davidsonville, see chapter of the establishment of that town elsewhere in this book.

The above was an account of the first court of old Lawrence County. Randolph has the distinction of possessing the site of the first court of two counties, Lawrence and of Randolph County proper, after it was organized. The first court held in the county after its organization was held at the home of James G. Russell, eight miles north of Pocahontas, on what was long known as the old Foster farm, now owned by Max Riggs. The date of convening was April 4, 1836. On the first page of book one of the records (county court) is this entry: "The judge did not appear; court adjourned until tomorrow morning." The next day the judge was present and the first term of Randolph County court was convened.

Peyton R. Pitman, for whom the village of Pitman and Pitman's Ferry was named, was the judge. His associate justices at this term were William Rice, the first resident of Warm Springs, Joseph Spikes, Benjamin Janes, and James Cooper. The first business transacted was the appointment of Jesse Spikes as constable for Columbia township, Jacob W. Shaver as constable for Current River township, George Glasscock as constable for Roanoke township and James Houston as constable for Demun.

The next business was the approving of the bond of William Black as sheriff and James Cooper as surveyor. James G. Russell was allowed ten dollars for advertising the election in 1835. In addition to the above, numerous citizens were appointed to mark out roads or were appointed as overseers for the various roads already marked out. This was the first term of county court in the county.

The first term of circuit court that was held in the county was held May 31, 1837, with Lewis B. Tulley as circuit judge. The following men were members of the first grand jury: George B. Croft, William Jarrett, William Spikes, Samuel Jordon, Ruben Rice, John Mansker, Fielden Stubblefield, William Marshall, Walter G. Hogan, John Welch, James Bigger, Isaac Blount, Lewis Edwards, John Shaver, Edward Mattix, James Luttrell, Amos Lively, Daniel Plott and Joseph Spikes.

The first petit jury was composed of the following: Isham F. Alcorn, Lemi Evans, Jesse Gray, Charles Hatcher, Jacob Shaver, William Crabtree, Isaac McDonald, William Mitchell, Charles Thompson, Isaac Everett, Daniel Lieb, and William Adair. Evans and Crabtree were fined for not appearing as jurymen after being summoned.

The majority of the first cases tried in this court were for assault and battery and gambling. The charge for gambling was entered on the record as "Betting at seven-up" in most cases, although a few were listed as "betting at a game called three-up." Thomas Johnson was the first prosecuting attorney. An interesting thing to be noted in the record of the first and second terms of Randolph County Circuit Court was the frequent appearance of the names of the leading citizens of that day on the docket. It seems that even though they occupied places of prominence in their communities and were often situated in responsible positions, they did not fail to defend their side of the questions involved, even to the extent of being hauled into court and charged with "assault and battery" and "creating an affray." The people who lived a hundred years ago were, of necessity, of the rough-and-ready type who often scorned conventional things and were not much for formality, relying a lot on impulses and looking at things for their true worth and nothing else.

Of the above list of the first grand and petit jurors who served in 1837, twenty-four of the names are still represented in Randolph County at the present time.

THE OLD MILITARY ROAD

What has been known as the "Old Military Road" for many years is that old road which entered Randolph County from Missouri at Pitman's Ferry and ran by way of Supply, Maynard, Attica, old Jackson and across Spring River into Lawrence County. This old road was first known as the Natchitoches Trail and had been used by the Indians from time immemorial in their travels from the north to the south and from the east to the west, as the route runs in a northeastern-southwestern direction. The route is a natural location for a road. It ran closely along the foothills of the Ozarks from the north to the south and is above the early flooded lowlands but near enough to be accessible to the Indian and wild animals to travel in going to and from the higher lands to the northwest.

After the coming of the white man the road was a general route of travel from St. Louis by way of the old French settlement of St. Genevieve to the southwest, across Arkansas into Texas and Mexico. Evidently it was used by early hunters and traders soon after the close of the Revolution. Some of the hardy pioneers of the east desired to explore the great unknown wilderness of the Mississippi Valley. After the Louisiana Purchase in 1803 quite a number of these people brought their families and settled in this section. Many years before this a road had been opened from the east to St. Genevieve, on the Mississippi south of St. Louis. The Military road is an extension of this road. Around 1800 a ferry was established at what is now Pitman by William Hix and was known as Hix's Ferry. This is ample proof that the old road was being used by enough travellers to make a ferry a profitable undertaking. A few years later the ferry was purchased, together with the farm, by P. R. Pitman, who later became the first county judge of Randolph County, and was known thereafter as Pitman's Ferry. About this time the route became known as the National road, but when Congress began to spend money to improve these frontier roads to be used for military purposes it became to be known as the "Military Road."

The first quarter of a century after this road and others like it were opened, there was no work done on them except what the travellers did as they went along. Sometimes they were changed as the conditions required, and as settlements grew up on or near them.

On March 2, 1831, Congress appropriated $15,000 to be used "on the road from Washington, Arkansas Territory, to Jackson in said Territory." On July 3, 1832, $20,000 more was set aside for this purpose. On February 24, 1835, another appropriation was made by Congress for work to be done on the old Military road. Lieut. R. D. C. Collins and Thomas Baker were given the contract to improve that part within the present Randolph County. The price for the work is recorded as follows "From Jackson to Elevenpoint, $14.00 per mile; from Elevenpoint to Fourche de Thomas, $18.75

per mile; from Fourche de Thomas to the Missouri state line, $8.50 per mile."

The present bridge at what is now known as the Foster Ford on Fourche creek is the third bridge at that point. This is the old Military crossing. The first two bridges were of wood. This is the old "Columbia" or "Fourche de Thomas" settlement (more will be said about this place later). The next crossing was on Elevenpoint River and a ferry was established here also. This ferry was established in 1815 or soon thereafter by David Black and is still known as Black's Ferry. The crossing on Spring River was at the place known in later years as the Miller Ford.

Some of the early maps show the road going by way of Davidsonville. The first road which was really the original Natchitoches trail did go by Davidsonville, but the road known and recognized as the National road or Southwest Trail and finally as the old Military road did not go by this, Randolph County's first postoffice. The lack of ferrying facilities and the flood plain on the south and west side of Davidsonville made it in a very hard spot to be located on an early road.

Many noted persons have travelled down this old road in the past century and a half, besides all the grand old pioneers who lived a life of usefulness "unhonored and unsung." Among the notables were Sam Houston, David Crockett, General John C. Fremont, Henry R. Schoolcraft, Nuttall the explorer; Moses Austin, his son, Stephen Austin, later to be known as the "Father of Texas"; Gen. Archibald Yell, Gov. James S. Conway, James Woodson Bates, Gen. Sterling Price, Gen. Joe Shelby, President U. S. Grant and many others. The first mail route in the state of Arkansas was over this route. Some historians say the route ran from St. Louis to Monroe, Louisiana, by way of Pitman, Fourche de Thomas (Columbia), Davidsonville, Polk Bayou (Batesville) and to Arkansas Post. Houck's History of Southeast Missouri states that the mail was first carried from Harrisonville, Illinois, by way of Potosi and Fredericktown, Mo., Pitman, Columbia and Davidsonville to stop at Batesville. This latter route evidently was of a later date than the St. Louis-Arkansas Post route. But at any rate both came through Randolph County and furnished mail to the county's first postoffices, Fourche de Thomas (Columbia) and Davidsonville, and possibly Pitman. After the decline of Davidsonville in 1829 when the county seat (of old Lawrence County) was moved to Jackson, a few miles northwest of the old town, the road was discontinued by Davidsonville to take the route described above. This mail was carried on horseback once a month. Taverns were built along the old road and many weary travellers, in the years after the road became well established, rested their weary bodies inside the walls of these buildings which were the forerunner of the modern hotel, or actually more like the tourist courts along our modern highways. From 1820 until the turn of the present century hundreds of families per year travelled over this old road in their trek south and west. Dr. Englemann, a noted German scientist who traveled this road from St. Louis to Little Rock in March, 1837, tells of spending one night and two days at Columbia (Fourche de Thomas) at the home of David Plott, waiting for the high water to run down. He states in his diary of the trip that several families of immigrants were detained at the same time and that in their haste to get across some of them drove their teams and wagons into the stream and the wagons were overturned by the swift current.

Many travellers from the east who had actually started to Texas or farther west, upon reaching this section decided to stop here and make it their home. This accounts in part for the fact that this section of the state was settled before that farther west and south. A few pushed on, and not finding what they wanted, came back and settled here. The first telegraph line to run through northeast Arkansas was strung along the old Military road. Only a few years ago a man living out northeast of Maynard told the writer about cutting a tree which had one of the old insulators imbedded in its trunk.

A branch of the Military road was opened in the early thirties from Jackson west, by way of Smithville and other points to Fayetteville. This is the road over which the Indians were taken in the removal from their home east of the Mississippi to the Indian Territory which is now the western part of Oklahoma. We have all heard of the hardships, cruelty and suffering borne by these Redmen at the hands of the Government agents who contracted to move them. They were paid sufficiently to have transported them in comfort and safety but the story persists that they were unscrupulous, hard-hearted fellows who drove them on, through bad weather, sickness, etc., which resulted in many deaths and much suffering.

If it were possible to project on a movie screen the vast panorama which moved along the old Military road during the years from 1820 until 1890, we would see depicted before us one of the greatest living dramas of all ages.

OTHER EARLY ROADS

Besides the old Military road described above, there were several other roads opened in Randolph County during the first years of settlement. On date of July 4, 1836, James Houston and Ransom Bettis reported to the county court that they had viewed the route from the west end of Broadway in the town of Pocahontas west seven miles to Black's Ferry, and recommended that this was the most practical route from Pocahontas to this ferry.

On this same date, John Boran, John Gullett and Daniel Plott were appointed to review the road from Stephen Eldridge's on Fourche at the Missouri state line over the most practical route towards Pocahontas "until it intersects the old road from Dr. Pitman's to Davidsonville," near the residence of Andrew Kelly (later at Daniel Plott's).

Ben Janes, Coleman Stubblefield and Joseph Spikes were appointed to lay out a road from the road between Cal Stubblefield's and the Spring Island ford on Elevenpoint, over the most direct route to the bridge on Fourche Dumas creek, on the Military road. All this was in July, 1836.

The next year a petition was filed by a number of citizens to the court, requesting that a road be opened from the ferry on Black River at Pocahontas down the east side of the river toward Litchfield, to the Lawrence County line. This road became later to be known as the Pocahontas-Jacksonport road. The first road mentioned above was what became known as the Smithville road and possibly earlier was the Black's Ferry road. The road from Stephen Eldridge's to the Military road was the old road which ran down the west side of Fourche creek and was later known as the old Belview road, although the route was changed in part in later years. This old road crossed the Military road a short distance west of the old Foster ford (or Fourche de Thomas military crossing) and ran on south to Pocahontas, coming into the road now travelled out of Pocahontas to the north exactly between the forks of the Warm Springs and Maynard road. This old road ran out by way of the old Kibler farm, the old Biggers farm on up across Mud creek at the "Dock Ingram ford." This is the old road which this writer travelled in coming to Pocahontas from western Siloam township when a child.

The road from Elevenpoint to Fourche bridge on the Military road was later replaced by a road which ran more directly east and west. It was located a few miles north of this road and was known as the Warm Springs-Corning road and crossed Fourche at the Phipps Mill ford.

The old Thomasville road, for which Thomasville Avenue in Pocahontas was named, ran from Pocahontas to Thomasville in Oregon County, Missouri. Its route was on the east side of Elevenpoint River. The very first road which ran up Elevenpoint travelled near this route but the road which connects Warm Springs and Pocahontas at the present time was used a great lot during the early days in travelling from the "Irish Wilderness" country on upper Fourche creek into Randolph County. Another old-time road ran down Janes creek to Ravenden Springs over much the same route that the present-day road travels. At one time, about the middle of the last century, the mail was carried from Doniphan by way of Dry Springs (which was a postoffice on the state line between Poynor, Missouri, and Middlebrook, Arkansas) across the hills to Janes' store on Janes creek, according to an old mail route record. Just how the route ran is not known. It possibly ran by way of the old Fourche de Thomas postoffice or the old Mud creek postoffice, which was on the old Mock homestead, and then across the hills to near the present town of Ravenden Springs. The 1836 term of Randolph County court licensed Ranson Bettis to operate a ferry at Pocahontas ($2.00 per year), Peyton R. Pitman at Pitman's ferry ($5.00 per year), and Thomas Black at Black's ferry ($2.00 per year). The fee charged would suggest that there was a lot more business at Pitman than at either of the other ferries. This was possibly caused by the heavy stream of emigrants who were moving over the old Military road on their long journey from the older states to the east and north to Texas, what is now Oklahoma and also the southern part of this state. Operating a ferry was one of the first industries in this section. We hear a lot at the present time about getting money from the tourist trade. The old river ferrymen of a century ago were the first to cash in on this source of revenue. However, the traveller of today is usually out on a business or pleasure trip, but the old pioneer largely made only a "one-way drive." He travelled over the road one time to stop at the end of the way, to establish a home for his family and live the remainder of his days at that end of the line. The part played by the early roads of our nation cannot be overestimated. Their importance and the stories and traditions associated with them almost make them ribbons of sacred soil criss-crossing our country, through lowlands and over hill and dale.

EARLY LINES OF TRANSPORTATION

The very first white man who came into this section of the nation, together with his family and possessions, came either by boat or overland in covered wagon. The easiest way to bring merchandise or household goods was to travel by flatboat. The routes usually followed was down the Ohio, then into the Mississippi. This built up such early settlements on the river as St. Genevieve, Cairo, New Madrid and others. With the coming of the steamboat they did not stop altogether on the Mississippi, but ran their boats up the smaller rivers. During the first days of settlement of Randolph County, Davidsonville was the chief river town in north Arkansas. Steamboats from the Mississippi River ports came here with merchandise for the settlers. Pocahontas became an early steamboat landing and many boats went on up Black River several miles and up Current River as far as the "Drew Farm" in Cherokee Bay, which was the present site of Biggers. Here Thomas Drew lived during the time he was county judge of Lawrence County and at the time he was elected Governor of Arkansas. Steamboats plied the rivers regularly until the coming of the first railroads. In later years, boats ran up Current and Black rivers much farther than stated above. In fact, since the writer can remember, boats came up Current River to Johnstontown on the river just west of the present town of Reyno and loaded bales of cotton bound for New Orleans and other southern ports. Tall stories of adventures and hardships of the early rivermen are a part of the literature of the nineteenth century. The rivers at that time were full of hidden dangers for the boatman. Snags, hidden rocks and shifting sandbars were often sudden death to proud rivercraft. In deed record number three of Randolph County is recorded the sinking of the river steamer *"Julia Dean"* in Black River fifteen miles below Pocahontas on April 30, 1853. Much valuable cargo was destroyed. The boat was on its way up the river to Pocahontas from Memphis. It had been making regular trips between these ports. Samuel Taylor was Master, S. D. Hancock was clerk, and Morgan Bateman was pilot. There was a rule in those days for the owners of the boat to carry cargo insurance, but if it could be proven by the insurance company that the boat's crew was negligent when fire or sinkings destroyed the cargo, the liability rested on the owner of the boat. On page 131 of this record is to be found a "protest to obtain insurance" for this loss. The location on the river where this sinking occurred ninety-three years ago is still known as the Julia Dean bar.

The first steamboat known to have come up Black River was the steamer *Laurel*, which came in 1829. Some of the later boats were the *Fairy Queen, Clara Inman, Hope, Miltharry, Bragg* and *Black Diamond*. The writer remembers seeing some furniture several years ago with a tag tacked on it which stated "shipped on the steamer *Hope*."

GENERAL HISTORY

As soon as the early trails were blazed out many settlers came in overland. The chief disadvantage of river transportation was that often it did not go where the traveller desired to go. To take care of this he cut out overland trails. The oldest trail to come into Randolph County is what is now known as the old Military road which entered the county from the north at Pitman's Ferry and ran toward the southwest by way of Maynard, Columbia (Jarrett), old Jackson and into Lawrence County near Imboden. (Much more will be said about this old road in a special chapter.) Two other old roads came down through the center of the county and were known as the Belview and Thomasville roads in later years. Principally all the early settlers of the county came here either overland on the old Military road or up Black River in an early steamboat. Most of those who came by boat settled at Davidsonville and around the mouth of Elevenpoint and Spring River. The rest of the county, especially the northeastern section, came in over the old road. This road was opened around 1800 and made Randolph County accessible to those pioneers pushing westward, at an earlier date than the counties farther south and west. Travel over these early trails was slow and hard. Often it was necessary to almost make a road as they went along. Streams had to be crossed, and when a large one was reached a raft had to be built which sometimes took days to construct. Camps had to be set up and breakdowns and sickness often happened on the way. Miles and miles of unbroken forests greeted the traveller and many long and lonesome nights were spent out under God's broad canopy of stars, amid the howls of wild animals and the knowledge that he was hundreds of miles from the home of his father's and with miles and miles of tortuous trail ahead of him. This early pioneer was truly to be compared with John of old. He prepared the way that those who came later might travel. And the wife and mother of this pioneer deserves much more credit than she has ever been accorded. It was she who made it possible for such movements in the long journey of man's upward climb to be accomplished.

EARLY SOCIAL AND RELIGIOUS LIFE

We often think of the life of the pioneer as being drab and monotonous. This would likely be true if we, of the present day, should be forced to live in the environment and surroundings which our grandparents lived. But they invented for themselves various ways and means of entertainment. We have heard more about the old time square dance or "hoe down," as it was often called. Most of the old-time ministers frowned upon it as a pastime, but to the majority of the inhabitants it was a genuine pleasure and afforded the chief source of public entertainment. When we look back upon the manner in which it was carried on we doubt very much if it could be classed with the modern dance, from a moral standpoint. To the majority who indulged, it afforded a wholesome, harmless sort of pleasure. The majority of girls who attended these old-time dances were "nice girls" and were highly respected and commanded respect and courtesy which was always accorded them, or their escort or one of the family pulled off his coat, rolled up his sleeves and proceeded to correct the matter. No one ever saw a lady drunk or heard her use the sort of language which we hear today. Smoking among the womenfolk was confined to the grandmothers with their old clay pipes.

The dancing of that day was generally carried on at the home of one of the inhabitants of the "neighborhood" and was attended by the neighbors for miles around. The fathers and mothers of the boys and girls were present and saw what was going on. This is different from our roadhouses and "honky-tonks" of the present day, with their attendant evils.

Pleasures were often associated with duties at hand. We have all heard of the quilting parties, spinning bees, house raisings, log rollings and other occasions when the neighbors were invited in to participate in the jobs that needed to be done. Often "races" were run and a friendly competition was engaged in, in the manner of seeing who could do the job the best or the fastest. All this was diversification for the folks who spent long lonely days in and around the log cabin in the small "clearing" in the woods, many miles from the nearest neighbor.

Church "socials," pie suppers, box suppers and other forms of entertainment were sponsored by the church, both for amusement and as a means of securing money to pay expenses. The schools did much the same way. "Exhibitions" were staged. Debating societies were organized and spelling and ciphering matches were held. All these afforded both entertainment and valuable educational training. There were other forms of entertainment which were both beneficial and monotony breaking for those who lived in Randolph County during the century which came to a close about the beginning of World War I.

The above constitutes a brief picture of the pioneer activities which would be classed as social. Religious activities of that day afforded another kind of diversification. We do not desire to appear sacriligious when we say that one of the major reasons for the organization of many churches during the early days was for the purpose of affording the settler, especially the young folks, "somewhere to go." It is a well known fact that people are going to go "somewhere." This is especially true of the younger folks. The pioneer "meeting house" helped solve this problem.

The church building of the early days was really a community building. It usually served the purpose of both schoolhouse and church building. It was also the scene of all other religious and social gatherings. It was also used as a place to hold elections, political speakings, etc.

But this old-time meeting house is best remembered as the place where the "big meeting," or revival was held. Once a month preaching was held. Along through the year and in some of the places Sunday school met regularly, but to many the major use was for the two or three weeks revival which was generally held "after crops were laid by." This was sometime during the months of July or August. The preacher, which was mostly of the "circuit rider" type, rode into the neighborhood some Saturday afternoon and services began that night and each night, and sometimes each day for some time. Here the plain unvarnished Gospel was fervently poured out of the mouth of the more or less "educated" man of God. What he lacked in Scriptural knowledge he made up in enthusiasm and religious fervor. People came in for miles around, on foot, in wagons and on horseback. On Sunday there was dinner on the ground. If he had accomplished his mission to a very great extent, there were several baptizings, at the most convenient creek. There was some division as to the teachings of the Scriptures, but most everyone attended and strong congregations were built up whose influence lives unto this day.

Some congregations held camp meetings which lasted several days. At these meetings the folks came and stayed for days.

The pioneer preacher was often poorly paid. When he was paid it was usually in farm products, etc. But it can be said to the everlasting honor and credit of this early man of God, he did his work for his Master and then found out what he was to receive in return, where, as it is with the modern preacher, he generally has to be guaranteed a certain sum or he does not serve. This is not true of all of our present-day ministers, but it is true of too many.

The good work done by the pioneer preacher has never been fully appreciated. He was truly like John of old, "He came forth to prepare a way for we who came later to follow."

GENERAL HISTORY

EARLY WATER MILLS

Water furnished the power for the first mills in the pioneer settlements. A few sawmills were operated by waterpower but this kind of power was more commonly used in operating burrs for grinding grain and for ginning cotton. To install a watermill it was necessary to build a dam across the stream and then install a "wheel and shaft" to produce this power. Some of the waterwheels were of the "overshot" type which ran the water to the top of a large wheel with boxes or cups to catch the water which started the wheel to turning by the weight of the water in the boxes as they revolved on the shaft, and came back around for refilling. The very oldest mills were built this way. Later mills were built with the power shaft upright and the power was produced by water from "flood gates" striking against a series of paddles built around the shaft like the spokes of a wheel. This power box and flood gate was built at the bottom of the dam and produced much more power, due to the pressure of the water in the mill pond behind the dam.

Along all the larger creeks and rivers can be seen the ruins of the old dams. The first one built in the county was built by Lewis DeMunn and his brothers, two miles below Pocahontas on what is still known as "Mill Creek," in 1822. The old stone abutments and some of the old logs can still be seen. The writer regrets that we do not have a complete list of all these old mill sites but below we name some of them.

One of the most noted, and possibly the last one, to cease operation was the old mill at Birdell. Built sometime during the first half of the past century, it was operated for half a century or more by John Carter. The Carters were related to the Perrins, Scotts and other families of this section. About 1880 Joseph Hufstedler purchased this mill and for over forty years it was known as the Hufstedler mill. Other mills were built on Elevenpoint River. This stream was especially well suited for the erection of mill dams as the banks are generally steep and the water swift. Lewis Dalton erected a watermill at Dalton about 1870 and ground grain and ginned cotton many years. Another very old mill site is at Brockett. It is listed on the road records of 1836 as "Ford's Mill" (was later known as Bollinger's mill), and it is said that there was once a three-story roller mill at this site. On Fourche de Mas were located a number of early watermills. Among them was the old Dalton mill, the old Keel mill, both just over the line in Missouri, Old Cedarville, just north of Middlebrook. The old stone burrs which were on display in the log cabin which used to stand on the Pocahontas fair ground were from the old Cedarville mill. The late Uncle Chas. G. Johnston had it moved here.

Another Fourche watermill was at Phipp's ford. It was in operation until about 1914. On Mud creek, at what is now the Price farm, was the Dock Ingram mill which was in operation for many years prior to 1900. The writer's grandfather operated a blacksmith shop here while my father was a boy at home. I have often heard the story told about an incident which happened at the shop. My grandfather was a very jovial man and sometimes carried his jokes possibly too far. The story goes that the late Uncle Tive Mock brought an axe into the shop which had "bursted" on one side of the "eye" and asked grandfather if he couldn't "lay" it some way. (The term "lay" was a process of welding one layer of metal over a break to bring the two parts together.) Grandfather looked the axe over and seeing that it was badly worn and hard to repair walked to the door of the shop and threw it far out into the mill pond. Turning to Uncle Tive, he remarked, "Tive that's the best way to 'lay' that axe that I know."

As stated above, we do not have a complete list of all the old mills which were built along the streams of Randolph County, as they were our first manufacturing plants.

The horsepower grist mill which John Janes operated on Janes' creek before 1822 was converted into a watermill in later years. Another, though later, on Janes' creek was the old Woodyard mill near where Ora Bailey now resides. W. W. Bailey, who dreamed of the famous Ravenden spring, operated a watermill on Janes' creek, a mile and one-half south of Ravenden Springs before 1880. It was at first a corn mill grinding only meal and feed, but later it was enlarged and "bolts" were added, making it a flour mill as well.

The farmer carried his wheat to these ancient mills and paid "toll" to get it ground. He received back in place of the wheat some flour, also "shorts" and "middlings" which was separated from the white center of the grain. This "middlings" was sometimes also used to make bread. It produced a dark loaf, somewhat like graham bread, and was very nourishing, although it didn't look too good.

Another early mill was the Johnson mill on Elevenpoint River. The story goes that the mill was small and ground very slowly. The operator would pour a bushel of corn into the hopper and go out in the field and work around a half day while the corn was being ground. One day he heard a dog barking at intervals in the vicinity of the mill. Thinking that someone might be bothering something, he decided to go see about it. Upon arriving at the mill he discovered that the dog was eating the meal as it ran out into the large wooden bowl placed there to receive it, and that he ate faster than the mill ground, and that he was barking for more when enough failed to run out.

Some of the first towns of the nation grew up from the site of an old watermill. Some early settler who lived on a stream which had a site suitable for the building of a dam, would do so, and install a mill. He may have been far back in the woods to begin with, but as his neighbors came to his mill a road would be opened up and the place become well known. Next probably would be a blacksmith shop. The settler would have his plows sharpened or his horse shod while he waited for his "turn" at the mill. Another enterprising neighbor would see that this should be a good "trading place" and would open up a trading post and carry the kinds of merchandise that the folks who came to the mill and the blacksmith shop would buy. Such is the story of the origin of towns and cities.

Another type of early power, although not water power as the title of this chapter suggests, was "horsepower." This is the origin of the term used today in measuring the power of all kinds of engines. There were different methods used to utilize horsepower. The sorghum mill method which caused the horse to travel in a circle, while a system of cogwheels increased the speed to the operating shaft. Another method was the treadmill. This sort of power was made possible by the stepping of the animals on a moving platform which was made to move because it was an incline which was a part of a large circular wheel or endless belt. The animal "walked all day but went nowhere." This was the old-time treadmill. Often yokes of oxen furnished the power instead of horses. Many of the early inland cotton gins were operated with this kind of power.

John Janes operated a horsepower grist mill on Janes creek before 1822. A flour mill was in operation on the Russell place about 1830, and Elijah Dalton and others operated a cotton gin at Warm Springs as late as 1880, on the treadmill plan. Many other horsepower mills were located in various places. All the first threshing machines which travelled over the country from farm to farm threshing the grain were horsepower, before the steam traction engine came into use in this section. The first steam engines to be used in this county were the stationary type. A firebox of stone or brick was built and the boiler placed upon it. Some of the first industrial casualties of the country were victims of early steam boiler explosions.

GENERAL HISTORY

EARLY CHURCHES OF THE COUNTY

Much has been said in the chapters dealing with the separate communities of the county concerning the early preachers. In relating the activities of these early men of God we have also been obliged to mention the places in which they carried on their work. But in doing this we do not feel that we have given the locations of the first churches enough prominence. In this article we will touch briefly upon this subject, and, of course, in doing so there will be some repetition of a portion of information already recorded in the book elsewhere.

As has been stated before, the old church which was established at the old Fourche de Thomas, or Columbia settlement, known as "Salem Church," was the first Baptist church in the state. It was established in 1818.

The first Methodist church in the county was built by William Spikes on Tennessee creek a short distance southwest of the present-day Ingram postoffice and called Mount Pisgah. The first building was of rough, unhewed poles and had a rock chimney at the end of the building. It is supposed to have been built around 1830. About ten years later Mr. Spikes built a large hewed log house close to the site of the first one and this building was used for many years as both a church and school. The third Mount Pisgah was built about 1885, just west of the present-day Spikes' cemetery. Jesse Spikes donated the site, James Hurn made the boards to cover the house, and a majority of the citizens of the neighborhood contributed time or money in the job of building it.

The old Methodist church at Siloam was built about 1840. A special article about this old church appears in this book, so we refer you to this article for further information regarding this place.

Not far from the same year, the Glaze Creek Church of Christ was established. A special article about this old church also appears elsewhere in this book.

Information is meager regarding the establishment of many other early churches in the county. Various churches and congregations have laid claim to being the first in the county or first in their respective neighborhood, but it is often very difficult for the historian who desires to secure as nearly accurate information as possible to decide which is actually correct.

The Mount Pleasant church at Pitman is reputed to have been established about 1825. There had been people living in this community around twenty years at that time, so it is likely that this is true. This was and still is a Missionary Baptist church.

Another early church of the county was the Cherokee Bay church. This old church was described in the early records as being a "United Baptist Church of Christ." Eld. Sherrod Winningham was ordained to preach for this church, June 7, 1834. There is a division of opinion as to just where the old church was actually located. It is likely that it was near the town of Old Reyno. There was an old "Round Track" church there in later years which may have been the old Cherokee Bay church.

During the early days there was an old church at the Hite cemetery. The old building standing in the cemetery at present is built from the logs of this old church, which was also used as a school. There was an early church in that section known as Union church. It was sponsored by Daniel Duckworth who lived just north of the present site of the Mississippi River Fuel Corporation pumping station. This church later became known as the "Yellow Hall." This church was established sometime about 1835 or 1840. although it may not have owned a building for some years.

Henry Slavens, who was a delegate to the Constitutional Convention from Randolph County in 1836, was ordained to preach at this church by Elders Henry McElmurry and Winningham, December 4, 1836.

The story of the first church activities in the Palestine-Ingram community is told in a special article. This community was one of the early strongholds of the early Church of Christ, as is told in that article. There was probably an organized congregation meeting at the homes in that community as early as 1825.

The old Antioch Baptist church which is located between Ingram and Hamil was organized sometime about 1850. The early records show that Samuel Reed was ordained to preach here May 20, 1859, by the church. There is no more known of this church until it was reorganized in 1873. On August 30 of that year a deed was made to the church by Surridge and Fisher for the property.

Not far from this place was another old church. On April 11, 1868, William F. Roach deeded the tract of land at what is now the Roach cemetery to the United Baptist church.

As is recorded elsewhere in this book, one of the first churches in the northeastern part of the county was built by Eld. Zera Allen of the Church of Christ, to be used both as a church and school. This building was used for many years. It stood on land located in section ten, township twenty-one, two east, and was deeded to the old Allen School district number two by Zera and Emaline Allen, April 6, 1871. Zera Allen is the grandfather of W. R. Allen of Supply at present.

Another old Church of Christ is the Hubble Creek church in the southwestern part of the county. Andrew Pace deeded the land for a church, September 1, 1868. It had been a more or less active church since 1852, the year it was first established. This and the Noland church are made up of the same families. John M. Lemmons is said to have been the first preacher here.

There is also an old Catholic church in this community, the only one in the county outside of Pocahontas and Engleberg. It was established sometime in the eighties and was built by the German families which settled here about the same time of the settlement at Engleberg.

The Catholic church at Engleberg was established about this same period. Our information is that Isaac DeBow and Tony Weisenbach were among the persons who were influential in the establishment of the church.

The churches at Ravenden Springs have been mentioned in the article about the village. There was a Methodist church organized at Walnut Hill before the former town came into existence. James Janes deeded land to this church in December, 1875.

Robert Marlin deeded the ground where the present-day Pentecostal church is located in the Blackwell community to the Methodist church November 23, 1875. It was then called Mount Vernon.

Thomas S. Simington deeded the land where the Attica Methodist church stands to that church, March 9, 1881. George W. Hibbard deeded the land where the Baptist church, known as Oak Grove, to that church January 16, 1882.

The present Church of Christ at Brakebill, two miles west of Middlebrook, was built here in 1930, but the original Brakebill church was organized about 1875, about a mile and one-half southwest of the present site. The first meeting place was in the old log house near the spring at the schoolhouse. The first members were the late Uncle Johnny Wilson, Uncle Billy Patton and others.

Another old church site of the county is Bethany, on Janes creek, above Ravenden Springs. Our information is that the first church here was a Missionary Baptist church, built in the seventies. After several years they moved to Yadkin, a few miles up the creek, and the Church of Christ built a building near this site, which is in use today by the latter church. The English, Higginbotham, Rogers, Kellett, Marriott, James, Davis, Bailey and other families reside in this community, and members of these families are identified with both churches.

The Shiloh Baptist church, five miles northwest of Pocahontas, was organized about 1875 by Rev. J. R. Pratt and others and is in a community which was settled around 1830. There is a likelihood that there was a church in this community many years before this church was organized. Early records show that the Shiloh, Antioch and Cherokee Bay churches joined the Bethel Association in 1857. So this tends to prove that there were earlier churches of these names before the present ones were built.

There are several "lost" congregations, or old churches, their location of which is not known. We know that there was a "Hurn's Chapel," an "Indian Lake" and a "Hopewell" church in Randolph County in the early days. The Indian Lake is supposed to be the old Cherokee Bay church. This is not definitely known. The records show that Isom Amos was ordained to preach at Hopewell in 1858. There are several others not known to the author which are known locally. We regret that we do not know the names of each dead and existing church that has ever been in the county.

There was a Janes Creek Church of Christ in existence in 1840. The records show that Eld. Samuel H. McCullah preached here and also Daniel Rose. Eld. McCullah married Sarah Alcorn in 1840. There is an entry on the records of December 4, 1842, where McCullah asked the church "on Fourche de Mas" for permission to preach at that church. Two of the elders of that church were W. Kellett and B. States.

There was a "County Line Baptist Church of Christ" somewhere in Randolph County before the Civil War. Levi Roberts, J. H. Leftchurch and William Martin were members. There is a possibility that this church may have been on the Sharp County line, somewhere along the western side of Randolph. On September 29, 1850, William Jones was ordained to preach at Concord church in Randolph County. The exact location of this church is not known.

There is supposed to have been a Spring River Baptist church at Old Jackson during the existence of the town, and possibly for several years afterward.

The author is well aware that there are other early churches which we have missed in this chapter. Possibly most of them are named here or in the stories of the towns or communities, but the reader must bear in mind that we have intended to name only those churches which have been established around fifty years or more. And in seeking information that is from one hundred down to fifty years old is no easy task.

But since writing the above we note that we have overlooked the old church at Birdell. Once known as Old Union, on the west side of Elevenpoint, it was one of the first churches built by the Christian people of the county. The Dunn, Hufstedler, Campbell, Lemmons, Perrin and other families have long been identified with this church.

Another old church of the county is the Baptist church at Sharum. This is an old community of the Black River bottom section of the county and the church has been in existence since before the War Between the States. The Dean, Luttrell, Brooks, Rogers and others, including the Shoffit and Staten families, have long been identified with this church and community. There are other congregations of the Methodist and Christian churches in this section which have been established many years.

GENERAL HISTORY

The history of churches and schools is a part of the story of any community. As stated above, some of the churches are mentioned only in the story of the community. The churches at Maynard and some other places is handled this way. The story of the churches of Pocahontas are like those of other places, more or less lost to the past. It is evident that there were established congregations of at least three or four of the predominating faiths in Pocahontas as early as 1840. There is no record of certain sites or activities until the town was around forty years of age.

Any person who knows the citizenry of Randolph County from the early days until the present time knows that there was religious activity here as soon as the community took form.

Tradition tells us that there was an old log Methodist church near the Dr. Hamil residence before the Civil War. This is probably true, as it is a fact that the old original town (starting with Bettis Bluff) was in that locality. The records show that Walter Lyles sold the Methodist church a site near the present building in 1853. A building is said to have been erected here but later moved across the street south of the present site. Later it was again moved back to the original place. The church at present occupies a nice brick building, built about 1922.

The Catholic church in Pocahontas had its origin through the efforts of Father J. P. O'Kean. This mission is said to have been opened by Bishop Edward Fitzgerald in 1868. The present church is located on ground donated by the Bishop. It was built in 1869 by James Hagan. Father O'Kean soon built up a thriving congregation. After he moved to Little Rock in 1871 the church saw a decline until 1880. At this time a large number of Catholic families emigrated from central Europe to Pocahontas and vicinity and this gave the church a strong boost. They have a nice stone building in Pocahontas at this time. Since 1880 the church has also maintained a school. The local church is known as St. Paul's Catholic Church.

A Catholic church was also established at Engleberg, a few miles northeast of Pocahontas, soon after the coming of the families from Germany. It is made up of members of some of the same families as those in the Pocahontas church. It is known as St. John's Catholic Church.

Information in regards to the first churches in Pocahontas is limited. The present Missionary Baptist church building was built about 1903. A large part of its membership is made up of the original families represented in the old Shiloh church, which we have already named. After the town began to grow, the close proximity of the Shiloh church caused many to start going to church at Pocahontas which had previously attended at Shiloh. In fact, we find that I. W. Standiford, who deeded the land for the Shiloh church, was one of the charter members of the Pocahontas church in 1902.

The church at present is housed in a medium size brick and wood building, but plans are being made to build a larger building in the near future. The Southern Baptist College, now located in the former community building on the Dalton road, is under the management of the local church. It was opened to the public in 1943. Rev. H. E. Williams is president of the college.

The Church of Christ in Pocahontas has been in existence since about 1885. If there was an early building, we have no records of such. Strong congregations of this church have existed near Birdell and at Palestine and Glaze Creek since about 1825, and at other places in the county for shorter lengths of time. The first meetings of the church were held in the courthouse and in an old building which formerly belonged to the Episcopal congregation. The present building, a nice brick building, was erected in 1913 and 1914. The location at that time was ideal for convenience, but since the city has grown the site is now almost "downtown" and there is a probability that in the near future a new building will be built farther out, away from the congested district.

At present the following Church of Christ ministers live in Pocahontas: Elders A. B. Shaver and Carroll C. Trent. The Baptist ministers are Rev. H. E. Williams and Rev. Harry Hunt. The Methodist minister is Rev. Hubert Pearce. The Catholic priest who has been with the local church died June 26, 1946, (the week this was written). He was Father Edward J. Yeager. His successor has not been announced.

The Pentecostal church has a nice stone building in the northwest part of the city which was built about 1937. Another church of this faith, a small frame building, is located in the southwestern part of the city.

The African Methodist church for the colored people has a frame building in the south part of town also. They have had a congregation and church building many years.

The Baptist church named above in this article is a Missionary Baptist church. The Freewill Baptists also have a nice sandstone building in the city. It was built about 1939. Eld. G. W. Million, Will S. White and others were sponsors of this church. Eld. Ralph Staten is the present minister, and the church has one of the largest memberships in the city.

Randolph County is well supplied with churches. The faiths listed above are the ones at this time which are represented in the county, in so far as meeting places are concerned. There are some members of certain churches in the county who do not maintain meeting places. Among these are the Presbyterians, Latter Day Saints, Seventh Day Adventists, etc.

There is very little antagonism between the different religious bodies in the county. They all get along pretty well. In fact, as time goes on, there is a trend toward unity in the basic principles of Christ's teachings.

MRS. ELIZA HOGAN'S SCHOOL
At the old Masonic Hall in Pocahontas about 1885

SOME OF RANDOLPH COUNTY'S TEACHERS IN THE 1880's
*Prof. and Mrs. John Hogan, center front row;
Kate Hogan, right end, front.*

GENERAL HISTORY

EARLY SCHOOLS AND EDUCATORS OF THE COUNTY

Along with the other information connected with the history of the various communities of the county has been mentioned the names of several of the leading educators of Randolph County. But due to the important part played by these people in the pioneer days, we feel that a more detailed article should be included concerning those who first dispensed the "three R's" within the present confines of our county.

Just who the first teacher was is not definitely known. Caleb Lindsey, who lived in the old Fourche de Thomas community before 1820, is reputed to have taught the first school in the state, in a cave near the present site of Ravenden Springs. If this story is accepted, this would make him our county's first educator.

There was very little educational activity in this section before the Civil War. Scattered communities had a few weeks of "subscription" school each year. This school was usually taught by the neighboring preacher.

B. J. Wiley, the first clerk of the county and the third county judge, is said to have been a teacher during the early thirties. He visited the established communities and agreed to teach for a price, which was usually paid in products of the farm and furs. Part of the price was the charge made by the family who boarded Mr. Wiley while he was living in the community. This was true of most of the first teachers.

Another early teacher was C. C. Elder, who was clerk of the county during the wartime sixties. Rev. Larkin Johnston was also a teacher during this period. He was the first tax assessor of the county, serving from 1862 to 1868. There were several more teachers in the county by this time and the author regrets that we do not have a more complete list.

During the period from the close of the War Between the States and 1880 conditions improved wonderfully in education. School districts were being laid out, houses built, and a general desire to have their children secure at least an elementary education was abroad in the land.

Most of the first houses built were to be used both as a school and "meeting house." This kind of building served the communities many years, and even unto this day many of the rural schoolhouses are used in this manner. Usually some "well fixed" man in the community would build a house and give it to the community. One such building was the old Allen schoolhouse which was built near Supply in Little Black township by Eld. Zera Allen. Desiring that the folks have a place to attend church and a place for the children to go to school, Eld. Allen, who was a Church of Christ minister, built this house and then donated it to the old District Number Three.

The old New Hope church and school, located on Mud creek, was another early school and church. The late Thomas D. Mock once told the author of teaching here in 1874. The house was an old one at that time.

Dr. Byrd built the first schoolhouse at Warm Springs. C. C. Elder, referred to above, was one of the first teachers here, followed by Mrs. Surridge and others.

At this place also taught Prof. and Mrs. Tilford and Prof. and Mrs. Hogan, possibly the best known teachers which have ever lived in Randolph County. Many citizens, past middle age, owe their education to these two couples who were in their prime from 1880 to around 1906.

Eli Abbott, early resident of Maynard, although uneducated himself, saw the need for a school of higher learning. To secure this, he built the school which was known as "Abbott's Institute." For many years it was attended by young folks from a wide radius. Some of the first teachers here are still living.

GENERAL HISTORY

It would be an interesting list indeed if it were possible to produce one which listed all the teachers of the county for the first fifty years of its existence. This is impossible. The meager list named above covers about all the known ones for this period. The period from 1860 until 1910 produced many fine educators for Randolph County. The list is too long to name all, but below we have a partial list of these. If there are those whose names should have been listed are not found herein, we wish to assure the reader that they were not intentionally omitted.

Here are the names of about forty of those which we can think of who belong to this list: W. T. Bispham, Prof. and Mrs. Tilford, Prof. Hogan and Mrs. Hogan, W. T. Stubblefield, S. A. Eaton, S. L. Johnston, William Henry Johnston, C. James Dalton, Ben F. Spikes, L. D. Hurn, Mrs. Surridge, J. L. Williford, W. E. Hibbard, J. T. Lomax, J. H. Skaggs, Martha Redwine Johnston, J. A. Ryburn, Nannie Wisner, C. E. Witt, Lula Witt, Tom W. Campbell, James Campbell, Kate Skinner, Henry Ator, H. M. Bishop, C. D. Bishop, J. Q. Pond, J. S. Anderson, Lucy Hill, Chas. H. Carter, John L. Fry, J. A. Galbraith, Sol M. White, Katie Jones White, Kate Hogan, James Wheat, Mrs. Lilly Roberts, Anna Jones, and Tell Thompson.

This does not take into consideration the long list of later teachers who have spent long years in the job of educating our boys and girls.

In this list we would find the names of Edgar Hulen, Birdie Hulen, John Hogan, Eugene Thompson, R. J. M. Wyatt, Hutch Phipps, Alma and Moina Spikes, Bertha Mock, Rufus A. Mock, Charles A. Dixon, Jess Redwine, Zadie L. Smith, Gertie Mock, Ed. Buxton, Mara and Myrtle Stubblefield, Minerva Simington, Myrt Bennett, Lucy Thomas, Virginia Henderson, Jeff Lawhon, Lawrence Stubblefield, Rufe Baker, Lindsey Miller, Dora King Spikes, Elva Magruder, Mayme Thomas and countless others who have taught in the schools of Randolph County during recent years.

Uncle Bert Grissom built a schoolhouse for the children in the community of western Siloam and eastern Warm Springs township about the close of the Civil War.

Other old schoolhouses of the period before the Civil War and the period just following, before the county was cut up into districts, were at Old Reyno, one near Yadkin, one just west of Birdell, one on Wells creek, and one in the vicinity of the McIlroy crossing on Elevenpoint River. There were others of which we do not know the location.

Of the educators who have lived in Randolph County, one of the best known was Rufus A. Mock, who was active in the educational field of the county from around 1910 until his death in 1934. For several years he was a teacher in different schools of the county, but later became the first county school superintendent. It was in this capacity that he did his most valuable service.

During this service he advocated consolidation, improvement of school buildings, bus transportation, school fairs, etc. In some of these he was "ahead of the times." He saw farther down the years than many. For this he met opposition and criticism. The system was made a political issue and the schools possibly suffered from the effects for a number of years.

However, as time passed the things advocated by Rufus Mock have been adopted and the wisdom of his ideas has been proven.

In justice to Rufus A. Mock, it must be said that if he were living today he would see most of the changes he advocated in effect, and many who strongly opposed his recommendations well pleased with the change.

There are seventy-one school districts in the county at the present time. The number of pupils of school age in the districts run from less than ten to a few over seven hundred in the Pocahontas district. Educational conditions in the county are gradually improving. But the good done by the early teacher must not be discounted. They built the foundation upon which we stand today, and did so under a lot more unfavorable conditions than we can realize. All honor to their memory!

RANDOLPH COUNTY'S ONLY GOVERNOR

Thomas Stephenson Drew

Thomas Stephenson Drew, the fourth Governor of the state of Arkansas, was a resident of Randolph County. He is the only governor the county has had. He was born near Lebanon, Wilson County, Tennessee, August 25, 1802. He was the son of Newton Drew who came to Tennessee from Southampton County, Virginia, in 1797.

Governor Drew first settled in Arkansas in Clark County in 1821. Here he served one term as county clerk, but did not ask for a second term. This was in 1823 to 1825.

After leaving the office of clerk of Clark County he embarked upon the business of an itinerant peddler. While doing this he made trips all over Arkansas Territory. While on one of these trips, which he made on horseback, he visited Pocahontas, which was then a small trading post and owned by Ransom Sutherland Bettis. Here he met Bettis' daughter, Cinderella, and they were married. The Bettis family was one of the first families of Randolph County, coming here from North Carolina.

After Thomas Drew married Cinderella Bettis her father gave her as her dowry eight hundred acres of land in Cherokee Bay. Here he and his bride moved and made their home for several years. He was elected to the office of county judge of Lawrence County, and served from 1832 to 1835, while residing at his plantation home, which was on the site of the present town of Biggers. The county seat of Lawrence County was at Old Jackson at that time.

THOMAS STEPHENSON DREW
Fourth governor of Arkansas. Elected from Randolph County.

The Territorial Legislature of 1835 cut off Randolph County from Lawrence County in October of that year. In 1836 a Constitutional Convention was called to meet in Little Rock, in January, to draw up a state constitution. Thomas S. Drew and Henry Slavens, both of Cherokee Bay in Randolph County, were chosen as two of the delegates from Lawrence and Randolph counties. Thus Thomas Drew helped write our first state constitution.

After this Drew lived the life of a planter on his farm and was not identified with public life until 1844 when the state

Democratic Convention nominated him for Governor. He was elected by a large majority over the Whig candidate. He served this term, which was for four years at that time, and did not announce for a second term. Nevertheless, he was elected for a second term without opposition in the state. A few days after the election, on November 10, 1848, Drew surprised his friends and constituents by announcing that he would not serve a second term.

While still in office, he appeared within the Senate chamber and read a letter announcing that he was resigning the office. The letter, in part, is as follows: "The overwhelming desire of friends, who believed they could do much, and no doubt intended to move in the matter, pledged me that every exertion would be made to raise my salary before the second term began, to a point sufficient at least to pay my expenses with my family at the seat of government, which the constitution of the state makes it imperative that the Executive shall reside. The failure to do this, or any attempt by those who had previously manifested so much interest in regard to this subject, placed me at once where I found that the time had elapsed in which it was possible to effect anything of the kind for my relief, under the prohibitions of the Constitution. The ceremonies of the inauguration were but just over when the determination was taken to resign, which I now do so, from the office of Governor of the State of Arkansas." So thus, only a few days over a month of his second term gone, Thomas Drew quit the office of Governor of Arkansas because the salary at that time was insufficient to "at least pay the expenses of the family" of the Chief Executive of the state.

Richard C. Byrd became acting Governor.

Being governor was not all the noteworthy things which Thomas S. Drew did during his lifetime. Besides being also county clerk of Clark County, county judge of Lawrence County and a member of the 1836 constitutional convention, he also has the distinction of being one of the founders of the city of Pocahontas. He and his father-in-law, Bettis, owned the land where the town is now located. As is recorded in another chapter of this book, Drew donated several parcels of land to the town. He also appeared in court at the 1837 term and acknowledged the execution of a bond to the county treasurer in the amount of $3,000.00, which was a donation

Monument at grave of Governor Drew in Masonic Cemetery in Pocahontas.

toward the building of a courthouse for Randolph County, "provided the building was located in Pocahontas." Bettis did likewise in the amount of one thousand dollars. March

17, 1841, Drew recorded in the deed record of Randolph County his "Drew's Addition" to the town of Pocahontas.

Just when the Drew family left the plantation home in Cherokee Bay is not known. It is supposed that they moved away when he was elected Governor. It appears that during the years that he was in Little Rock that he suffered severe financial losses. The records show that Drew and his wife "deeded" considerable real estate and several slaves to his mother-in-law, Mary Bettis, on June 1, 1850, "For money borrowed April 1, 1846, in the amount of $4,100.00." Mrs. Bettis lived in Desha County, Arkansas, at that time. Ransom S. Bettis died about 1841 or early 1842. Drew was appointed as his administrator April 13, 1842.

Mrs. Drew's mother died at Lake Providence, Louisiana, June 23, 1852. Mrs. Drew inherited considerable property from her mother at that time. But it seems that the family had become so deeply in debt that they never recovered from the effects.

On October 23, 1849, a large assembly of men from many states of the Union met at Memphis for the first meeting of the proposed Memphis Railroad. This was a proposed railroad from San Diego, California, on the Pacific coast to end at Memphis. Thomas S. Drew was the representative from Arkansas, being one of the vice-presidents elected at the convention. Others from Arkansas were in attendance.

April 7, 1853, Thomas S. Drew was appointed by the President of the United States to the office of superintendent of Indian affairs for the Southern Division, with an office at Van Buren. He was not an applicant for the place. No record can be found where he ever took over the office. It is doubtful that he did, since the local records show various activities of his in Randolph County all along during this period.

In the election of 1858, Drew was a candidate for Congress from the Second Congressional District on the Independent ticket. Albert Rust was the Democratic candidate. Rust won the election by a large majority. Just why Drew ran as an Independent is not known. It is possible that he had lost his popularity and failed to be chosen as the regular democratic candidate and ran as an Independent, hoping to gain his former support.

One noteworthy act of Governor Drew while in that office was his proclamation which set aside Thursday, December 9, 1847, as a day of Thanksgiving. This was the first Thanksgiving ever observed in Arkansas. Although the day had been observed in New England for many years, it had not been generally observed in the South prior to this time.

After 1858 Drew seems to have ceased to take a very active part in public affairs. His name is mentioned locally during this period, mostly by deed records, where he and his wife disposed of some of their holdings.

He was employed in the general store of Green R. Jones in Pocahontas as bookkeeper at a salary of $200 per month in 1866. Soon after this he resigned and opened an office as attorney. He is said to have had a very good legal mind. A portion of this salary as bookkeeper was credited to Drew's account at the Jones store. He seems to have been badly in debt at this time. When William H. Jarrett came to Pocahontas from Columbia in 1866, he also got a job in Jones' store. After Drew resigned, Jones and Drew made an agreement that Jarrett was to board with the Drew family for a price of twenty-five dollars per month, this amount to be taken off Jarrett's salary and applied on Drew's account at the store. Jarrett remained with the family four years.

Thomas S. Drew and Cinderella Bettis Drew had five children living at that time. Their names were Joe, James and Ransom, boys, and Emma and Sadie, the girls. The girls both married Federal officers, although the family was sympathetic toward the cause of the Confederacy. Evidently this did not meet the approval of the neighbors who were bitter toward the North. A letter written at the time of the marriage of Emma to the northern army officer from some young lady residing in Pocahontas to a friend elsewhere stated: "You asked about Emma Drew's marriage to the Yankee; well, that is about all you could expect of her," was the belittling reply. We understand that this letter is in the possession of Mrs. H. M. Jacoway of Little Rock at this time.

Both the Drew girls were musicians.

Nothing is known of the Drew family after 1870. Some writers have stated that they moved to Texas "soon after the close of the war." This is incorrect, as shown above. It is likely that they did remove to that state about 1871 or 1872. Thomas Drew died there at Lipan, Hood County, Texas, in 1879. Here his remains lay in an unmarked grave until 1923, when a number of interested Randolph County citizens asked W. A. Jackson, who was state senator from this district at that time, to ask the Legislature to appropriate one thousand dollars to be used to move the remains of Governor Drew from Texas for re-interment in the Masonic cemetery in Pocahontas.

This was done and a committee composed of Senator Jackson, R. N. Hamil and Judge J. W. Meeks was appointed to go to Texas for this purpose. The ashes of Arkansas' third governor was deposited with fitting ceremonies in the cemetery named above on Decoration day, May 30, 1923. One of the largest crowds ever assembled in Pocahontas up to that time attended the ceremony.

Thus comes to a close the story of Randolph County's only citizen who up to the present has occupied the office of Governor of Arkansas.

An appropriate marble shaft stands on the spot of the last resting place of this noted man, who was not only a governor of a great state, but one of the first citizens of Cherokee Bay, one of the first county officials of Lawrence and Clark counties, one of the founders of the city of Pocahontas, and the only man who ever resigned as governor of the state because the salary was too low to support his family.

Quoting the words of the late William Jarrett who, as stated above, lived in the Drew home four years, "Thomas Drew was small in stature, had a kindly, friendly smile, and was one of the gentlest, most patient men you ever saw."

POCAHONTAS' THREE COURTHOUSES

The first courthouse which was built in what is now Randolph County was, as is well known, at Davidsonville. Here the seat of justice remained until 1829, when it was moved to Jackson.

At Jackson was the site of the second courthouse in Randolph County. Both these were courthouses to serve old Lawrence County, of which Randolph was a part. In 1835, when Randolph County was cut off from Lawrence, the county seat of Lawrence County was moved to Smithville. This left Randolph without a county seat. Just why Jackson was not considered as the county seat of the new county is not known.

It can be said of the pioneer who chose the sites for the early towns that his judgment was usually good when it came to picking out places for the county seat. While Lawrence County was not so fortunate, Randolph has the distinction of having had only one county seat, although it possesses the site of three.

As is known, the site of Pocahontas was known as Bettis Bluff at the time Randolph County was formed. Ransom S. Bettis, the father-in-law of Thomas S. Drew, lived on the site and there was a small trading center here.

GENERAL HISTORY

As is related in the Fourche de Thomas article, the decision as to what place would be the county seat was left to a vote of the people.

Old Columbia, or Fourche de Thomas, was a strong contender for the place, and some say that if it had not been for the fact that Pocahontas was located on a navigable stream, which was a very important advantage at that time, Columbia would have won.

But the fact is, the chief reason Pocahontas won in the election was due to the fact that Bettis and Drew owned the site of the town of Pocahontas and when the election was advertised they also advertised a big free barbecue and picnic to be held at Pocahontas on that date, and a majority of the voters of the county attended. Eats were plentiful and liquor flowed freely. After partaking of the eats and drinking the free liquor of the sponsors, the crowd, so we are told, felt much invigorated and also kindly toward Drew and Bettis and were easily persuaded to vote for Pocahontas.

Anyway, Pocahontas won, and the county seat has remained here ever since. The first major job for the new county and town was the building of a courthouse, the story of which follows. In fact the following account gives you the story of the building of the three courthouses which the county has had since the county was formed in 1835.

The first courthouse was built between 1837 and 1839. It was a two-story building forty feet square. Thomas O. Marr was the contractor and he received twenty-four hundred dollars for the job. Daniel Lieb, Thomas Holderby, John R. Vance, James Rowland and Ransom Bettis were securities to the contract which Marr gave to the building committee which was appointed to supervise the building. This contract was signed April 21, 1838. A. W. McKinney and E. D. Pitman were witnesses to the deal. Marr was to be paid eight hundred dollars within six months, "or sooner if collected,"

RANDOLPH COUNTY'S SECOND COURTHOUSE
Now called the "Old Courthouse"

RANDOLPH COUNTY'S PRESENT COURTHOUSE
A modern fireproof building, erected in 1940

and sixteen hundred dollars within twelve months, "or sooner if collected."

Daniel Lieb, Joseph Spikes, Fielding Stubblefield and John R. Vance were appointed as commissioners "to superintend buildings, receive donations, etc."

July 27, 1837, Thomas S. Drew donated to the commissioners the following lands in the town of Pocahontas, to be used by said commissioners for the purpose of building a courthouse and other public buildings:

"All of blocks 18, 19, 26, 27, 28, 29, 30, 31, 35, 36, 37, 38, 39, 42, 43, and the east part of lot one in blocks 44, and 45, lot 6 in block 45. Lots 35 and 36 in block 34, and part of lots 3 and 4 in block 17. North part of lot 4 in block 15, and all of block 20 and lot 1 in block 21 and lot 1 in block 22. Lot no. 4 in block 34. Lot 2 in block 43, together with the triangular fractions in the northwest and northeast corners of the west half of the southwest quarter of the northwest quarter of section 27, township 19, north range, one east, and the north fractional part of the public square which is marked block number 32. Also lot no. 32 in block 44, all lying east of Broadway street in the town of Pocahontas."

The deed to the commissioners was signed by Thomas S. Drew and his wife, Cinderella Drew, and witnessed by Casper Schmick, who was a justice of the peace, and Ransom S. Bettis, Drew's father-in-law.

This property was transferred to James S. Conway, who was Governor of Arkansas at that time, by the commissioners, to become public owned property. The courthouse built on this land stood until about 1870, when it collapsed due to structural weakness. It had become unsafe for occupancy, and as early as 1868 a new courthouse had been talked about.

THE SECOND COURTHOUSE

The second courthouse in Pocahontas is the building in the public square and which is now known as the "old courthouse." It was used during the recent war as an entertainment center for the boys in service located at the local airbase. It now houses the county library, the city officials' office and the upstairs is still used for entertainment purposes.

This building was completed early in 1875. After the first old courthouse was declared unsafe for occupancy, quarters were rented for use as a courthouse. On April 15, 1872, the court ordered the clerk's office to be moved to the lower floor of the county jail. Also, the lower part of the jail was to be used as a place to hold county and probate court "until further notice." June 8, 1874, M. D. Baber, as commissioner of public buildings, rented the store building of J. P. Black & Co. for use as a courthouse. The building is described as "containing five rooms, a shed and cistern attached, also containing a stove and pipe." The rent was fifty dollars per month, to be paid in county warrants, or "if paid in greenback, fifty cents on the dollar would be accepted as full payment." This contract was to run until April, 1875. Just when the old house was abandoned as a courthouse is not known, but on October 18, 1865, the St. Charles Hotel was rented as a courthouse. From this it appears that the offices were moved around considerable between the time the old house was condemned and the new one was built. The Black store is supposed to have been located about where the present Pocahontas postoffice building stands.

The first steps taken toward building the second courthouse appears to have been on May 19, 1869, when Thomas L. Martin, who was then commissioner of public buildings, was ordered by the court to advertise for bids for the construction of the building. For some reason, no contract was awarded to anyone until April 15, 1872, when the commissioner at that time, one Josiah Fisher, awarded the contract for the construction of a courthouse to John A. McKay of Helena. The contract price was $39,865.00, to be paid in payments as the construction progressed, the work to be completed by April 1, 1873. McKay was to accept the old building as a $1,000 payment.

The contractor was unsatisfactory. A lot of delay and disagreements came about. The commissioner paid McKay more money than he was supposed to have done and yet the building was far from being finished when the expiration date came, April 1, 1873. Three men were appointed as building supervisors, and they in turn appointed a new commissioner in the place of Josiah Fisher. The supervisors were John P. Black, Green R. Jones and Jacob Hufstedler. They appointed Thomas Simington as commissioner and ordered him to advertise in the *Randolph Republican* newspaper for somebody to take the job of finishing the job which McKay had fallen down on. There seems to have been a compromise effected between the commissioners and McKay wherein he did go ahead and finish the building, although under an amended contract.

This did not work out very satisfactory, either, and after several disputes with McKay over the matter of settlement, in January, 1875, court proceedings were started to take the newly constructed building out of the hands of McKay, who had forbid the county to take possession until his claims had been paid in full. Evidently the county won out in the suit, as we find that on April 7, 1875, the county and circuit clerk (There was only one clerk's office at that time) had been ordered by the county judge to oversee the moving of all offices into the new building.

On April the nineteenth of the same year County Judge Isham Russell and the various justices of the peace of the county met and appropriated funds to be used in purchasing furniture and fixtures for the new courthouse.

In June after this the law firm of Baber and Henderson was employed by the county to go to Helena and represent the county in a suit in court in which McKay was still attempting to collect on his claims. The matter was settled by a compromise, but it appears that neither the county nor the contractor was satisfied with the deal. Such is the story of the building of the second courthouse of Randolph County, which stands today in the center of the "square," just north of the present courthouse.

THE THIRD COURTHOUSE

After sixty years of service to the county the building described above was thought by many to be out of date and no longer satisfactory as a courthouse. Those favoring the erection of a new building arranged for an election to be held in the county to determine whether the majority of taxpayers wanted a new building. The election was held and a majority was in favor of the move. Joe S. Decker, the county judge at that time—1940—appointed a group of men to make up an advisory board, which would assist him in the preliminaries of getting the project under way. The board was made up of the following: J. B. Weaver, Oscar Prince, Lantie Martin, A. J. Cooper, R. E. Sallee, George Promberger, Sr., F. W. Cox and Harry Hite.

The contract for the construction of the new building was awarded to E. V. Bird Construction Co.

Judge Decker appointed five former county judges as building commissioners. They were Ben A. Brown, G. W. Million, Joe Snodgrass, Dee Mock and C. H. Brooks. Eugene John Stern was the architect.

The contract price for the erection of the courthouse was $68,763.50. The contract price for the erection of the cobblestone jail was awarded to Henry Dust, of Pocahontas, for the sum of $2,547.00.

GENERAL HISTORY

Ninety-two thousand dollars worth of bonds were sold to finance the whole project. A three-story fireproof building was erected which is a credit to the county. This building is one of the finest and most substantial county courthouses in the state. Such is the condensed history of the building of Randolph County's three courthouses.

In the one hundred and a few years of this county's existence, since the first settler came, court has been held at five different places in the county.

LIFE IN RANDOLPH COUNTY PRIOR TO THE CIVIL WAR

Living conditions and customs among the people who first came here and those who lived here during the first three quarters of a century remained about the same. Modern conveniences and the mode of living was about the same for the family who saw the clouds of the War of Secession gather and the family which first stopped besides the old Southwest Trail. Up until this time no railroad had reached our section. No telephone or telegraph line has come to us, in fact the telephone was as yet unknown. Our only connection with the outside world was by contact with the small stream of immigrants who came trickling into our county from the east and by the few steamboats which braved the snags and sandbars of our uncharted rivers. As we know, the first mail came overland by horseback rider from St. Louis. The first mail route ran the old Military road from St. Louis via. St. Genevieve, Pitman, Davidsonville and Arkansas Post to Monroe, Louisiana, once a month. High water, bad roads, bad weather, etc., made the trips hazardous and uncertain. We of today who become impatient if the mail happens to be thirty minutes late cannot grasp the contrasts along this line of one hundred years ago.

Life in the home was a very simple procedure, yet carried with it long hours of arduous toil and handicaps. The first homes were usually one-room log cabins; sometimes a "lean-to" side room made of clapboards, provided an extra room used as a kitchen. A huge stone or "stick and dirt" chimney furnished the heat for both the comfort of the family and for cooking. Many of the first log homes were eighteen to twenty feet square and contained everything the family owned in the way of household furnishings. Usually the back of the room was occupied by two or three bedsteads, generally home-made. In the middle of the room or near the one window was the "stand-table" on which was found the lamp of whatever method of lighting that was used— grease lamp, candles, or in later years the first kerosene burners. High upon the back or side wall were usually found huge "enlarged" pictures of grandfather, grandmother or some other older member of the family, in the years after the coming of the first photographs. Above the fireplace was the "mantleboard, upon which was located the clock and other necessary articles that lasted best out of the reach of the smaller children. Above this, or over the door, were placed two forks, whittled from a small tree, upon which was placed the trusty family rifle. On one side of the fireplace usually hung the "shot pouch and powder horn." On the other side father or grandfather usually had hung a few "hands" of choice large leaves of tobacco to "cure" for immediate use. Back under the bed or in a remote corner was found the family trunk, which held as its precious contents the entire family wardrobe, plus a few heirlooms, odd keepsakes, etc. In one corner, or sometimes along one wall as a permanent shelf, stood the dining table, upon which rested all the family's chinaware, silverware and cooking utensils that could not be hung upon pegs along the wall. At mealtime a temporary removal was effected, the table cleared and the meal was spread. The family sat around the table, usually upon a long bench. In front of the fireplace was a wide hearth made of a flat rock. "Live" coals of fire were drawn out on this and the food that was fried was placed in a "spider" or frying pan and cooked upon this fire. Boiled food was placed in a huge black iron kettle and hung on a "crane" which swung out above the fire, which was made of large sticks of wood with a huge backlog behind it. Bread was baked by placing it in a large cast iron skillet which had a protruding iron lid. A bed of coals was drawn out upon the hearth and the skillet placed on them and a big shovelful of them heaped upon the lid. Here, between these two pieces of ancient cast-iron, was cooked some of the sweetest "staff of life" that was ever eaten by man!

Back in that dim and distant day the problem of courtship was a lot more complicated than it is in the present day of parlor, sport coupe and roadhouses. The bashful boy of that day had to face the whole family a greater part of the time he spent with his girl friend. They usually sat on the trunk or back on the side of the bed and "whispered sweet nothings" into each other's ears while the rest of the family sat in a circle around the open fireplace, if the occasion was during the winter.

The list of foods which provided sustenance for the pioneer and his family was small. All of it was grown on the farm upon which he resided except the wild game, etc., which came from the nearby forest. Bread was principally made of corn meal before the days of the roller mill which brought into popular use the bread made of wheat and some other small grains. The corn meal was "grated" during the early autumn before it became too hard. After this it was pounded into meal with a mortar and pestle—Indian style. Lots of fruit and vegetables were "dried" during the late summer, before the use of jars came into common use. Some vegetables and potatoes were stored in the cellar or "holed up." Much corn was utilized for food by being made into "lye hominy." The old saying of "living on hog and hominy" had its origin from the fact that it was often the case, especially during a hard winter, that the early settler's family did live on the generally plentiful supply of pork and corn from his crib as their main source of food. We hear a lot during depression years of the family "live at home" program. The pioneer practiced this to the fullest extent.

Today we go to the local store for all such things as soap, sugar, pepper, spices, etc. One hundred years and less ago folks couldn't do this. They had to "manage for them," or do without. It is true that they often did the latter; but their ability to find the things needed would be a task that we of the present day would probably fail in. Wild honey furnished our first families their first and chief source of sweetening. Soap was made by the ash-hopper method of distilling lye from wood ashes and combining this with meat scraps to produce the semi-liquid brown soap which elderly people (and a few of the present time) can remember as being the contents of a large unsightly barrel in the woodshed or smokehouse. The field of spices and pepper was obtained mostly by growing red pepper and onions in the garden. Horseradish, garlic and other like plants were sometimes included.

The clothing of the pioneer was home-made. Home-made "jeans," which was woven on the huge loom, was the principal source of men's clothing and a part of the women's. Lucky indeed was the lady who owned a "store-bought dress" from the East. Shoes were made at home and some local man was a hatter. Hose for both men and women were knitted by the womenfolk of the family from wool sheared from the sheep and spun into yarn on the old spinning wheel.

The above description of pioneer living depicts the first methods. With the coming of better means of communication and transportation conditions gradually changed. Pioneer living is a far cry from our modern ways, but the rugged old backswoodsman, possibly through necessity, proved his skill at meeting and solving many problems that we, his grandsons, would most likely fail to accomplish. Pioneer life moved steadily along, and when an emergency or tough times came along they rolled up their sleeves and tackled the job and did not wait for an edict from Washington as we do today.

Social life on the frontier was limited, yet colorful. The house-raisings, play parties, old-time square dances, husking and spinning bees, candy-breakings and box suppers were the chief sources of diversification and entertainment for both young and old. Horse races, picnics and barbecues, not to mention fish fries, charivaris, etc., were also a part of the social activities, especially during the summer months. All this flourished until the turn of the present century and is not entirely extinct even today in the rural sections.

Business and finance was carried on in a limited way. The medium of exchange was principally by barter and trade. Very little actual cash found its way into the pockets of Randolph countians during the first years of its existence. On the old records of the county can often be found recordings of trades wherein one man bought livestock, slaves or household goods, paying for same with a certain number of coonskins, oxen, a negro boy or so many bushels of corn. Occasionally a father would hire his son out to a neighbor "to work all dry days from April 1 to July 4" for "seventy-five bushels of corn, in addition to his board, work clothing and washing." The early school teachers and preachers were paid in "pork, feathers and homespun cloth."

THE CIVIL WAR

As is true of the entire nation, especially the Southland, Randolph County played her part in the regrettable War Between the States. We who live at this time, when we look back through almost a century of time, are prone to think of this war inside our own nation, between our own folks, as a very unnecessary occurrence. In fact the same could be said of all wars. Yet there was a very distinct issue at stake. Time has mellowed the scene. Old hatreds and sectional differences have subsided to the stage where we, of the second and third generation, can never feel the sting which our grandfathers felt when the "Yankees" told them what they "must" do. Of course, as is generally known, the slavery question was the root of all the trouble. The North wanted to free the slaves; the South wanted to keep them. The South sought to pull away from the North, and by so doing "could handle their own affairs without Northern interference." The North, in order to preserve the union of states, would not agree to this. So here was the direct and immediate cause which started actual conflict. When the North told the South that "you cannot secede" the pride and independence which burned deep in the rugged old southerners blood just "couldn't take it"—to use present-day slang in stating this. While no doubt at this time it would be hard to find a person, even in the "deep South," that is not glad that the North won, yet we of the South are proud of the independent spirit and pride which our people displayed during this dark period of our nation's history.

It cannot be denied that both sides had a selfish motive in their stand on the slavery question. The southern slave-owners needed the negroes to help them in much the same manner that we need teams, tractors, etc., at this time to assist us. It was grave financial and economic loss to the South to part with this practice. On the other hand, the North did not need slave labor, since it had no plantations, and the negro at that time did not make a satisfactory industrial worker. In order to sway public sentiment, the North made a moral issue of slavery. While we do know that slavery is morally wrong, as a Southerner, we do not believe we are prejudiced when we say that we do not believe this would have been considered any more in the North than in the South if the slave had been of equal advantage in that section.

It is not the desire of the author at this time to bring forth a discussion of the moral and economic reasons behind the Civil War, but only to briefly explain the setting of the stage which produced the tragic drama of civil strife which resulted in the greatest blight which has ever spread over our fair land.

After the break had spread beyond repair and the states of the South had begun to withdraw from the Union, Arkansas followed suit. The Secession Convention, which resulted in Arkansas joining the Confederacy, met in Little Rock, March 4, 1861. James W. Crenshaw was the delegate from Randolph County. The state actually withdrew from the Union May 6, 1861. On May 13 a Military Board was appointed at Little Rock for the purpose of organizing the state for actual combat service. The first action was to organize five regiments of men. This was quickly done. Ten thousand men were assembled and, according to the records, "they rendezvoused at Pocahontas as soon as they were ready to march." This step was taken as a safeguard from invasion from the north. Missouri as yet was undecided as to what stand she was to take and there were northern sympathizers within "three days" marching time of the northern borders of Arkansas, of sufficient strength to threaten the safety of this section, should they decide to make a bold strike, which they never did.

On August 29, 1861, General William J. Hardee landed at Pocahontas to take charge of the troops assembled here. The troops were stationed chiefly to the south and west of town. Excavations along the south banks of Mill creek in the vicinity of "Cypress Springs," just outside of the southwestern corner of the present city limits, can still be seen. Many men died while encamped here and are buried in the woods in that vicinity and in the old burying ground north of town.

The camp is known in some of the military records as "Camp Shaver," presumably named for Col. Robert G. Shaver who was stationed here for some time.

On October 7 Gen. Hardee was promoted to the rank of major general, by which time he had about completed the work of transferring the Arkansas troops and organizing an army, which was composed of the following regiments: Second Arkansas Confederate, under Col. Thomas C. Hindman. The first Arkansas Confederate regiment of infantry, under Col. James F. Fagan, had already departed for Virginia. The Third under Col. Albert Rust, the Fourth under Col. Evander McNair, the Fifth under Col. David C. Cross, the Sixth under Col. Richard Lyon, the Seventh under Col. Robert G. Shaver, the Eighth under Col. William K. Patterson. There were other regiments and batallions of artillery too numerous to mention. Solond Borland, former United States senator, was appointed by the Confederate government to supervise the job of assembling clothing and food for the troops in camp at Pocahontas, September 12, 1861. Different regiments were assembled here for removal to the points which they were needed most. General Earl VanDorn was also stationed at Pocahontas for some time. We do not have the dates of the movements in and out of the county during the four years of activity here. Governor Rector issued a statement in January of 1862 to the public in which he stated: "To all men, who by state law are subject to military duty, are hereby directed to report, on or before March 5," to General Van Dorn at Pocahontas.

According to one record in existence there were eight companies of men organized in Randolph County, of Randolph County men. They were under the command of the following men: Joseph Martin, Eli Hufstedler, Mahlon McNabb, T. J. Mellon, Albert Kelsey, William A. Black, Isaac Schmick and John Mitchell.

There was also a camp of soldiers at Pitman Ferry for several months. General Hardee was there awhile after moving from Pocahontas. His camp was across the river from Pitman, just south of old "Buckskull," on the bank of Current River. Gen. Jeff Thompson and his men were in camp exactly on the line between what is now Clay and Randolph County, just south of the old Pitman ferry. On July 20, 1862, a real battle was fought here between the soldiers who had been ordered to move from Pocahontas to Greenville, Missouri, up the old Military road by way of Pitman. After this battle they are reputed to have drove the Federals away and went on to Greenville, where they were ordered back on account of a threat of invading forces of Federals from the northwest. Here they again met in an engagement, November 25, 1863. A large portion of the troops which spent some time at Pitman and at Pocahontas finally were ordered to Bowling Green, Kentucky, going up by way of Bird's Point on the Mississippi, just south of Cairo, Illinois. They finally reached Bowling Green after a small battle at Bird's Point. A number of families in the county today have relatives who fell in the major battle at Bowling Green.

August 22, 1863, a band of Federals attacked the forces at Pocahontas, and in September, 1863, a band of men under Col. Reeves attacked a group of Federals under Col. Leeper, and several men were killed in the engagement in Cherokee Bay, on the old Herron farm. General Steel of the northern army occupied Pocahontas several months in 1862, after the recruiting camp here was abandoned. This was all the activity in the county except by "bushwhackers" or roving bands who sought to waylay the opposition and attack them by surprise. A band of this kind from each side met at the "Tom Pulliam Spring" sometime in 1862 and a skirmish ensued. This was about five miles northeast of Warm Springs, just over the line in Missouri.

A lot of damage was done by roving bands of bushwhackers who killed and stole in many sections of the country. Such a band of Federals killed Henry Wythe, the blind brother of Judge James Martin's wife, at their home at what is now known as Martin Springs, in Columbia township.

Sometime during the war a band of Federals surprised the congregation at Siloam church and captured a number of men during church. Rev. Larkin F. Johnston was preaching. William Swindle was wounded in the attack.

The Seventh Infantry, mentioned above, moved east of the Mississippi and participated in the bloody battle of Shiloh, one of the major battles of the entire war. It was afterwards known as the "Bloody Seventh." Henry M. Stanley, noted African explorer, joined this regiment at Pocahontas.

The fifteenth Arkansas regiment, which was in the engagements at Pitman, Greenville and Bird's Point, was finally placed under Gen. Albert Sidney Johnston at Bowling Green, Kentucky.

There are many stories of other encounters with the "Yankees," as the natives called the northern soldiers in derision. The war years and the years immediately following the close were hard, bitter years for the people of the South. While there was quite a bit of activity in Randolph County during the war, we escaped the destruction of property which fell the lot of many places in the Southern States. Many of the fine young men of the county lost their lives in combat and several came home to live the balance of their lives as cripples, but, generally, the close of hostilities found our section ready to take up the duties of providing for their families at the same place and in the same way as before the war, except for the "hard times" which was upon them.

The writer remembers hearing our grandfather make the remark many times that he made a crop the first year after the close of the war "on grass and buttermilk." The men who came home from battle faced a hard immediate future. Their livestock had been killed or stolen. Their buildings and fences in sad state of repair. No money. No credit in the country. Nowhere to go for help. It was really a time for application of the old adage to "root hog or die." When we see the thousands of today who look to Washington, D. C., for help every time they hit a little tough spot we often think about how our grandfathers and grandmothers handled a like problem. Grandmother once told us that the year the war closed her mother, who was a widow, had nothing in the way of food left when spring came except "a few bushels of bread corn" which she had kept hidden all winter from the marauding bands of soldiers, straggling groups from both sides. She relates that often their evening meal consisted of a piece of "plain" cornbread and "what wild onions we could find growing along the spring branch." But with all this, the southern people handed down to us a great lesson in industry, thrift and hope in the way they met and solved the hardships of that distant dark period of time just following the close of the Civil War.

STREAMS OF RANDOLPH COUNTY

The rivers and creeks of a country have a great influence upon the early settlement. The streams which are large enough for boats to navigate are actually the first "roads" travelled in the settlement of a frontier country. Also the fertile lands along such streams afford much farming lands; but in this respect the smaller streams' bottomland is usually cleared first on account of the ease in getting it ready for cultivation. Another feature along this line are the springs along the creeks. The first settlers' source of drinking water came largely from springs which were located along the hillsides of the valleys.

The largest stream in Randolph County is Black River —named this because the first settlers found the water dark and sluggish. Black River flows down out of the hills of upper southeast Missouri, through Clay County, Arkansas, into this county. Among the towns along Black River Poplar Bluff, Missouri, Corning and Pocahontas in Arkansas are the most important. Lead miners under the leadership of the Frenchman Renault and others settled on upper Black River, some as early as 1725. Other early families, mostly French, who, not liking the swampy lands around New Madrid, moved west to the hills which were the headwater source of Black River. The French also made a settlement at what is now known as Peach Orchard in Clay County, on Black River. Pierre LeMieux called the place "Petit Baril," which is supposed to be Peach Orchard in French. Pocahontas is known to have been a French trading post in 1790, and some writers place the date back as far as 1760. Then comes the old towns on Black River of Davidsonville and Powhatan. From here the river flows south to unite with White River at Newport. Old Jacksonport was another old river town which died when Newport was born.

Next river in importance in Randolph County is Current River, named so by the first hunters because of the swiftness of its water. Current River finds its source high in the hills of central southern Missouri. Dent County, Missouri, divides its rainfall between Black, Current and Merrimac rivers. Black and Current carry their water far southward to White River, which finally empties into the Mississippi only about sixty miles north of the Louisiana state line. The Merrimac carries its liquid load north to empty into the Father of Waters just south of the city limits of St. Louis. Current River is noted far and wide for its fishing, especially the upper portion. Eminence, Van Buren, and Doniphan in Missouri, are the leading towns on this river.

In Randolph County, on Current River, is located the ancient river crossing at Pitman, first known as Hix's Ferry, which was opened soon after 1803 and later as Pitman's Ferry. The early Gaines, Perkins, Duckworth and other ferries were on Current River, as were Shoemaker, Sims and Johnstontown steamboat "landings." Current River empties into Black near Skaggs' old ferry, about six miles above Pocahontas.

Another river of the county is Elevenpoint, so named because its source is made up of "eleven different creeks." It runs down out of Oregon County, Missouri. Along the banks of Elevenpoint River settled some of the first settlers in northeast Arkansas. The Stubblefields, McIlroys, Looneys, Wells, Whites, Bakers and others were here soon after the Louisiana Purchase. Elm Store, Dalton and Birdell are early towns along this stream. The old Carter Mill (now known as the Hufstedler Mill) was one of the first water mills in this section of the state. While the bottom along Elevenpoint is not wide, it is very fertile. Some of the best farm land in Arkansas is on this river. Elevenpoint River empties into Spring River only a short distance above the mouth of Spring River itself. Right here could almost be called the "Garden of Eden" of Lawrence and Randolph counties. Here in this immediate vicinity was located the "House of Solomon Hewitt," and a short distance away "the new house of Richard Murphy," where the two first terms of court were held for old Lawrence County in 1815.

Spring River flows along the western boundary of Randolph County. While it really is not in the county, the east side of its valley is. Originating from Mammoth Spring, the largest fresh water spring in the nation, this stream is one of the most beautiful mountain rivers in the state.

Along this stream settled many of the first settlers in this section. Mammoth Spring, Hardy, Williford, Ravenden and Imboden are the chief towns along this stream. The Wells, Sloan, Wyatt, Fortenberry, Taylor, Wayland and other early families first stopped in this valley.

Other smaller streams of the county are Janes Creek, Fourche du Mas and several other "creeks," such as Glaze Creek, Dry Creek (two of them), Camp, Tennessee, Mud, Wells and several others of lesser importance.

Janes Creek has as its source a number of small creeks which come into Arkansas southwest of Myrtle, Missouri, and flows south by way of Ravenden Springs to empty into Spring River. The "dream town" of Ravenden Springs, noted as a local health resort, is located near this creek. It was on this creek that John Janes settled in 1809. It was also on this creek that Caleb Lindsey is supposed to have taught the first school in the state, in a cave.

(Author's note: The name *Fourche du Mas* is the way it appears on the early maps of this section.)

Fourche du Mas flows down out of Ripley County, Missouri, into Randolph County a short distance north of Middlebrook. From here it runs in a southeasterly direction by way of the old "Fourche de Thomas" or Columbia settlement where the Military road crosses, on down by Brockett, which in early days was known as Bollinger's Mill, to empty into Black River a short distance above Pocahontas. This stream is supposed to have been first visited by Frenchmen who gave it the name of Fourche de Maux, or de Mas. Later it was called Fourche de Thomas, or Thomas fork. It is so listed on the early maps, and the community around the Military crossing, which is now known as Jarrett, was first called Fourche de Thomas, and at one time had a postoffice by that name. For some reason the name reverted back to the French, and it has long been known as Fourche du Mas. Some of the first settlers of north Arkansas settled along this stream.

Dry Creek which flows into Elevenpoint below Oconee and Dry Creek which flows into Fourche du Mas near the ancient Eldridge ford in Siloam township are the two smaller streams of the same name in the county. Mud Creek, which flows down by the village of Warm Springs, is another noted creek. On this creek settled the Shavers, Mocks, Morris, Fletcher, Holt and other early families. On the old homestead of the late Thomas D. Mock the grandfather of Mr. Mock settled in 1815 and a postoffice with Matthias Mock as postmaster was established here in 1836 and called Mud Creek. Mud Creek flows into Fourche at the old Dock Ingram farm, now known as the Price place.

Glaze Creek has its head in the low hills between Middlebrook and Supply, near the Missouri-Arkansas state line, to state it roughly. It is a short stream which empties into Current River not far from the old Pitman ferry. Near this creek is located Glaze Creek Church of Christ, which is one of the oldest churches of this faith in northeast Arkansas. On this creek, which was known in the early records as "Glaze Kenon" creek, were located "improvements" and pre-emption claims as early as 1812. The villages of Supply, Minorca and Pitman are all located near this creek.

Wells creek got its name from the early Wells family who settled along its banks in the first quarter of the nineteenth century. Dial's Creek in northwest Randolph County also got its name from an early family. Wells Creek is in the western part of the county.

Camp Creek, Tennessee Creek and Tattle Creek all flow into Fourche from the west side and are located near the center of the county. Camp Creek got its name from the Camp family. Tennessee Creek got its name because so many of the early settlers along its bank came from that state. Just how Tattle Creek obtained its name is not known to the writer. Mansker Creek, which flows along the north city limits of Pocahontas, got its name from George Mansker who settled here about 1817. Mansker had a large family which later located mostly in the Maynard and Little Black communities. Many of the early families of the central part of the county intermarried in this family. Among these were the Mock, Ingram, Richardson, Rice, Lindsey and Fisher families.

There are many lesser important streams in the county, but practically all the early families settled along these streams before they moved into the larger river bottoms which were universally called "swamps" by these first settlers.

OUR NOTED SPRINGS IN RANDOLPH COUNTY

At Warm Springs and Ravenden Springs are located noted springs. While they are undeveloped, especially at Warm Springs, they have mineral content which makes them valuable as a health resort.

From 1870 to about 1905 many people in bad health, especially from the lowlands, spent several weeks each year vacationing at Warm Springs. At one time there was a forty-room hotel on the site of the springs and the town saw a boom which lasted several years. At Ravenden Springs is the spring which contains mineral properties which are reputed to be a big help in some forms of stomach trouble. This was supposed to have been discovered by a man's dream. More will be said about both of these towns in the proper chapter. The county abounds in a lot more gushing cold springs which afford some of the best water in the nation.

RAILROADS OF RANDOLPH COUNTY

The actual history of railroad building in so far as it concerns Randolph County "almost" started as early as October, 1849. In that month the first survey started from the U. S. Arsenal in St. Louis and was made from there to the "big bend" in Red River at Fulton in south Arkansas. The work was supervised by Capt. Josiah Barney of the U. S. Topographical Engineering Corps. The movement was sponsored by the United States government in an effort to promote interest in the settlement of the new state of Texas.

Captain Barney originally planned a railroad route from St. Louis to Iron Mountain and then down some tributary of Black River to Poplar Bluff and on down through Randolph County to the southern destination. He planned that if it was too difficult to follow Black River closely to cross the divide between Black and Current River and run down Current to Black River and Pocahontas. Either route would have ran through Pocahontas. This was the birth of the movement that finally resulted in the building of the railroad now known as the Missouri Pacific.

The story comes to us that Capt. Barney made an error in his calculations for crossing the "Coppermine ridge" between St. Louis and Iron Mountain and ran his survey too far south. This route would have required a long tunnel. He tried another survey and ran down St. Francis valley to the lowlands at old Indian Ford. Here he crossed over to Poplar Bluff and ran straight from Poplar Bluff to Fulton. This survey ran down the present route of the Missouri Pacific. He crossed the corner of Randolph County in July, 1850. But no railroad was built from his survey.

In 1852 the St. Louis, Iron Mountain Railway Co. was chartered and a survey made by J. H. Morley. This was the survey adopted and it ran the same route as Barney's from Poplar Bluff south, touching Randolph County only at the extreme southeast corner, at O'Kean.

The Iron Mountain line actually only ran to the Missouri line. The line from the state line south to Fulton was known as the Cairo and Fulton. It was chartered in 1853. Roswell Beebe was the first president. This road was sponsored principally by men in Little Rock.

The first through train over this track, which was the first train through Randolph County, was in December, 1872, twenty-three years after the first survey was made and two years after the first shovel of dirt was handled in the actual construction. In 1874 the Cairo and Fulton and the St. Louis-Iron Mountain was consolidated. In 1917 the name was changed to the Missouri Pacific. This was Randolph County's first railroad, although it only crossed the county a distance of two and one-half miles.

The next railroad to touch the county was the Kansas City, Fort Scott and Memphis road which was built between 1872 and 1882 from Memphis to Kansas City.

After crossing the level land from Memphis to Jonesboro, it crossed over Crowley's Ridge there and ran in a northwesterly direction by way of Hoxie to start its long upward climb through the Ozarks, at Black Rock. Here it entered the Spring River valley which it followed to Mammoth Spring. After leaving Mammoth Spring, the line starts a steady climb up through the Ozark foothills to reach the table land near Springfield, which slopes away to the Kansas prairies.

The exact date of the first survey along this route is not known to the author. Some preliminary work was done in 1872. Several surveys were made. At one time a route up Elevenpoint River by way of Thomasville in Oregon County, Missouri, was considered. The high hills of the watershed between Elevenpoint and Current River were an obstacle to this route. The Myatt's creek valley and the long gently sloping basin in the vicinity of West Plains proved to be an easier way of reaching the tableland, referred to above. The road was completed in 1882. This road crosses a tiny neck of Randolph County, in the extreme southwest corner. Slightly over eleven hundred feet of track is assessed to the Wyatt School District No. 67 of Randolph County. The road missed Ravenden Springs six miles and the town of Ravenden, first known as "Ravenden Junction," just across the line in Lawrence County, sprang up as a result. Another survey for this road ran up Janes creek, but met the same fate as the Elevenpoint route.

The third and most important railroad in Randolph County, in so far as the county itself is concerned, is the present Frisco line, known at this time as the Cape Girardeau-Hoxie branch of the St. Louis-San Francisco.

The first part of this line was begun in 1896, after several surveys had been made. This was the line from Pocahontas to Hoxie and was known as the Hoxie-Pocahontas and Northern Railway Company. It was sponsored by local people, with the help of eastern capital. Six years later the line from Poplar Bluff to Pocahontas was completed. It was known as the South Missouri and Arkansas Railroad. The northeastern end of the line had been built in 1901 down to Poplar Bluff. For a period of about six years the trains ran up to Pocahontas from Hoxie, and back. But this was a wonderful day for the town when it was completed. Merchandise, etc., shipped from Memphis, St. Louis, Little Rock, Kansas City and other places came "to our very door," as one resident of the time stated. Merchants in the northern part of the county who had been going to Harviell, on the main line of the St. Louis-Iron Mountain line since 1872 for their merchandise, (until the branch line of the St. Louis-Iron Mountain was built from Neelyville to Doniphan about 1885) could now come to their own county seat for their merchandise which was "shipped in."

The story of the building of the Frisco through the county is pretty well known. That part from Hoxie to Pocahontas was built with very little change in the first survey. But that part from Success, in Clay County, by way of the towns of Reyno and Biggers to Pocahontas, was the source of much "wire pulling." Several surveys were made. The first survey considered going only to Corning on the Iron Mountain line. This did not materialize. The chief idea seemed to be to come south from Poplar Bluff to Pocahontas. The first survey with this in mind, ran by way of the town of Reyno. The town that was known as Reyno at that time was on the site of what is now known as the "Old Reyno" community, where the Biggers Auxiliary Airfield was built during World War II. After passing Old Reyno the survey ran down the middle of Cherokee Bay to cross Current River near the present Highway 67 bridge, then called McIlroy's Ferry, and on across the swamplands to Pocahontas. If this survey had been used, it is very probable that a large town would have grown up on the site of Old Reyno instead of two smaller ones at Reyno and Biggers.

This survey ran south of Biggers some distance. There was no town here at that time, but the late B. F. Biggers and others owned land along the river and improvements had been made here. The second survey pulled the line away from Old Reyno to the north, running as close to the river at what is now Biggers as possible. The citizens of Old Reyno protested vigorously, but to no avail. The road was built as we see it today, missing Old Reyno about two miles. The result was that the town of Biggers soon started building. Not to be outdone, the folks living at Old Reyno moved to the new railroad, two miles due north, and started a town for themselves with the same name. Whole buildings were rolled to the new location. This resulted in the birth of the towns of Reyno and Biggers on the railroad and the death of Old Reyno and Johnstontown on the river.

This line runs a distance of a little over twenty-two miles in Randolph County. Such is the story of our county's railroads.

The coming of the railroads saw the decline of the steamboats.

Pocahontas has the distinction of being the only town in the county which was both an important river town and also a leading spot on the new railroad. The first means of transportation into this section was the old Military road. The next the steamboat. Next came the railroad. We now have motor truck freight lines and passenger bus lines. How long will it be until we have freight and passengers transported by regular scheduled air lines?

THE CATHOLIC CHURCH IN RANDOLPH COUNTY

The following article, which is a nice outline of the work of establishing and maintaining the Catholic Church in Randolph County, was written by Mrs. Mary Wyllie Monday. It gives the reader a list of the names, etc., of the first families of this church who came to the county.

"Although the assertion is supported more by tradition than by documentary evidence, Catholicy has existed in what is now Randolph County since that era when pioneer settlers were pressing ever westward and southward in the early days of the American nation. Drifting down from Ohio, Illinois and upper Missouri; from the hills of Kentucky and Tennessee and the far-away fields of Georgia. Also, up the river road from Louisiana to the now long-vanished town of Davidsonville came Spanish and French families, lured by the promise of new lands.

"True, it was not the definitely organized Catholicy that followed the advent of Fathers O'Kean, Weibel and Saettle, rather it was an adherence to the Church as a point of family history by individuals who, despite their inability to practice the main parts of their creed, retained the name and at least some of the more familiar practices—the sign of the cross and recitation of certain typifying prayers. A generation ago there were still natives of the county who could recall that their forebears came 'from across the waters,' and whom they guessed to be Catholics because they had a rosary, prayer book or a Catholic Bible.

"Further evidence arguing the presence of Catholics in the county is found in the history of the ghost-town of Davidsonville, once seat of justice for all northern Arkansas and southern Missouri and site of the first postoffice in Arkansas. The story of the once flourishing little town recounts the presence of French and Spanish Catholics among its several hundred citizens and records a visit in 1824 of two Jesuit priests, Fathers Odin and Timon, from Boise Brulle, near St. Louis.

"Irregularly, until the establishment of the Diocese of Little Rock, Randolph County was attended by priests from New Madrid, Missouri. That Pocahontas was the only Catholic mission in the region is indicated by the fact that Catholics from the 'Irish Wilderness' in southern Missouri brought their dead to be buried in the little cemetery on the western outskirt of the little village.

"In 1867 Father James P. O'Kean of Memphis, Tenn., an Irishman and a Confederate veteran, while a passenger on a Mississippi River steamer, joined a group of business men from Pocahontas. During the course of their conversation these men invited Father O'Kean to hold a series of lectures in Pocahontas, promising to secure a building for the meeting place. Father O'Kean agreed to request permission of his Bishop to come to Pocahontas and conduct a series of lectures explaining Catholic doctrine. At the close of the services, held in a vacant store building near the court square, the citizens, eager to secure for their town the stabilizing influence of another church, offered to build a church for him. Colonel Marvin made a deed conveying a tract of land on the heights on the west side of town to the Diocese of Little Rock. Volunteer donations of money and free labor, principally by Protestants and Jews (there being less than a dozen Catholics in the county at the time), only a year later had the little frame building ready for the soldier-priest. Among the original members of the tiny parish, which Father O'Kean dedicated to St. Paul the Apostle, were Nicholas Bach, his sister, Mrs. Cizert, and her son, Nicholas; the family of John Bossiere and a Mr. Hogan.

"The family of Dr. James Campbell Esselman; his niece, Miss Nannie Lansdale; a nephew, George Esselman; Dan Monday; Dr. Putnam's family; Miss M. E. Smith and William Jarrett are among the first names registered in the baptismal record of the new parish.

"When Father O'Kean left, four years later, to become Rector of St. Andrew's Cathedral in Little Rock, he left a parish of about one hundred members.

"From 1872 to 1879 Father Thomas Reilly was pastor of St. Paul's.

"In 1879 Father Eugene Weibel, a Benedictine monk from the University of Einsedeln, Switzerland, was appointed to fill the pastorate.

"A vigorous impetuous to the growth of the parish and to the county came in the early '80's, when Father Weibel secured for Pocahontas a representative part of the great tide of immigrants flowing into the United States from Europe and the British Isles. From Germany, Switzerland, Holland, Belgium, Saxony and Bavaria; from Ireland and Scotland they came to build their homes and sink their roots deep into the soil of Randolph County. The annals of Randolph's progress records such names as Walters, Peters, Worms, DeClerk, Spinnenweber, Geiser, Frenken, Derris, Hellmond, Winkels, Shippers, Gergardt, Jansen, Martin, Wyllie, Brodel, Rager, Monday, Schneider, Throesch, Walterscheid, Ungerank, Liebhaber, Reiner, Sparber, Pfeiffer, Gerlach, Brunner, Thilemeier, Lesmeister, Baltz, Meier, Hauseman, Blissenbach, Frangenberg, Frenkenberger, Schaechtel, Wurtz,

Jaeger, Zitzelberger, Scheid, Barthel, Dachs, Thiele, Seibold, Gschwend, Hollenstein, Doman, Junkersfeld, Hoffman, Hoelcher, Muyres, Thennes, Weisenbach, Neff, Geisinger, Seilers, Kronsiedler, Sense, Rothsinger, Ohlenforst, Dangler, Eckstein, Eich, Weibel, Roellen, Graf, Linder, Keifer, Mattingly, Knoch, Steimel, Mons, Ausman, Bauer, Koechner, Zosso, Bergmann and Maasen.

"The foreign immigrants experienced almost insurmountable difficulties—ignorance of the language and customs, fast dwindling finances, climatic conditions, many of them falling victims to the dreaded 'swamp fever.' The mortality rate among the children was appalling. Many of the newcomers quickly disposed of their property and left the county. Those who remained, by their thrift and progressiveness, exercised a marked influence for good in the development of the county. The suspicion and often open hostility that had been directed at them in the beginning gave way to friendliness and fellowship. They brought about an almost revolutionary change in the agricultural system of the county. In fact, this change in farming methods had been one of the openly voiced objections to acceptance of the foreigners, as some of the native sons, accustomed to living off the land with a minimum of effort, complained: 'These Dutchmen,' (all foreign-speaking people were indiscriminately classified as 'Dutchmen') are going to ruin the country with their plowing and fencing. First thing we know there won't be a tract of land left for hunting or for our stock to forage in. Life for the indolent of that day was a simple matter of fishing, hunting, raising a few sweet potatoes and a 'little jag' of corn for bread. Deer, wild turkeys and game of all sorts were plentiful. When a man established a 'meat claim' by placing a pair or two of hogs in the vast acreage of cane brakes in the lush river bottoms, all he had to do was drive into the brakes in the fall and kill enough hogs for all the meat and lard his family would require. Quite naturally he resented the intrusion into his Utopia by the foreigners.

GENERAL HISTORY

"Today Randolph stands proudly in the front ranks of agriculture in the state and many of the homesteads of these immigrants are among the finest farms in the county.

"In 1884 Father Weibel opened a grammar school in Pocahontas and placed it in charge of a quartette of Benedictine nuns from Conception, Missouri, Sister Beatrice, Sister Agnes, Sister Frances and Sister Walburga.

"Prior to the coming of the Benedictine Sisters, four Sisters of the Dominican Order came to Pocahontas but did not remain long.

"Soon the Sisters built a commodious convent and quite a community of nuns and novices lived in Pocahontas, in the Convent Maria Stein, where they taught school, music, needlecraft and painting. Later they opened an academy and boarding school for girls. Young men and young ladies of the city were accepted as day students.

"In 1886 Father Weibel built the church of St. John the Baptist in Engelberg in Columbia township, for the convenience of the large number of Catholics who had settled in the fertile lands watered by Fourche du Mas and Current rivers. The rural parish flourished and soon outgrew the capacity of the little church. Father A. G. Haeringer, while pastor of St. John's built the handsome church and school on the parish property in Engelberg. A comfortable home for the sisters who teach the school occupies a part of the spacious lawn. A rectory of native fieldstone was added to the parish property by Rev. H. W. Nix about 1939.

"Frequently, for months at a time, St. Paul's and St. John's parishes were without a resident pastor, priests from other parts of the state filling the vacancies.

"In 1889 The Rev. Henry Fuerst was pastor of St. Paul's. A musician of no small range, he soon organized a St. Cecilia Society in the parish, and a short time had trained a credible choir among its members. Father Fuerst's pastorate extended to 1898.

"From 1898 to 1908 Father Mathew Saettle, O.S.B., was pastor of St. Paul's. Through his powerful efforts the beautiful church crowning 'Catholic Hill' in Pocahontas, was built. Of native limestone, hand-hewn, it stands a living monument to the humble Benedictine monk. During the time of his pastorate in Pocahontas, Father Mathew built a small church in Noland, in East Roanoke township. The churches in Noland and Engelberg were attended by the pastor of St. Paul's in Pocahontas for many years. The little church in Noland was destroyed by fire some years later.

In 1908 Father Joseph Froitzheim succeeded Father Mathew in Pocahontas. A scholar and an executive, Father Froitzheim recognizing the value of concentrated effort, organized several powerful units in the parish. The Young People's Society, the Ladies' Club, the Holy Name Society for men and a council of the Knights of Columbus. A large parish hall was built and equipped for social activities. In 1922 a two-year Junior High course was added to the parochial school.

" 'Father' Froitzheim, as he preferred to be called, although wearing the ecclesiastical purple of the Monsignori, was pastor of St. Paul's until July 13, 1930, when he succumbed to a heart attack.

"The Rev. Monsignor A. G. Haeringer was appointed to succeed Monsignor Froitzheim, serving as pastor from July, 1930, to June, 1939. One of the first movements he inaugurated in the parish was the erection of a suitable monument to the memory of Monsignor Froitzheim. With his approval the local Knights of Columbus built a grotto on the site of the first Catholic church in Pocahontas. It is one of the finest reproductions of the famous shrine in Lourdes, France, to be found in America.

GENERAL HISTORY

"The Rev. Edward J. Yeager was appointed pastor of St. Paul's in June, 1939. A progressor for nine years in Catholic High School in Little Rock, Father Yeager accomplished marvelous improvements for the parochial school in Pocahontas. He replaced the two-year Junior class with a complete four-year high school course, housing it temporarily in the auditorium of the parish hall. Partitions ingeniously fashioned to fold out of the way when the auditorium was needed for social activities, segregated the class rooms. Father Yeager was completing plans for a new and modern school building and a completely equipped hospital for Pocahontas at the time of his death, June 26, 1946. Father Thomas Kennedy, assistant rector of St. Paul's, is continuing the work begun by Father Yeager.

"The little parish established in 1868 is now recognized as one of the outstanding parishes of Arkansas."

RANDOLPH COUNTY NEWSPAPERS

Randolph County has had many newspapers in the years since the first one was established in 1858. In that year two newspapers were started. The *Herald,* which was published by Prof. Norman and Dr. Boshears, and the *Weekly Advertiser,* published by Joseph T. Fisher. Two years later, in 1860, James T. Martin became owner of both papers and consolidated the plants to publish one paper called the *Advertiser and Herald.* It was destroyed by Federal soldiers in 1863.

In 1865 Edwin Rockwell established the *Courier.* He sold the paper in 1867 to T. J. Ratcliffe and J. H. Purkins, who changed the name of the paper to the *Black River Standard.* The paper ceased publication one year later and the equipment was purchased by Thomas L. Martin, a Republican, who started the *Randolph County Express* in July, 1868. The same month Edwin Rockwell and Joseph Hufstedler established the *Randolph County Courier* which was consolidated with the *Express* a short time later. This paper died in 1873.

In 1869 the *Randolph Republican* was started but was unsuccessful. It appears that this was on account of the citizens of that day "just wouldn't have anything that was Republican." It was in this paper that the advertisements appeared, advertising for bids for the construction of the second courthouse, now called the old courthouse.

Later the Scalpel was established by J. H. Purkins and Edwin Rockwell. J. A. C. Jackson purchased an interest in this paper after the death of Rockwell, and continued to be active in the publication until 1882 when he sold out to W. A. Lucas. Soon after Lucas became owner the plant burned and the paper was not revived.

In 1881 the *Herald* was established at Ravenden Springs by C. W. and L. A. Dunifer. Prior to this time all papers had been printed at Pocahontas. In June, 1882, the *Herald* was moved to Pocahontas, and the name changed to the *Randolph Herald*. J. N. Bolen bought the *Randolph Herald* from the Dunifers in 1885. Sometime during this period B. B. Morton established a paper in Pocahontas and called it the *Pocahontas Free Press*. This paper was sold to Bolen soon after it was started.

In 1895 Prof. R. L. Williford and S. O. Penick started a paper at Maynard and called it the *Pilot*. Williford sold his interest to Rufus Lindsey. Penick and Lindsey moved the paper to Pocahontas. A few months after the paper was moved to Pocahontas the owners bought out the *Randolph Herald* and changed the name to the *Herald-Pilot*. Lindsey sold out to Penick and moved back to Maynard where he established the *Northeast Arkansas Enterprise* in 1897. Three years later Mr. Lindsey died and the paper was sold to parties at Doniphan, Missouri. The first newspaper which the author remembers was the well known "Boom Edition" of the Maynard *Enterprise* which was published by Mr. Lindsey a short time before his death, which was a year before this writer was born. This edition was a boost for Randolph County, Arkansas, and Ripley County, Missouri, and contained the names of many persons living today who were active in business at that date.

S. O. Penick, who owned the *Herald-Pilot* after Lindsey went back to Maynard, sold out to J. N. Bolen, the former owner, who changed the name back to *Randolph Herald*. Bolen sold out once more in 1898 to A. T. Hull, who sold it to C. E. Spiller in 1899. Spiller died in 1900. L. F. Blankenship bought the paper in 1901 and the paper has been owned by the Blankenship family ever since. However, there has been several changes and partnerships.

In 1902 Earl W. Hodges moved the *Spring River News* to Pocahontas and changed the name to *Pocahontas News*. The *Herald* and *News* were consolidated in 1903 and the name *News-Herald* was adopted.

J. N. Bolen once more entered the newspaper field in 1902 when he and J. A. C. Jackson established the *Randolph County Democrat*, but this paper was discontinued in a few months. The Hodges-Blankenship partnership lasted until 1904 when Hodges moved to Little Rock to become printing clerk in the statehouse. The *Pocahontas Star* was consolidated with the *News-Herald* in 1907. V. G. Hinton, who was the owner of the *News-Herald*, became a partner with L. F. Blankenship and the name of the paper was changed to *Star-Herald*, which it has held until the present time. David Lindsey and Oscar Wyatt held interest in the *Star-Herald* for some time but for several years the sole owners have been the Blankenship family, since the death of Mr. Blankenship in 1930.

Other papers which have been established in Randolph County are the *Maynard Backlog*, in 1907; the *Enterprise* at Biggers in 1904; the *Current River Banner* at Biggers in 1906. The editors of the above named papers were W. T.

Warren, V. G. Hinton, J. N. Davenport and D. A. Lindsey. The *Sentinel* at Maynard in 1907, by R. J. Wyatt; the *Eye-Opener* at Ravenden Springs in 1899, by W. F. Lemmons (name changed to the *Hustler* with John Chun as owner); the *Cherokee Headlight*, by L. F. Blankenship, at Biggers in 1910; another Ravenden Springs *Hustler* in 1911 by R. L. Byrne; the Ravenden Springs *Weekly News* by Chas. A. Dixon in 1908; the *Randolph County Clipper* by Roy Elliott in 1909; the *Pocahontas Times* in 1912 by R. N. Schoonover and later H. B. Dixon; the *Randolph Democrat* in 1917 by A. H. Chapin, later by A. J. Lewis, and still later by Neal Douglass, Orto Finley and W. S. Tussey; the *Randolph County Democrat* by James W. Case in 1931. The *Democrat* was published from 1931 until 1937.

RANDOLPH COUNTY'S PART IN WAR

There was no white man known to have been living in Randolph County at the time of the Revolutionary war. A scattered population was here when the War of 1812 was fought. No one went from this section to see action in this war. The chief influence of the War of 1812 on Randolph County was the influx of population which came west as soon as hostilities had ceased and the new United States could turn its mind toward things of peace and development. The early deed records show where a few soldiers of that war received land grants here, given them by the government for their services in this second fight with the British.

Of course, as has been stated before in this book, there were a few men who had served in the Revolution who came west and established homes in this county. We wish that we had the names of all these, but this is impossible. Some of those we know were Edmund Hudson, John Janes, Daniel Lieb, John Dalton, John Davidson and others.

GENERAL HISTORY

We have already written a separate chapter on the part our county played in the Civil War, so we will refer the reader to that section if more is desired to be known about the period of that conflict.

In 1898, although almost one-half a century ago now, was the year of the conflict with Spain. This short war was known as the Spanish-American War. Several citizens of the county at this time were soldiers in this war. It was in this war that the island of Cuba was freed of Spanish bondage and made a free nation. It was in this war that we came into possession of the Philippine Islands. These valuable tropical islands lie off the coast of Asia and were the scene of much hard fighting during the days following December 7, 1941. While a valuable addition to the United States from a commercial standpoint, they are a liability from a military standpoint. Some may disagree with the author in this, but during the days following the Spanish-American War one noted statesman who opposed the seizure of the islands by the United States said that some day they would be the cause of us becoming involved in a major war. This prophecy came true at the beginning of the last war. Jealousy, greed and competition between our nation and the Japanese over affairs connected with the Philippines brought on the Pearl Harbor attack.

Almost one-fifth of a century elapsed after the war with Spain before we again became involved in another major war. (This does not count the flare-up with Mexico in 1915.)

We have here passed up the war with Mexico during the 1840's when several of our early settlers went down on the border to help Texas win her independence from that nation. It was in this conflict that we remember Davy Crockett, Archibald Yell and others, the latter from Arkansas.

Nineteen years after Admiral Dewey steamed into Manila Bay to clean up the Spanish fleet we find our nation once more on the brink of a major war which became known as the first World War.

The war in continental Europe which had been going on since June, 1914, had finally found us involved. The story which leads up to our participation is well known. First was the various recommendations and regulations imposed by the belligerent nations upon neutrals which were shipping food and war material to the enemy. Then came the blockade in which we were told to "stay out" of certain waters, etc. The final blow came with the sinking of the Lusitania, with many Americans on board. This was practically an act of war. The Germans denied the sinkings. The English who were needing our help desperately fanned the fires of hatred between our country and Germany for purely selfish reasons. Time may yet expose some startling things yet unrevealed in the affairs of international relations involving Britain and other nations during this time of strained relations. Just who did sink the great vessel may never be known, but we do know that it did have the effect of bringing us abruptly into the war when we were attempting to remain neutral.

The remainder of the story is still imprinted deeply on our minds. On February 3, 1917, we severed diplomatic relations with Germany. On April 4 we declared war. On June 5 we called our young men in to register under the Conscription Act. In a few days we began to see them called into army camps scattered throughout the nation and a few months found them fighting in the trenches of France, Belgium and other countries of continental Europe. Many of our sons and brothers made the supreme sacrifice "on Flanders Field" and other places. After a little over a year in the fighting we saw Kaiser Wilhelm abdicate the throne and flee to Holland. On November 11, 1918, we saw the war come to a close. The world accepted the peace with joy. They said the boys had just fought "the war to end wars," and everybody was happy.

The slow moving boats began to bring our fighters home. Wartime inflation had begun to take its toll industrially and domestically. Natives of Europe who no longer needed our men began to complain and turn a cold shoulder to our men. Wartime obligations began to mature. France, Britain and a few smaller nations turned a cold shoulder to our requests for payments due us for loans which spelled their very existence. Twenty-eight years have passed and they are still unpaid. Why? Why loan them more?

Then came the lean years. After that the New Deal, and after that another world war. The all-over picture of the conditions of the last war were strikingly similar to the first one.

We all remember the conditions which came about which brought on World War II. Jealousy between the British empire and Hitler's expanding European empire was kindling enough to start any conflagration.

The zero hour came when the armies of Germany began to overrun Poland over the protest of several major powers, including France.

With this came open warfare between the big nations of Europe, excepting Russia, which remained neutral for a time, her attitude and sympathy swaying back and forth between the two warring sides. Finally Hitler, thinking that he was going to win anyway, decided to attack Russia and whip her along with the British and French and have the job done, when the war finally ended. He made one grave mistake—he judged correctly when he decided that Russia was weak industrially and financially, but she was strong numerically. All she needed was tools with which to fight. She had plenty of men to use them.

Jealousy between the United States and Japan was kindled by secret underground forces backed by Hitler. Hitler's men spread propaganda in Japan against our country, and British and French spies and undercover men added their bit of the same tactics, except on the other side. Hard tense feelings grew up between our country and Japan, and it only needed a spark to set off the fire. This came when our nation made various recommendations and demands on Japan in regards to her off-color movements in the East Indies. The representatives of the Japanese government and high officials in Washington were supposed to be working on the problem of a peaceful settlement of the differences between the two nations when the Japanese attacked us in Hawaii at Pearl Harbor on that never-to-be-forgotten December 7, 1941. The balance of the story is known to all.

Everything went into the big job of winning the war. All commercial and industrial plants in the nation were converted into war plants. Our young men from 18 to 45 years of age were ordered to register (those who had not done so previously in the first peace-time conscription our nation ever had, September 16, 1938). Many in this group were called. Something over twelve hundred from Randolph County actually saw service in some branch of the army or navy. The actual figures are not available at this time. About forty-five made the supreme sacrifice. As was typical of the whole nation, Randolph County went "all out" for war, and besides furnishing the cream of our young manhood, we also furnished hundreds of thousands of dollars in cash in the various war bond drives and other wartime calls, including the Red Cross, war relief, etc. In fact, at this time we are still sending thousands of dollars in food, clothing, etc., to war-torn Europe and other parts of the world—a year after the close of the first part of the conflict.

Our nation was engaged in actual warfare a period of three years, eight months and seven days from the day Pearl Harbor was attacked to the day Japan surrendered. Germany went down three months and six days sooner.

These were bitter years for many Randolph County folks. Fathers who had been married several years and were sober, settled men engaged in making a living for their families were jerked up and sent away to foreign soil, away from their families. Youths still in school were taken to the camps and subjected to the same rules and regulations as the hardened regular.

Rationing was placed on almost every necessary commodity. Wartime mushroom prosperity appeared to undermine the stable peacetime economic and financial structure. General unrest spread over the country. Folks became used to easy money—high wages—and other unnatural conditions which wartime brings.

All this is a part of war. Human life and welfare is the uppermost concern in any war, but there are a lot of bad things which go with war besides actual combat and death. War has no rightful place in a civilized world. War is always "justified" during the period of actual fighting, but there is no true justification for war. The reader may disagree with the author but it is a fact that war is the most destructive and demoralizing agent which mankind is heir to. It not only kills and maims; it destroys morals, initiative; upsets normal living and bankrupts the nations involved, and works hardships on the world at large.

It will be a bright day for the nation and the world as well when we have men in our legislative and diplomatic departments of our government who work continually for a world of peace instead of bickering and manipulating in the affairs of international importance—men who will sit down at a table and work out the differences and petty jealousies instead of supporting a drove of undercover men who do nothing but stir up strife.

Envy and greed are the underlying causes of almost all wars. Another serious cause of war is agreements, treaties, etc. Our forefathers who founded this nation warned us about "entangling foreign alliances." If we had heeded their warning we would have saved ourselves untold grief and loss.

We hope the time is near when the world will realize that it is far better to get along peacefully than to fight.

Miscellaneous

Part Two

OFFICIALS OF RANDOLPH COUNTY SINCE ITS FORMATION

Date	Representative	County Judge	Circuit Clerk	County Clerk	Sheriff	Treasurer	Assessor
1835-1836	L. J. Anthony	P. R. Pitman	B. J. Wiley	None	Wm. Black	None	None
1836-1838	W. Pilbourn	P. R. Pitman	B. J. Wiley	None	Wm. Black	B. M. Simpson	None
1838-1840	None	P. R. Pitman	B. J. Wiley	None	Wm. Black	J. Newland	None
1840-1842	W. A. Houston	P. R. Pitman	J. H. Imboden	None	J. H. Imboden	J. Newland	None
1842-1844	W. M. Mitchell	James Martin	T. O. Marr	None	J. Spikes	J. Newland	None
1844-1846	J. B. Anthony	James Martin	T. O. Marr	None	J. Spikes	J. Newland	None
1846-1848	B. R. Baker	B. J. Wiley	T. O. Marr	None	J. Spikes	W. L. Rice	None
1848-1850	H. McIlroy	B. J. Wiley	L. F. Johnston	None	John Chandler	W. L. Rice	None
1850-1852	James Martin	James Martin	J. F. Walker	None	W. G. Murphy	W. L. Rice	None
1852-1854	W. R. Hunter	W. R. Hunter	E. L. Urmston	None	W. G. Murphy	J. D. Cross	None
1854-1856	W. R. Cain	J. P. Ingram	E. L. Urmston	None	W. G. Murphy	J. D. Cross	None
1856-1858	Michael Beshoars	J. P. Ingram	J. B. Kelsey	None	D. C. Black	J. D. Cross	None
1858-1860	J. H. Purkins	J. P. Ingram	J. B. Kelsey	None	D. C. Black	W. W. Douthitt	None
1860-1862	None	Wm. Thompson	C. C. Elder	None	Mahlon McNabb	W. W. Douthitt	L. F. Johnston
1862-1864	J. F. Harrison	Henry Cockrum	C. C. Elder	None	S. M. Truly	Thomas Foster	L. F. Johnston
1864-1866	J. Hufstedler	Henry Cockrum	Edwin Rockwell	None	D. C. Black	Thomas Foster	L. F. Johnston
1866-1868	W. G. Matheney	Henry Cockrum	J. T. Robinson	None	G. A. Eaton	A. J. Pace	D. C. Downey
1868-1872	J. Dodson	G. V. Corey	J. T. Robinson	None	J. T. Fisher	T. S. Bennett	J. D. Wyatt
1872-1874	P. Pierce	Commissioners	J. Schoonover	None	J. F. Spikes	J. W. Slayton	S. H. Richardson
1874-1876	R. H. Black	Isham Russell	J. Schoonover	None	D. C. Black	A. H. Kibler	J. H. Richardson
1876-1878	Thomas Foster	J. H. Purkins	J. Schoonover	None	Wibb Conner	A. H. Kibler	J. H. Richardson
1878-1880	R. C. Mack	S. J. Johnson	J. T. Robinson	None	Wibb Conner	A. H. Kibler	W. H. Johnston
1880-1882	Perry Nettle	S. J. Johnson	W. T. Bispham	None	A. J. Witt	J. R. Chambers	M. D. Bowers
1882-1884	C. G. Johnston	J. H. Richardson	W. T. Bispham	None	Ben F. Spikes	J. R. Chambers	M. D. Bowers
1884-1886	Perry Nettle	Dan Wyatt	W. S. Tanner	None	Ben F. Spikes	J. R. Chambers	Gid Thompson
1886-1888	John C. Wisner	A. J. Witt	J. T. Robinson	None	W. M. Hogan	S. M. White	Gid Thompson
1888-1890	A. J. Witt	A. J. Witt	J. T. Robinson	None	W. M. Hogan	S. M. White	L. H. Jones
1890-1892	M. D. Bowers	D. C. Black	Ben A. Brown	None	M. R. Armstrong	J. W. Presley	W. T. Stubblefield
1892-1894	C. H. Henderson	H. M. Bishop	Ben A. Brown	None	M. R. Armstrong	J. W. Presley	J. D. Gossett
1894-1896	T. W. Campbell	Wibb Conner	M. R. Armstrong	J. T. Robinson	L. H. Jones	J. N. Gossett	J. L. Fry
1896-1898	H. E. Ruff	J. B. DuVall	M. R. Armstrong	Ben F. Spikes	W. R. Russell	I. N. Sorrell	Tobe Chastian
1898-1900	H. E. Ruff	J. B. DuVall	J. J. Lewis	M. R. Armstrong	W. R. Russell	I. N. Sorrell	J. H. Bennett
1900-1902	A. M. Doss	R. H. Black	J. J. Lewis	M. R. Armstrong	W. A. Jackson	I. N. Sorrell	R. L. Higginbotham
1902-1904	W. A. Jackson	Ben A. Brown	J. W. Going	Ben Johnston	Sam Brown	J. A. Parker	R. L. Higginbotham
1904-1906	W. L. Pope	S. M. White	Dee Mock	Ben Johnston	Sam Brown	J. A. Parker	H. Hollowell
1906-1908	E. N. Ellis	S. M. White	Dee Mock	E. T. Harrison	A. J. Cole	H. L. Haynes	Mason Stacy
1908-1910	J. J. Lewis	Joe Hufstedler	B. B. Raglin	E. T. Harrison	W. R. Russell	Clarence Abbott	Mason Stacy
1910-1912	E. E. Du Bois	M. R. Armstrong	B. B. Raglin	W. H. Phipps	W. R. Russell	Ben F. Spikes	D. D. Mondy
1913-1914	H. M. Crockett	Sam Brown	Ed. R. Hicks	W. H. Phipps	R. H. Gullett	Ben F. Spikes	D. D. Mondy
1915-1916	C. Higginbotham	Dee Mock	Ed. R. Hicks	W. H. Phipps	R. H. Gullett	J. A. White	D. H. Holder
1917-1918	Elijah Dalton	Dee Mock	Ben F. Mays	W. H. Phipps	W. H. Perren	Will S. White	D. H. Holder
1919-1920	A. J. Cole	G. W. Million	Ben F. Mays	Rufus K. Baker	J. P. Spikes	Will S. White	W. E. Tiner
1921-1922	J. E. Smith	Rector Pickett	Joe Snodgrass	Rufus K. Baker	J. P. Spikes	H. L. Haynes	Wesley Brown
1923-1924	J. E. Smith	Joe S. Decker	Joe Snodgrass	Myrt Waldron	C. H. Brooks	H. L. Haynes	Wesley Brown
1925-1926	J. E. Smith	Joe Snodgrass	Rufus K. Baker	Myrt Waldron	C. H. Brooks	John J. Moore	Luther Harnden
1927-1928	H. H. Price	C. H. Brooks	Jeff Lawhon	Jim Shivley	J. T. Thompson	John J. Moore	Luther Harnden
1929-1930	J. E. Smith	Joe S. Decker	Jeff Lawhon	Jim Shivley	J. T. Thompson	Jeff Lawhon	Rex E. Jolly
1931-1932	Rufus K. Baker	Rex E. Jolly	Jack Thomas	Harry Talbott	Roland Morris	Edgar Poe	Rex E. Jolly
1933-1934	Alvin Burrow	Rex E. Jolly	Jack Thomas	Harry Talbott	Roland Morris	Edgar Poe	Walter Jackson
1935-1936	Walter Jackson	Oscar Prince	Carl Brown	Wesley Nibert	Guy Amos	Lawrence Dalton	Earle Tilley
1937-1938			Carl Brown	Wesley Nibert	Guy Amos		

THE POCAHONTAS "COURTHOUSE GANG" IN 1946

The folks who work in the courthouse in Pocahontas are no different and no better than a lot of other folks in Randolph County, and the fact is they do not deserve any more notice except for the fact that they happen to be the ones with whom the author worked during the past two years. This is during the time we have been engaged in the job of being the county treasurer and writing a history of the county on the side.

For the above reason we thought it would not be out of line to record for the future just who composed the "Courthouse Gang" in 1945 and 1946. So here goes:

John L. Bledsoe is judge of the Sixteenth Judicial District of Arkansas. He and his family came to Pocahontas from Izard County about twenty years ago. His wife was a member of a well known family of that section.

Harrell Simpson is the prosecuting attorney for the same district. He came here about six years ago from Sharp County. His wife is a daughter of Mr. and Mrs. F. E. Belford. Belfords have been long time residents of Cherokee Bay and her maternal relatives are the Hatley and Johnston families who have been residents of the county almost a century.

County Judge Oscar Prince is a native of Janes Creek township and is a member of the related Prince-Higginbotham-Bloodworth families of that section. Mrs. Prince is a daughter of the late John D. Campbell, a member of one of the first families who came to Lawrence County.

Walter W. Jackson, Randolph County representative in the state Legislature, hails from the Hamil community and is a member of an early family of the county. His wife was a Tyler, another family which has been in the county since about 1840.

MISCELLANEOUS

Sheriff and Collector Guy Amos came to Pocahontas from the Shiloh community. He is a member of the Amos, Haynes, McIlroy, Pratt and other families of the county. Mrs. Amos was a Going and her mother a Looney. Both are early families of the county, the Looney family being one of the first to settle on Elevenpoint River.

Earle Tilley, tax assessor, is a native of Richardson township and is a member of the related Tilley, Kerley, Redwine and Ingram families of eastern Randolph County. His wife was an Evans, another family of the same community.

Circuit Clerk Carl Brown is a member of one of the early Brown families of western Randolph County. His wife was a Fry. The Fry family was one of the first settlers in the Ravenden Springs community.

Wesley Nibert, county clerk, is a native of Columbia township, a few miles north of Pocahontas. His mother was a Hall. His wife was a Rice. The Rices, Stubblefields, McIlroys and Looneys were related families who settled on Elevenpoint River very early.

Lawrence Dalton, county treasurer and author of this book, is a native of Siloam township. The Daltons settled near the Arkansas-Missouri state line about 1812. His mother was a Marlette, native of Indiana. His wife was a Lamb, a descendant of the early Hatley, Ingram and Lamb families of Little Black township.

County School Supervisor Earl Smith is a member of one of the early Smith families of central Randolph County. His mother was a Brown, one of the early families of the Jackson township section. Mrs. Smith was a Doyle, one of the early Lawrence County families. Her mother was a Lindsey, of one of the early Lindsey families of Randolph County.

Mrs. Lula Cole, of the County Welfare office, is a member of the Thomas family which came to Warm Springs township from Illinois about forty years ago. She is the widow of the late Jack Cole who was related to the Holt and Phillips families of Warm Springs.

Mrs. Cole's assistant, Mrs. Frank Wallace, was a Barden and related to the Hufstedler and Barden families of Roanoke township. The Wallaces came here from eastern Clay County.

In the Federal offices in the courthouse are Mrs. Mildred Dalton, Mrs. Bill Bates and several "newcomers." Mrs. Dalton is the wife of Mack Dalton of Dalton. She was a Hughes. Mrs. Bates is a member of the Keith-Lindsey family.

Uncle Dan Bates, who keeps the lawn mowed so nicely and the inside of the courthouse so spick and span, came to Pocahontas many years ago from the southwestern part of the county. His wife was a Hancock. They reared a large family of boys and girls who are all grown and doing all right for themselves.

The deputies in the offices of the county officials are Oscar Burrow, in the sheriff's office. He is a member of the Burrow family, early residents of Warm Springs. His mother was a Hubbs. Oscar's wife was Mrs. Virginia McGlothlin from Little Rock.

In the tax assessor's office, Green G. Davis is a deputy. He is of the Shaver-Davis family of Ingram township, early residents of the county. Mr. Davis' wife died a few years ago. She was a Starling.

The deputy circuit clerk is Laura Hogan, daughter of Mr. and Mrs. Will Hogan of Pocahontas. Both her parents are from the Ingram-Vernon community. Mrs. Hogan was an Early.

The deputy county clerk is Mrs. Gene Pierce, wife of Douglas Pierce. She was a Holt and related to the early Holt, Moore and Howard families. Her husband is of the Pierce and Farrow families of near Water Valley. Betty, daughter of County Clerk Nibert, also assists in that office.

MISCELLANEOUS

The state revenue collector for Randolph County is John Shivley, Jr. His family came to the Pitman community many years ago. His mother was a Hawkins. His wife was a Parish, all early families of eastern Randolph County.

Charlcie Burr, who works part time in the sheriff's office, is the wife of Charles Burr. She is a member of the Crismon Sago families who have resided in Columbia township a long time.

Ila Fowler, who is Earl Smith's assistant in the county supervisor's office, is a daughter of Mr. and Mrs. Sherman Fowler and a member of two of the oldest families of Little Black township, the Fowlers and the Parishs.

In the recent primary election Carl Brown was nominated for the office of sheriff and collector, Clifford Massey for tax assessor, Earl Chester for circuit clerk, and Bob Harvester for county clerk.

They will go into office January 1, 1947, and together with the two second-termers, Oscar Prince, county judge, and Lawrence Dalton, county treasurer, they will make up the "Courthouse Gang" for the years of 1947-48, if nothing unforseen happens.

Chester comes from Elm Store township; Carl Brown comes from the circuit clerk's office, where he has served two terms; Clifford Massey comes from Jackson township, and Bob Harvester lives in Pocahontas.

Walter Jackson, representative; John L. Bledsoe, circuit judge, and Harrell Simpson are also holdovers from their present offices. Dr. J. E. Smith is state senator from this district, composed of Randolph, Lawrence and Sharp counties.

ODDS AND ENDS OF RANDOLPH COUNTY HISTORY

In writin the history of any community or nation there are a number of incidents which do not seem to fit in with any certain subject or chapter. The same is true of this history. Below we are relating various stories and interesting incidents which are of a miscellaneous nature.

WEATHER

First we will talk of the weather. Weather plays a major role in the life and welfare of the human race. Floods, storms and drouth are the three great destroyers, but extreme hot and cold come in for a part in the show. This section has been visited by a number of destructive tornadoes, or cyclones, as they are most generally called in this country. About ten years before the Civil War a very destructive tornado passed through Randolph County. Coming into the county near Imboden, it travelled by way of the present-day villages of Attica and Maynard and crossed Current River near Success. This path has been followed very closely several times within the memory of living persons. About 1916 a storm travelled across the county a few miles north of this path, and among other damage done, blew away the Methodist church at Siloam and the Church of Christ building at Glaze Creek. A number of people were injured and a few killed by this storm. On May 9, 1927, the worst tornado of recent years crossed the county and killed a number of people and did a lot of damage. This was the storm which tore up the town of Hoxie in Lawrence County and killed around three hundred persons at Poplar Bluff. This storm passed just south of Maynard and tore a path across the country from near Attica, across Richardson and Little Black townships and destroyed a lot of property and killed several people along the way.

MISCELLANEOUS

About forty-five years ago—between 1895 and 1900—there came the worst hail storm which this section possibly ever erperienced. It was of a local nature, occurring mostly in a strip through Siloam township and the lower part of Missouri, near by. Older citizens tell us that slugs of ice fell which were as large as large cabbage heads, only irregular in size and shape. A picnic was being held at Phipps Mill just west of Middlebrook that day and many almost incredible stories were told by different citizens about just what happened. Holes as large as a wash basin were torn through good board roofs. Some livestock was killed, and one man related that one stone struck his wagon tongue and broke it like it was a straw. On Fourche Creek, near the Joseph Dalton farm, some eight miles above the state line in Missouri, so much hail fell on the ground and was washed into the stream by the accompanying rainfall that it filled the stream with the ice and the fish were washed out onto the shoals and gravel bars while numb from the cold. They were picked up in large numbers after the storm subsided. Drifts of ice were still to be seen at noon the next day, although it was in June when this occurred.

Tradition tells us that about 1840 all the streams in the country rose higher than ever before. There have been a number of times when we had high water along the larger streams. In May, 1882, after several days of rain, which greatly damaged the uplands, the rivers became very high. The same thing occurred again in 1890. In 1915 came the "August overflow" which many still remember. After a week of almost incessant rain, all creeks and rivers rose to the highest stage ever known, and thousands of acres of fine crops were destroyed and a lot of livestock was lost. Many people along Current and Black River were forced to leave home, and general destruction was in evidence. In February, March and April, 1927, there was a series of overflows which did much damage, although not as much as the one in 1915, on account of the time of year. This year is remembered as a very wet one. Many farmers in the lowlands had no crop in sight June 1.

The coldest weather which we have record was about the winter 1899. A big sleet, which stayed on the ground about forty-five days, fell during the months of January and February, 1901. The deepest snow that has fallen in this section since its settlement was in the winter of 1886. It is said to have been three feet deep on the level. The winter of 1917-18 is remembered as being the coldest and having the deepest snowfall of recent years. The snow began falling December 7, 1917, and was still on the ground to some extent the latter part of February.

TIMBER WORK AND SAWMILLING

An industry which flourished during the early days of settlement, after the first roads were built and steam power came into general use, was the cutting and sawmilling of the millions of feet of lumber. Our virgin forests were not to be excelled in the South. Some of the finest white oak trees in the United States grew in Randolph County. Sad to relate, much of this fine timber was wasted because of the cheapness and through necessity in the clearing of the fields. The first mills cut only the lumber which was needed locally as there was no market within reach of this section. After the coming of the railroads the story changed. Outside interests came here and bought large tracts of timber and cut the timber into stave and heading stocks, railroad ties, and later into furniture material.

Before the railroads, much timber was "rafted" down the streams. This became quite an industry on the larger streams from about 1890 to 1910. Success (in Clay County), Biggers, Pocahontas (in Randolph County), and Black Rock (in Lawrence County) became known as important mill towns during this period. Other smaller towns sprung up like mushrooms during this period, only to die when the virgin timber supply ran out. Keller, Poluca and Running Lake, in the lowlands between Pocahontas and Biggers, were towns of this kind.

Timber cutting, hauling and sawmilling was hard, dangerous work. The hauling was often done with oxen. Sometimes when the timber was close to the mill, instead of using wagons, "lizards" were used to drag the logs in. These lizards were forked pieces of timber upon which the end of the log was tied and the timber was "skidded" in. This was true principally of the bottom country where the ground was usually damp and "slick." The early steam boilers had their weakness and imperfections. Sometimes they "blew up" and scalded the workers. Among the pulleys, carriages and lines of the unprotected machinery danger lurked. But the timber industry had its lighter side. Lumber camps were established, usually in the bottom country, and a number of men would live here several months and work out the surrounding timber. Old-time dances, shooting matches and other pioneer sports were indulged in. This sort of life was carried on for many years along the lowlands adjacent to our larger rivers. Many families grew up in this work. The Switzer family is especially remembered as being "timbermen" along the west side of Black and Current River, from Pocahontas to Downey's Ferry, during the first years of the present century. But this era has passed. What timber work that is in operation at this time is made up mostly of small sawmills which cut small timber and saw it into railroad ties or small dimension lumber. This is hauled to market by the many trucks which are owned locally, and the bolt-cutter who hauls his short length timber to the local handle mill to be manufactured into various kinds of handles.

ORIGIN OF NAMES OF PLACES

While possibly not historically important, the origin of names is an interesting study, especially when it applies to towns, communities, etc. We have a number of interesting names in Randolph County. The name Pocahontas, for instance, already explained in the chapter devoted to the history of the town and also in the Fourche de Thomas article. Supply is named thus because the early storekeeper who secured a postoffice wanted the public to know that he always had a "supply' of merchandise. There are several communities in the nation of this name. Ingram, located in the central part of the county, was named first for the late G. H. (Dock) Ingram when the name applied at what is now the Price farm on Mud creek. The Ingram of today is located around five miles from the original place so named. The places called Ingram have had various other names, such as "Henpeck" and "Gooberhull." Just wehere these names originated is not known. School District No. 52 (now known as Oak Hill), west of Elevenpoint River, was formerly known as "Hot Corner," and the rural community in the southwest corner of Warm Springs township used to be known as "Warm Corner." The original school house in District No. 2 was located on a level section of land, yet it was named "High Point." It was in this old building that the author learned from McGuffey's that "The Cat sat on the Mat." Many places in the county are named for the family which established the settlement or were local residents. The village of Birdell was named by Joseph Hufstedler for two of his daughters, Birdie and Ella. The postoffice at Noland was named for a young lady, Nova Pyland, who lived in the community at the time the office was named. The original postoffice at what is now Elevenpoint was called "Lima." This is interesting from the fact that Daniel W. McIlroy was the postmaster at that office before he became postmaster at "Peru" in Cherokee Bay in 1883. Mr. McIlroy evidently liked South American names. Just why these offices were thus named is not known. Cedars have been remembered in the naming of many places in the county. School Districts Nos. 26 and 81 are both named "Cedar Grove." One is on the road between Pocahontas and Maynard and the other is on Janes creek above Ravenden Springs. Cedar Ridge School District is located on the western side of Old Davidsonville, and Cedar Bluff school is on Janes creek in Union township. Several names are of biblical origin. Some of them are Palestine School, Siloam Church; there is also a Palestine Church, Antioch Church, Mount Pisgah Church, Shiloh Church. There are two New Home churches and two New Hope schools in the county; also two Ring Schools. There used to be a Macedonia School just west of Warm Springs. Water comes in for its part in the naming of places in the county. We have Warm Springs, Ravenden Springs, Bluff Springs, Spring Hill, Running Lake, Water Valley, to say nothing of all the "creeks." Hills come in for a few names also, such as Allen Hill, Spring Hill, Oak Hill, Union Hill, High Point, Clearview, Fairview, Pleasant Hill, Cedar Ridge, Bald Knob, and Mount Pisgah.

Several communities and towns in Randolph County are named for early families. Among these are Maynard, Dalton, Biggers, Reyno (lds), Pitman, Hamil, Mock, Ingram, Ring, Foster, Debow, Shannon, Holmes, Sharum, Fender and Lesterville. Poynor and Burr (ow), Missouri, just over the state line, are both named for Randolph County families.

ONE HUNDRED YEAR CLUB

The following named families, and possibly others, have resided in the county over a century: Johnston, Bigger, Mock, Shaver, Dalton, Dunn, Hufstedler, Perrin, Sparkman, McIlroy, Stubblefield, Davis, Sloan, White, King, Murphy, Moore, Jarrett, Foster, Lindsey, Ingram, Pitman, Duff, Cockrum, Mansker, Rapert, Carter, Lewis, Reeves, Morris, Wiley, Dean, Crabtree, Miller, Cox, Eldridge, Looney, Black, Janes, James, Martin, McNabb, Nettles, O'Neal, Hudson, Holt, Bailey, Phillips, Spikes, McCarroll, Campbell, Haas, Carroll, Vandergriff.

LAWBREAKERS

Every community suffers some from the activities of the law-breakers. Randolph County is no exception to this rule.

While we believe that this county has been as free from "gangs" or organized criminals as any county in the state, yet we have had our share of individual bad men. There have been a number of murders in the county. Some have been caught and punished for the killings, but from one cause or another some have never paid for their crimes. The first murder of which we have a record is that of Mrs. Polly Hillhouse who was slain by a slave. The slave was hanged at Old Jackson in 1831, the year after the murder. Four or five men have been executed in the county, and one or two have been subjected to the supreme penalty elsewhere for crimes committed in this county. One case of lynching was performed in the county, in Pocahontas. The victim was hanged on the old steel bridge, still standing on the west side of the concrete highway culvert on Highway 67 between the old court square and the Black River bridge. No sheriff or deputy has ever lost his life in the performance of his duty.

So far as we can learn the county has had only one bank robbery in daylight (at Maynard in 1917). The robber was never apprehended. The bank at Reyno was burglarized about 1926, but was unsuccessful. The burglar was discovered, and as he came out of the building was ordered to halt, but instead dropped his loot and ran away. He was never captured. There have been a number of postoffice burglarizing cases. So far as we can learn there has never been a mail or train robbery.

DESTRUCTIVE FIRES

The county has experienced a number of disastrous fires. Pocahontas has had a number which destroyed a large section of the city. The last big fire was about 1914, when the entire block from what is now the bank corner to Johnston's drug store corner was burned out. However, the city has a number of buildings standing in it today which date around seventy to eighty years old. Warm Springs suffered a blow when the forty-room hotel was destroyed at the springs there about fifty-five years ago. Reyno has had a number of destructive fires for a town of its size. During the period from 1924 to 1930 the greater portion of the business section and about fifteen residences were destroyed by fire.

EPIDEMICS

Randolph County has been spared the blight of any epidemic since the days when Old Davidsonville is supposed to have been practically wiped out by yellow fever, except for the influenza epidemic during the winter of 1918-19 when a large number of citizens of the county died of this disease, soon after the close of the first World War.

DROUTHS AND DEPRESSIONS

Randolph County has experienced several severe drouths during the past century. The one we hear most about from the oldest citizens is the year 1881. In that year practically nothing was grown on the farms. Older citizezns tell of the hardships endured by the people as a result of this crop failure. In 1901 the county went through another extreme dry year. There was scarcely any rain from April until September, and the hill land was a total failure. The only crops grown were in the low bottoms along the larger streams, and this was short. The years of 1930 and 1934 were very dry. Hot winds blew which seared the growing crops, even where they were on soil that contained moisture. 1930 is especially remembered since the country was already in the grip of a nation-wide economic depression. This made conditions very bad for all. The farmer failed to produce crops to sustain and support him and the laborer was out of work. Much hardships was endured. The condition was so severe that it appeared that outside help must come in the way of governmental assistance. This did come. It cannot be denied that this was necessary in many cases, but it started a practice which has been held to be entirely too much since that time. Many folks who were self-supporting before this period seem to have "lost their grip," as the pioneer used to say, and have formed the habit of looking to the government many times when they could help themselves. At any rate, the drouths were the "straw which broke the camel's back" and the nation sank into a depression which lasted until the second World War came along to lift it out. There appears, to the writer, to be something radically wrong with our economic set-up when it becomes a fact that the only thing that will (or has) brought our country out of economic stagnation is a bloody war which takes the lives of many of our noble sons.

We hope, for the sake of future generations, that it will be a long, long time before we have another destructive drouth, a serious depression or a bloody war.

They are within themselves a terrible blight upon the wellbeing of the human family, to say nothing of the aftermath which does nothing towards the upbuilding of the people. This is especially true of war.

INTERESTING ITEMS FROM HERE AND THERE

In doing any historical research work we find many interesting items which do not belong in any certain chapter, but are a vital part of the story of any country. This is true of Randolph County history. In this article the writer will include such, beginning with the following: Governor Archibald Yell married Maria Ficklin at Pocahontas, July 7, 1836. Stephen F. Austin, known as the "Father of Texas" and Alamo fame, was appointed by Territorial Governor Miller to the office of judge of the first territorial court which was held July 15, 1820. On the land records, dated September 24, 1818, Richard Woods sold to Joseph Janes a preemption claim on Janes creek "located west of Lot Davis." Stephen F. Austin was a witness to the transaction. Austin possibly resided in Randolph County at this time.

January 9, 1820, Daniel Ashabranner sold a claim on Glaze Kenon creek to Bernard Rogan. Rogan and Daniel

Cheek were the men who laid out the town of Currenton in 1820. Ashabranner is listed as being the operator of a lead mine in Madison County, Missouri, during the period around 1925-30.

George Mansker made a will December 21, 1822, at Greenville, Mo., and James S. Conway, later Governor of Arkansas, was a witness to his signature.

There was not much formality in the first records of the county. The story is well known of the rivalry between old Columbia and Pocahontas over the location of the Randolph county seat in 1835. But the same was true of Davidsonville and this community, although it was known as Fourche de Thomas at that time, when the first county seat of old Lawrence County was established in 1815.

The records show that Basil Boran of the Fourche de Thomas community was accused by Lewis De Munn and others of stating that De Munn and the other members of the courthouse commissioners had double-crossed the citizens of the north part of the county when they decided in favor of Davidsonville. On the date of May 31, 1816, Boran appeared in court and signed a "lie bill," or retraction, to the effect that he knew nothing dishonorable of De Munn and the others and that the charge that he had said these things was untrue.

In another entry a certain man and woman were married and the next record entry is a statement by the man that he was the legitimate father of the woman's five children, and that in the future they were to bear his name.

In one of the first land record entries is that of a grant made by the United States to a soldier of the War of 1812, but the record left off the range in the description and it is impossible to locate it today.

Other interesting stories of happenings in the county during the early days are found in the marriage records. In one instance John Brown applied for a license to marry Mary Jones. (This is not their real names. They have descendants in the county at the present time.) Two days later she married Bill Smith. On the records, two days later, is written: "Miss Jones sacked John Brown and married Bill Smith."

In another instance there is recorded this statement in the space for parental consent if needed: "Mr. County Clerk, please let Bill White have license to marry my daughter by my say so," signed John Doe.

In the marriage records during the time the late Jos. T. Robinson was county clerk, in recording one marriage Mr. Robinson wrote in "Silver and gold I have none, but this couple have my best wishes."

In organizing the first Territorial Legislature in Arkansas at Arkansas Post, February 7, 1820, Edward McDonald, who resided in what is now Little Black township, Randolph County, was elected president of the body. Richard Searvy was elected secretary and Joseph Hardin, speaker. Hardin and Searcy both lived at Davidsonville. This is quite an honor for Randolph County, although this was known as the "delegation from Lawrence County." These men—all three— lived in what is now Randolph County. William Stephenson of Hempstead County was first elected speaker but after serving one day resigned. The story goes that after looking the "rough and ready" assembly of frontiersmen over, he stated that "I had rather shoot then be shot at," presuming that if trouble arose in the session shooting would probably be done first and questions asked afterwards. When Harden took his place he remarked that he had been shot at by the British in 1778 and was not afraid of any of the members and "their small arms."

Mrs. Sallie Pickett, a former resident of Pocahontas who was a granddaughter of Col. John Miller (the father of Gov. William R. Miller), tells of an incident which happened while Colonel Miller ran a store at Davidsonville. A fellow who lived in that vicinity came to Miller's store one day to buy a barrel of liquor. In a few days he was back after another barrel. Colonel Miller questioned the man about using so much liquor in such a short time, thereupon the fellow drawled, "Wall, I don't know as that is so bad bein's there is ten of us in family and we ain't got no cow."

Court was often held out in the open in the summer time. The story goes that often the witness was "stolen" from court to keep him from appearing and that sometimes court was adjourned so that the members could go off on a bear chase that had developed suddenly.

WHERE OUR PEOPLE CAME FROM

It is interesting to observe the ancestry of the folks who make up the present population of Randolph County.

We are prone to think of them as being of English descent, except the families who are descended from the European immigrants who settled in Pocahontas and at Engleberg in 1880 and the years following. This is not altogether true. Our first settlers came principally from the older states of the east or from the sons and daughters of the early settlers who pushed across the Appalachians with Sevier, Harrod and Daniel Boone.

This does not mean that they were English. The Plott family which settled on Fourche was of Pennsylvania German stock. Lewis De Munn, who was the first clerk of old Lawrence County, was of a French family who fled from the mother country during the French Revolution. The same is true of the Garrett family which was related to the Stubblefields and other settlers on Elevenpoint. David Black, who settled at Black's Ferry in 1815, was a grandson of a native of Amsterdam, Holland, of the same name. Dr. J. C. Esselman, who was the grandfather of Mrs. Kate Skinner and Mrs. M. M. Carter of Pocahontas, was a native of Scotland and served through the Revolution as a captain in the British army. Isaac Hurst, the father of Mrs. Lena Black, also of Pocahontas, was a native of Greece. The Simington and Hollowell families are of Scotch ancestry. The Hufstedler family is descended from a German family which came to America about 1775. The Knotts family is Welsh.

The paternal family of this writer is Irish, and the maternal ancestors were Pennsylvania "Dutchmen."

The large group of citizens of the county which are generally thought of as being Germans are not all of that nationality. During the period from 1870 to 1900, or later, we received many good citizens who left the older countries of continental Europe due to political and social dissatisfaction. In this group are Bavarians, Prussians, Austrians, Dutch, French and a few Irish, all generally referred to as either German or Dutchmen. There are very few true English people in this section.

The colored population of Randolph County is not over one hundred and fifty at present, and practically all of these are native descendants of native slaves. This can be proven by most of the family names. Some of these names are as follows: Taylor, Mansker, Duckworth, McCarroll, Oakes, James, Pitman, White, Johnson, etc.

There are no Chinese, Japanese, Italian, Spanish or Greeks in the county. We have some local natives who have Indian blood in their veins, but we do not have anyone who would actually rate as a Redman in the county.

WHO LIVES IN RANDOLPH COUNTY?

The question of "Who lives in Randolph County?" brings to mind a lot of things. We hear of some communities which are peopled with "foreigners." Just what implication this word means varies in different communities. It is a fact that all of us are descended from foreigners. When our forefathers landed in America we were not natives of this land. But, generally, the word means "fresh from some place else," as the little boy once said.

The early settlers of Randolph County came mostly from the older states of the North and East. Some of the best blood that has ever lived in this county, however, came almost directly from some of the countries of Europe.

But, as is true of most early settled sections, we had a number of families which came early and down through the years have occupied a position somewhat like the "First Families of Virginia." They had a feeling that since they were here first that they had a "priority" (to use a word which has come into general use of late) on things. We all re member the time when one of the qualifications for being a choice candidate for public office was that of being born in a log cabin. We all appreciate these conditions and sentiment to some extent. The fact was, as one early settler once stated it, the early comers resented to some extent the intrusion of the ones who came in later. This early settler said, "We ain't aimin' to let these upstarts come in and take over our churches and politics after our daddies and granddaddies started them and done the dirty, hard part."

This condition was true of all pioneer communities. It has faded away during the years, going the way of other sectional differences.

We can remember when the man from the lowlands was a "foreigner" to the inhabitant of the hills and vice versa. The author grew up in the hills of western Siloam township, in the north central part of Randolph County. We remember when the greatest insult that could be hurled our way was being called a "hillbilly" by a resident of Cherokee Bay or Black River bottoms. We retaliated by calling them "swamp angels" and "sandlappers." Stories were circulated in the years past and gone by one faction at the expense of the other. Some of these stories were told by the man in the lowlands to the effect that in the backwoods hills there existed a long, lean, hungry class of hillbillies who never "heard a train whistle," didn't know one letter from another, and who went barefooted nine months out of the year, but who could knock a squirrel out of the top of the highest tree "at one throw." When the hillmen heard these stories they would picture the resident of the bottoms as being "a poor mosquito-bitten, yellow-faced, pot-bellied, malaria-infected sap who didn't know how a well man felt." Adding such explanations of the conditions in the lowlands as "drinking frog soup all summer and wading mud knee deep all winter."

While the lowlanders bragged of the tall corn, big pumpkins and bale-to-the-acre cotton which they grew, the hillmen said it was left to them to gather the crop for them. This statement was made from the fact that each fall many families from the hills would move over into the bottoms and spend the autumn season picking cotton. This was, at that time, the chief source of cash for many hill families.

The hillfolk brought back stories of how the bottoms people "lived out of a paper poke" while making the big cotton crops, and how when fall came the credit merchant "got all they made." There was a much more "live at home" program in effect in the hills than in the bottoms.

The radical resident of the lowlands who said that the hills "looked like starvation" to him was met with the statement that "Hot or cold, wet or dry, you always found plenty to eat on the table any time you stopped for a meal in the hills." With the story of how many dollars a good cotton crop would bring the grower came the rebuttal, "We may not have as much money as you do sometimes, but we stay out of debt."

So on and on the story goes. With the coming of better roads and auto transportation both sections "came closer together." Each Saturday now the folks from O'Kean and

Manson mix and mingle with the folks from Union township, Little Black and Reyno in the large crowd which is always in town (Pocahontas) on that day. This has brought about a better understanding between the different communities, especially the hills and bottoms. Another thing which has had a strong influence on this difference has been the migration from the hills to the bottoms.

The first settlements were in the hills, and for many years before the lowlands were cleared and drained and while the hill land was fresh, people had little desire to move into the bottom sections. With the time arriving that a lot of the hill land had become worn out (before the days of rotation, diversification and other soil conservation practices), the overflow of population naturally looked to the fertile bottom land for homes. The result was the first settlers of this section soon found themselves surrounded by people from the hills. And in the future, if the hillsmen talked about the "sandlapper," he was likely talking about his brother or sister, and after a few years of fusion of the two "kinds" of people in the bottoms there ceased to be much talking about the "hillbilly" because he was somebody's uncle or grandfather "back home."

This is the story of the disappearance of the "hillbilly and sandlapper."

"CARRY ME BACK TO OLD VIRGINIA"

We who live today will never know the loneliness and homesickness which our foreparents felt at times. Moving to a new land, far away from the land of their fathers, carried with it a certain amount of sorrow and regret. After landing in the new community, if things went well, attractions for and memories of the mother country or childhood home faded gradually; but if hardships and privations appeared, which was often the case, a longing for the old home left behind was a natural attraction.

The author of "Carry Me Back to Old Virginia," "West Virginia Hills," "On the Banks of the Wabash," "Old Kentucky Home" and many other songs written during the period of early settlement expresses the feelings of those whose old home was "far, far away."

We who have lived far back enough to have known some of the original settlers who came here from the older states of the East know about this attraction for the old home which remained with these immigrants, some of whom were our grandparents, throughout their lives.

While they lived their lives in their new homes, many of these early-comers remained loyal to the land of their birth; and although they loved their adopted state, nothing here was ever quite as good as it was "back in Old Kaintuck." In their estimation a native of Old Virginia or Kentucky, or some other state from which they came, was just a little superior to other folks. There was just a little more "blue blood" in their veins than possessed by other people. As one writer has said, "The corn grew a little taller, the grass was a little greener and the maidens a lot prettier back home."

The story goes that a few years ago a citizen of a certain community in Randolph County, a natural comic and not too bright mentally, tiring of hearing a certain old fellow of the neighborhood bragging about his old home state of Kentucky, asked the old fellow if there were actually a lot of good folks in that state. "Oh, yes, sir," replied the old fellow, "best people in the world." "I thought so," replied the comic, "because none of them ever moved anywhere else."

Of course this was not really true, as many of the finest families of our county and state came from Kentucky and the other eastern states. But this fellow's statement explains the feelings of many of the "natives" of this section toward those who "brought too much of their old home with them."

Mother Nature has planted in the souls of we humans that feeling and conviction that a lot of things were "a little bigger and a whole lot better" back during our childhood days.

This explains the matter discussed above. There is no water in the world today that "tastes as good" or quenches our thirst like that old spring we can remember at grandfather's or Uncle Elijah's or some other place near our old childhood home. We can see it today—the water boiling up from under a limestone rock and flowing down through the spring lot over a clean, gravelly bottom with peppermint growing along both sides of the water. No one in the world can bake biscuits "like mother used to bake," and Uncle Dan Bates, only yesterday, was telling us that the "best bread in the world" was the "salt-rising" variety which mothers used to make "back in the good old days."

Rivers looked larger, trees were bigger, the "bottom field" looked a lot larger and the corn rows a lot longer, especially when we looked down them over the back of old Jack while we walked along between the handles of a one-horse double shovel. (Evidently they would have looked a lot shorter from the seat of a tractor.)

All this rambling along the subject of homesickness, the memories of youth, etc., may not belong in a county history, but the word "history" itself is truly just "his history," and at last only a story of life. Life is generally thought of as the activities and the peculiar plan of things which Nature created to work in conjunction with that elusive product called "time." And actually history is the recordings of events performed by individuals at certain places, at certain times. All this sounds vague and very abstract, but is a part of the grain or chaff of this book.

But, at last, this subject is bound up in the thought which some writer expressed in printed words when he said:

"Memory, like the ivy, clings
To olden times, and ways, and things."

"OLD TIME RELIGION"

Thousands of pages have been written to record the deeds of those who have been politically prominent in the past. Tons of paper has been used to tell about the activities of military men and record the story of bloody battles. Scores of books have been written to acquaint the reader with the struggles and hardships of the hardy pioneer who pushed into the virgin forests to hew out a home for himself and family.

All this is a part of the huge task of recording history. In fact it has been the major part of practically all histories which have been written.

But there is a class of men who played a leading part in the great drama of pioneer history of Randolph County and the nation who have not been given the space and credit which they deserve. These men are the pioneer preachers. Quite a lot has been said about the early "circuit riders." They were the preachers who travelled around over the land, going from one isolated community to another at regular intervals to preach to the congregations which assembled on these dates. The crowd was made up of the families of the adjacent "neighborhood" which was often ten miles across. Eli Lindsey, pioneer Methodist preacher who lived in this section around 1815, was possibly the best known of the circuit rider class. There were others who belonged in this class, among which was John Young Lindsey, a nephew of Eli, who was an early Baptist preacher who is reputed to have been one of the organizers of old Salem church at Jarrett schoolhouse, Randolph County, which was the first Baptist church in the state. One of the first preachers of the Church of Christ was Samuel McCullah who, according to the records, applied to the elders of his church "at the home of Brother B. States on Fourche de Mas," December 4, 1942, for "written credentials to preach the gospel of the Lord as an evangelist wherever God and his Providence did cast my lot." The credentials were signed by Eld. William Kellett.

Henry Slavens, who was a delegate to the Constitutional Convention in Little Rock from Randolph County, January 4, 1836, was ordained to preach at "Cherokee Bay Baptist Church of Christ" December 4, 1836. Sherrod Winningham and Henry McElmurry were listed as elders. Prior to this, June 7, 1834, Winningham was ordained to preach by William Macon and Henry McElmurry as elders.

During the period from 1815 to 1835 two Catholic missionaries, John Odin and John Timon, did missionary work among the Indians and early settlers around Davidsonville and Jackson.

These were the first preachers, so far as we know, who came to this section to spread the Gospel in the pioneer settlements. There is in existence a long list of preachers who appeared during the period from 1835 to the period of the Civil War. Some of these are referred to even unto this day. Space forbids the naming of many of these old and early men of God. Many who lived and labored and went to their graves "unhonored and unsung" were really greater man in the sight of their Maker than those we hear a lot about.

Below we will list a few of the names of preachers whose names appear on the early records prior to 1860. Among these were John Hovenaugh, Green Moore, Daniel Rose, William Taylor, Joshua Bumpass, Samuel Hutchinson, Mordecai Haliburton, Gideon Shockley, Elisha Landers, James Ferrill, James Garrett, Reuben Black, Jess Burrow, Theopolius Garrett, Abner Garrison and Peter Watson.

The above is only a partial list of the early preachers before 1860.

The following list is made up of some who really belonged in the list above, together with some who labored in the vineyard of the Lord until recently. The second list is as follows: David Sharp, Parson James, M. D. Bowers, Martin Hogan, Peter Shaver, John Yarbrough, John Rush, David Presley, W. S. Southworth, Demps King, William Shaver, Larkin Johnston, Jessie Roach, W. A. Downing, W. A. Goodwin, Arthur Conner, Zera Allen, Isaac Witt, Jesse Robinson, D. M. Robinson, J. F. Armstrong, R. F. Carroll, J. R. Pratt, J. A. Lemmons, Eld. Hollowell, W. T. Shoffit, Father O'Kean, Alec Fowler, E. T. Lincoln, and a lot of others which should be listed here who are not remembered at this time.

A third list which brings us down to the present, although only the ones of long service in Randolph County are listed, is as follows: S. L. Johnston, A. B. Shaver, Know Belew, J. Will Henley, J. A. Spence, J. A. Allison, W. W. Bailey, O. H. L. Cunningham, Craven Wilson, Bynum Black, F. C. Neely, Amos Lemmons, John H. Harper.

Only a few of the first ones named at the beginning of this chapter were really "circuit riders." Most of them were men who lived at a certain town or community and preached at various places as they were called, or went on their own accord, to build up the various congregations of their affiliations.

There is no other profession that has done more good for less pay than the pioneer preacher. He has repeated the story of John of old a thousand times by going out and "preparing a way for others to follow."

In most pioneer frontier communities he was the next man to come into the settlement after the settler arrived with his family. He often served as both preacher and school teacher. Many times he went out and with his own hands built the first church building, a rough log cabin, but here he proclaimed to all the world that there was a Divine Being "from whom all blessings flow," and who in return for these blessings expected mortal man to love and respect him and to live lives according to the rules laid down in his book.

The old-time protracted meeting, which has been mentioned before, was a valuable institution of the early settlements. It not only provided a place for the folks to enjoy themselves socially, it builded up the morals of the settler and instilled in him the precepts of the Golden Rule.

This protracted meeting could never have happened if there had not been a self-sacrificing preacher "at the head of things." He often labored for weeks at a time with the congregation, and in return received only whatever pay the folks felt disposed to pay him. The pay was usually not enough to provide a living for his family and he had to work in the field or shop throughout the week to "splice out" his ministerial salary to the point where it provided the necessary food and shelter for his family.

Many have been the instances where the early preacher has walked or ridden horseback many miles to preach "over Saturday night and Sunday" and was not paid one cent, or possibly given a few old clothing for his family or a piece of home-cured bacon or a "poke of meal." To many of we who live today who are used to seeing a lot of our preachers set their own price which, if they are not paid this, will not work for us, cannot fully appreciate the conditions under which the early preacher labored. But, in fairness to all, we know that there are possibly very great extremes in both cases.

Isaac Witt, one of the pioneer Baptist preachers of central Randolph County, whose family was related to the writer's father, used to work all week in the fields with his children and on Sunday put on his starched, studded front shirt and homespun suit and start out over a road, sometimes several miles long, to preach twice that day and return home that night. The trip was usually made in an old-time one-horse buggy which was pulled by one of his ponies which had been hitched to a plow all week. Stuffed snugly in behind the seat was a few ears of corn or a sheaf of oats, because Parson Isaac never knew for sure that he would be invited home by some brother who had "hoss feed." Monday morning would find him again at the handles of the plow. This story was true of many other such early preachers. But Parson Witt, like a lot more of these grand old men of God, made his mark. The Baptist church at Maynard is today known as Witt's Chapel, in his honor.

The story goes that Rev. L. F. Johnston, one of the early Methodist preachers of the county, would walk for miles to preach to the settlers around Siloam, Old Mount Pisgah and other early communities. He reared a large family and accumulated some property while doing so. Ben Johnston, now living in Pocahontas, who is the grandson of the above-named pioneer minister, once stated to this writer that his grandfather on his mother's side of the family built a church-house for his grandfather on his father's side to preach in. This is true since the old Mount Pisgah church which was located just west of the present Ingram postoffice was built largely through the efforts of William Spikes several years before the Civil War. William Spikes was the father of the late Martha Spikes Johnston, mother of Ben Johnston.

Eld. Joe H. Blue, veteran minister of the Church of Christ, once told the writer that he preached a whole year once for less than fifty dollars. During this year he states that he made long trips through snow and rain and conducted many funeral services, wedding ceremonies, etc., besides preaching at several different churches.

Many other old preachers devoted long years of service in the task of spreading Christian influence in a new land. Such men as Uncle Peter Shaver, David Sharp, S. L. Johnston, J. Will Henley, David Presley, Arthur Conner, William Shaver, Demps King, J. F. Armstrong, J. Amos Lemmons and countless others whom we would like to name here left their footprints on the sands of time. The amount of good they did can never be measured. While their work here possibly was never appreciated enough, evidently "a crown is laid up in Heaven" for them.

The families of these men are not to be forgotten, especially the wife and mother. It was she who stayed behind and "kept the home fires burning" while her husband went forth to work for their Master. Her task was not easy.

The churches of the county were divided principally between the Methodist, Baptist and Church of Christ during the early days although there were several Presbyterians, Catholics and scattered groups of Church of God or Holiness. Many communities had a "meeting house" where all sects and beliefs were welcome to come and preach. While this was true in some communities, the line was usually drawn as to who the church building belonged to. Of the early rural communities usually one belief predominated pretty strongly until modern days. With better roads, improved means of travel and outside influence, some of the communities which were once practically "one hundred per cent" strong in one church are now greatly mixed. One belief during the early days "ran through the family" in many cases. This is an exception today.

THE OLD-TIME COUNTRY STORE

Possibly this article does not belong in a book which is supposed to be devoted to the task of recording the happenings of historical importance of our people, but since time and space has been given to other institutions we feel that the old-time country store, with the proverbial "pot-bellied stove and open cracker barrel," should be given some notice.

The first store which was "opened for business" in this section during the days of early settlement was the "trading post," located on a larger stream, where the boats brought him coffee, calico, spices and several other items which were not obtainable locally. The operator of the trading post exchanged his merchandise for furs which the hunters brought to him. In some places beeswax, which had been obtained from robbing bee trees in the forests and "bear grease" which was rendered from the flesh of bears killed locally, was also used in place of cash in buying their needs. Very little money was used as a medium of exchange.

This first merchant knew nothing of the art of display and merchandising. The procedure was very simple. He received his wares from the boatmen and traded them to the neighbors for their produce, and the boatmen picked up the produce and brought him some more wares.

After the establishment of "settlements" some enterprising settler built a log house and announced to the public that he was opening up a store which would carry in stock "the latest pieces of wearing material and silks from New Orleans," or maybe it was Pittsburgh. Occasionally some merchandise found its way into the frontier from New York. But even with this type of merchandise available at times, for many, many years the pioneer mother manufactured the clothing for the family at home.

The inside of one of these early-day stores presented a varied picture. All kinds of food products which we now buy in packages was sold in bulk from bins. Soda, salt, sulphur and many items in the drug line was sold by the ounce or pound. There were no paper bags, so the article was wrapped up in paper. The first scales were a far cry from our automatic electric calculating ones. At first "balances" were used. They were made like the picture you sometimes see today in drug advertisements. Everything was placed on one side and the proper size weight was placed on the opposite side and the commodity was "weighed in the balance." After this came the old scoop and beam weight scales. Thousands of items which are very commonplace today were unheard of even until the turn of the last century. Of the dozens of breakfast foods on the market today, fifty years ago and before there usually was nothing but unpolished rice, and it was not always available. Then came rolled oats. The early store did not have canned foods. There are many folks living today who, when they were children, never saw anything canned come from the store unless it happened to be a can of peaches which father bought for a sick member of the family the year following a "peach failure." One of the first dry goods items to come into popular use, which was purchased at the local store, was a coarse, unbleached cotton cloth, generally called "factory," because it had been made at a "factory" instead of at home. This material was the forerunner of our present-day "domestic" and sheetings. This material was woven in the mills of New England and came to this section over the long route by water down the Atlantic coast to New Orleans and up the Mississippi and our smaller streams by steamboat. It was in the latter half of the past century before meat was sold in the stores, except an occasional extra "side of bacon" which a local prosperous farmer had "to spare" along during the late summer from his smokehouse, which he wished to dispose of before "hog-killing time," about November. The first packing house lard which came to the stores of Randolph County came in "hogsheads" or large wooden barrels. It was sold in bulk. The customer brought along his container and bought any amount he wished. You could generally tell whether the storekeeper was right- or left-handed by which side of his coat was the "greasiest," where he had leaned over the edge of the barrel when he was dipping out the lard. The first shoes to come to our local stores were the old split-leather type "brogans." After becoming wet a few times the leather grew as stiff and hard as sheet metal, and many of our prominent men past middle age today know how it feels to have his ankles chaffed by the top of the old brogans. To make children's shoes last longer, a toekick made of a strip of copper or brass was placed around the toe of the shoe. This addition to the split-leather product did not add materially to the comfort of the article. Hosiery was made at home, for both men and women. Many a righteous mother, during the days of forty and fifty years ago, charged that her "modern" daughter-in-law was "too onery to do her duty" when she went to the store to buy the black-ribbed cotton hose for her children instead of knitting them herself. The nice, smoothly-milled cotton hose available today, which the present-day lady "wouldn't be caught out in the dark with a pair on," would have been a luxury when grandmother was a girl. One of the most profitable departments in the early general store was the drug section. The early "elixirs" which were recommended to cure almost every ill which the human is heir to, found ready sale to the early settler, especially during the days before the country doctors were close enough to call or consult. The many "quack" remedies which produced unfavorable results, and the passing of tighter drug laws to curb them, slowed this line down some.

A popular type of early-day store was the "furnishing store." We think of such a store today as being a large business which deals with heavy merchandise, especially furniture. This was not true of the early store of this description. It was a store which extended "gin whistling" terms, or spring to fall credit to farmers mostly, who in turn gave the merchant a mortgage on "about everything except the old lady and the kids," as one fellow stated it. About March the first the papers were fixed up for a certain amount, due about October the first. This kind of credit was expensive on the customer. Prices, through necessity, were high. A part of this increase in price was due to the fact that the merchant had his capital tied up in mortgages for two-thirds of the year. And, of course, there were some credit losses due to short crops, etc.; but since the man obtaining the credit was bound to the merchant, he was more or less at the mercy of said merchant, and if the latter desired to place too high a profit on the merchandise, there was little the customer could do about it. This was often true, but, strange to say, many people would patronize this kind of store year after year, and as a result oftentimes drift into the class who just really worked all the year for what his credit was worth at the store. Of course this was not always true. Some merchants of this kind of store were really and truly benefactors to the population, especially during the lean years. They "carried" the people over until better times enabled them to become self-supporting and pay out also. This type of store flourished during the years before the coming of modern credit agencies which finance the farmer on reasonable rates and moderate terms. This enables him to pay cash and take advantage of competitive prices.

The country store, all through the years, has become an American institution. Here the citizens gathered before the days of daily mail and radio to discuss the weather, the issues of the day, and to trade horses and other activities. Some of these were to pitch horseshoes out under the neighboring trees or play ball or marbles. This was often done while waiting for their "grinding," as often the neighborhood grist mill was located near the store. Here was usually held the candidate speakings, the elections, and many other forms of community get-togethers.

The modern store is more attractive. It is more sanitary. It is more convenient and complete, but it has lost something which is hard to define, which the old-time crossroads store possessed.

OLD-TIME SINGING

There possibly are those who may think that singing is of such unimportance that it has no place in the recordings of the past. We differ with those who believe this. One leading jurist has said that when you find a community with a good singing class you found a good community, morally.

The pioneer who, after laboring in the fields and forests for six days, received spiritual and physical contentment and relaxation through the singing of songs of praise to his Master on the Sabbath day.

Possibly the best known vocal music teacher the county has produced was J. E. Wilson, who taught classes in many communities of the county, especially in the vicinity of Pitman, Supply and Maynard, during the period from 1880 until about 1905.

When the Old Folks Singing holds it annual convention at Maynard each year, in September, old Professor Wilson is always remembered. Others who were identified with this institution who have passed on are John D. Campbell and L. F. Blankenship.

Other early singing teachers of that period were a Mr. Tracy and a Mr. Lillard. Lillard was from the vicinity of old Walnut Hill. They both taught schools in different places.

The first method of singing was what we would call the "Read, Repeat and Sing" method. The leader would stand before the class and read from the book, which was usually the old "Christian Harmony" or "Class, Choir and Congregation" book, and the class would repeat the words after him. This was done a verse at a time, and then they would sing the words and music.

We do not have a complete list of those who were song and class leaders during the days before the coming of modern music and "round notes." However, we do know of some of them. There are others of later dates who really belong in this class, but the following are among the leaders who were active during the days when the "old-time singing" was the current style used, and some of these are still active today: Calloway Pringle, Steadman Johnston, T. R. Roberson, Granville Wright, Lee Farrow, Mr. Gannoway, Albert Taylor, Ozzie Templeton, Jack Cole, Noah Phillips, John R. Holt and others we do not know about. Wright, Farrow, Pringle, Phillips, Gannoway, Cole and Templeton are deceased.

The good done by these pioneers on vocal music is not to be belittled. Working in connection with the early ministers and teachers of the county, they did much to build up the moral and educational side of life for those who lived during the days when our country was in its formative period.

THE KU KLUX KLAN IN RANDOLPH COUNTY

The story of the Ku Klux Klan or "Ku Klux," as we have heard them called, is a familiar story in this section, even though at this date there are very few persons who were members or even remember the activities of the original Ku Klux.

This was an organization of local citizens, organized and operated in secret, during the days of Reconstruction following the Civil War. It was born of a desire of the local citizens to secure control of their communities from the more or less unscrupulous individuals who had come into the country from the North at the close of the war Another plan of the Ku Klux was to act as a check on the colored people who lately having obtained their freedom might become unruly and abusive. Very little evidence of the latter was in evidence. Actually, the chief activity of the organization turned out to be the warning and often punishing of wrongdoers in the country, many of which were the low moral and "ne'er do well" type of native citizens.

If a local citizen was suspicioned of stealing corn from his neighbor's crib, or had been cruel to his family, or a man or woman had been known to have lived in adultry, etc., they were called upon during the dark hours around midnight or later and given dire warnings. If he stopped the doing of what he was accused, no other visits were made. If he persisted in the offense, he usually found himself being bound over a convenient log and "horse-whipped." One whipping, which was administered by some pretty strong-armed citizen, usually was enough.

The members of the Klan had certain meeting places and at these meetings, which were held in the dead of the night in some remote section before a huge log fire, the general moral and political condition of the neighborhood was discussed. If it was found that some citizen in the community needed "attending to," the group proceeded to his home and performed the task, as described above.

They were usually clad in long white robes which covered them from head to foot, and often carried lighted torches and other paraphernalia which was used to bring terror to the heart of the wrongdoer. The chief source of the strength of the Ku Klux was the secrecy of who made up the members of the organization. Those who were not members did not know who was "looking at them," as one darky explained.

There was a lot of good done during this unsettled period by the Ku Kluxs, but, as is true of many organizations, churches, etc., some of the wrong kind of people became members, and there were cases where unfortunate incidents occurred which were committed by undesirable characters and the Ku Klux were given credit for the deed which finally caused it to lose its popularity and prestige.

SLAVERY

The question of slavery was discussed in brief in the chapter about the Civil War, but we desire to go into the matter further due to the fact that it was a very vital issue and a serious proposition with the first people who came to Randolph County.

There has possibly been more prejudiced statements been made on the question of slavery than any other subject in our history. The stories of extreme cruelty imposed on the blacks were badly exaggerated. There is no doubt that some owners were cruel to their slaves, but the majority were given fair treatment, and many were the tears shed both by master and slave when either passed away. Some men are mean to their families. Some men are cruel to their livestock, and some army officers were lowdown enough to mistreat the private in the army under the disguise of "army discipline." The same was true of the slaveowner. It all depended on what sort of man he was. We all have heard how many former slaves came to the "big house" of their master when they heard about Lincoln's Emancipation Proclamation and assured them of their loyalty. The writer's own paternal grandfather's life was saved during the battle of Prairie Grove by a faithful black man who carried him out of the thick of the battle after he had been wounded.

The wife whose husband was away at war during the sixties many times tucked her little ones to bed at night satisfied with the thought that no one could harm her brood so long as old Mose or Rastus remained in his cabin close by. One writer said that a few thousand torches in the hands of the blacks left at home would have ended the war in thirty days, to the sorrow of the South, but not one was lighted.

Such was the picture, except in obscure instances, of the loyalty and bond of affection between master and slave.

Many interesting stories are handed down to us concerning the colored folks during and after this period. J. B. Weaver tells a story which came to him from his grandfather. He states that in the years before the war a family lived on the farm now owned and occupied by Robert Vann and family out east of Maynard which owned some slaves, among which was a negro woman who was extremely fleshy, weighing around seven hundred pounds. The owner decided to sell his slaves and offered the fat woman for sale and had no bidders. She was considered too fat to work. She was again offered for sale and a fellow bought her. He was told that she was useless. He remarked that she had been allowed to sit around and eat and that he had a different remedy, remarking that "she will be able to chop cotton next spring." The story goes that he took her home and put her on a diet of bread and water, and Dinah lost the extra avordupois, her health improved and she did chop cotton the next spring.

The colored man has been the victim of much abuse and discrimination in the past. A noted educator has said that if the white man of today, regardless of nationality and creed, had been subject to the things which the negro had during the past three hundred years, he doubted if they would now present within their ranks one man who was as good a citizen as hundreds of colored people are today.

During the political campaign of 1944, when the subject of negroes voting in state primaries was a heated issue, a highly respected colored man and landowner of Cherokee Bay was discussing the matter with the writer. Among his remarks he stated: "All the meanness which we colored folks know was taught us by you white folks, as we were totally ignorant when we were brought over here from Africa." This statement impressed me. There is a thought behind this statement.

Anyway, the negro was at one time a very valuable piece of property. He was looked upon in the same light as a horse or cow. The plantation owner felt that dire calamity stalked his door any time his slaves were taken from him. Financial and social standing was measured according to the number of slaves the planter owned during the first half of the nineteenth century. Slave ownership was general. Practically every man of means, and especially those who did farming extensively, owned one to twenty slaves of different ages. When the issue was attacked from a moral standpoint, some few liberated their negroes. Some who had slaves considered it a "necessary evil," but with most owners little thought was given to this angle. A few folks today, in speaking of their ancestors, are inclined to leave the impression that "my grandfather was not a slaveowner," but we find that most of them were. By checking the early records we find that most of the early preachers were slaveholders. In fact, we find recorded where Eli Lindsey, who was one of the first "circuit riders" of Arkansas, owned slaves while residing in Randolph County. On page 383 of the old record book "B" of old Lawrence County is recorded a transaction wherein Benjamin Williams sold to Eli Lindsey "One negro woman named Penny, one negro boy named Tom, one negro boy named Frank, and a negro girl named Mary." This was September 10, 1822. Lindsey afterwards sold these slaves to John Hinds.

Practically all of the civilized world today is free of slavery. We are all glad that this problem is settled and that the practice has been abolished for all time. Yet during that colorful era, when slavery flourished, we find that it was practiced and generally accepted by the peoples of the entire civilized world.

SOME OF RANDOLPH COUNTY'S NOTED MEN OF THE PAST

In writing a history of the nation, or of a state,, the historian invariably includes a list of the "Ten Greatest Men" of the nation or state, although the number is not always ten.

This list is usually secured by referring to the Hall of Fame or by a "straw vote" from the people. This is not such a hard task where miles of terra firma spread between the author and those whose friends and kinsmen were not included. The story is different with the poor historian of a county. Here he is placed "face to face" with all the people and with a list which would put the current "Who's Who" or "The Four Hundred" to shame, and with the unpleasant (and possibly unwise) task of attempting to choose a limited number of names from a long list of illustrious citizens of our own native county. But here goes, "so help me God."

The three "first citizens" of the county are like the story of the fellow who, upon imbibing too freely of the "spirits which invigorate," when asked who the toughest character in town was, replied, "There's just two of them and I'm both of 'em."

JOHN JANES

The "first citizen" of Randolph County cannot be designated. John Janes, who, as Shinn's History states, settled on Janes creek in 1809, is given recognizance by that historian as being the first man to locate in the county. Janes was a Revolutionary soldier who was in the battle of Yorktown. Soon after the close of the Revolution he came west, stopping at the post of St. Louis for awhile and then coming on down into this section. Certain members of the family claim as early as 1805. His place of settlement is said to have been on what is known as the Bridges farm, about one mile above the present J. J. Brooks farm, near a large spring. His son, Jim Janes, father of Mrs. Belle Galbraith, now living in Pocahontas, built what is probably the oldest house still standing in the county, in 1840. This old house is just south of Ravenden Springs. At any rate, John Janes is one of the first citizens of Randolph County. He married Mary Black, daughter of David Black, who settled on Elevenpoint in 1815. The Janes family intermarried with the Wells, Black, Galbraith and Wayland families early.

Matthias Mock

Next on the list of firsts is Matthias Mock, mentioned a number of times elsewhere in this book. He settled on Mud creek in 1815, and Reynolds in his history of Arkansas gives him credit as being the county's first settler. Mock married Leah Shaver, a daughter of John Shaver, another early settler on this creek, as his first wife, and after her death he married Margaret Mansker, June 24, 1828, a daughter of George Mansker who settled on the creek named for him, just north of the city of Pocahontas, in 1817. Mocks third wife was Amanda Rasberry. Mock was the father of a large family, and from these there are legions of descendants scattered over the South and West at the present time. There is within the county at the present time at least a hundred families who trace their ancestry to Matthias Mock.

Dr. William Jarrett

Third on the list of "first" citizens is Dr. William Jarrett. His descendants say that he came to the community where the present-day Jarrett schoolhouse is located about 1800. He is reputed to have purchased a land claim from Richard Fletcher in 1801, in this community. Richard Fletcher was the father of John Gould Fletcher who lies buried in the old Lindseyville cemetery, and who was the father of the first Fletchers in Arkansas. If this claim could be proven, it would establish William Jarrett as the first known settler in the county. Fletcher was one of the original settlers at Watauga, the first settlement in Tennessee, and it may be that he owned a claim here before the family came, otherwise that family would come in for consideration as the first family of the county.

Dr. Jarrett married Hannah Seavers, who was a daughter of Martin Miller. Martin Miller owned land in this community during the first years after 1800, and in 1821 he made a will giving a part of this to Mrs. Jarrett. Mrs. Jarrett first married Gabriel Seavers, a soldier of the War of 1812, and who was wounded at the battle of New Orleans.

Dr. Jarrett was a physician, possibly the first one in Randolph County. He is mentioned in the writings of Englemann, the German scientist who made a trip from St. Louis to Little Rock in 1837. Dr. Jarrett was the father of Henry Conway Jarrett and other children. Henry Conway was the father of Uncle Joe Jarrett who lives on the old homestead at this time, and also other children.

Dr. Peyton R. Pitman

Dr. Peyton R. Pitman settled at what is now known as the old Pitman Ferry on Current River about 1811 or 1812. He was a physician and also justice of the peace for many years. When the county was formed in 1835, he was chosen as the first county judge. For many years his name figured prominently in the affairs of the county. He was at one time postmaster at the old Fourche de Thomas postoffice, and it is possible that he lived at that place even though he owned and operated the ferry and his large plantation on Current River. Erasmus D. Pitman was his son, and a number of people in the county at this time are his descendants. When Dr. Englemann passed down the old Military road in 1837 he states that the doctor (Pitman) had a very fine home and broad acres of fertile land on both sides of the river. Elsewhere in this book is a picture of the old ferry place as it appears today.

BURWELL J. WILEY

Burwell J. Wiley, who was the first clerk of Randolph County for a period of seven years and the third county judge for four years, was one of the best known men of the county during the first days of settlement.

He was a school teacher, justice of the peace, and was prominent in all public affairs for many years. He was the father of Henry Wiley and other children. A number of Henry Wiley's children reside in Pocahontas at this time. Wiley township was named for this family.

On the records of the county, book number one, page one, dated April 19, 1852, is recorded what is known in the records of Randolph County as the "Genesis of Randolph County." It concerns the activities of B. J. Wiley and its author is unknown, possibly written by a contemporary official.

The "Genesis" is as follows: "In the beginning was B. J. Wiley and B. J. Wiley was the clerk, and the clerk was B. J. Wiley, so sayeth the law. This is the book of the generation of Randolph County. The Territory of Arkansas begat Lawrence County and Lawrence County begat Randolph County. Randolph County was in existence three hundred and sixty-five days and begat B. J. Wiley. B. J. Wiley reigned fifteen years, during which time he labored hard in the services of his country and begat sons and daughters. And after B. J. Wiley had lived forty and seven years, in the fifteenth year of his reign, there came a voice from his subjects (the people) saying: 'B. J. Wiley, thou good and faithful servant, in whom we are well pleased, thou has labored long and faithful, thou has done mighty deeds, thou voice was heard in the council halls of they state, thou name has been enrolled on the escutcheons of fame and safely filed in the archives of the halls of the legislature of your adopted state, there to remain a monument to future generations.'

"Then our beloved and favorite son, thou wearied mind and toiling limbs must have rest and refreshments; retire from thy labor, enter into private and perfect retreat, and let thy gray hairs go down in peace to they grave. And when thou art dead, thy body laid beneath the green sod, then will we rear a monument over thy remains and wear the usual badge of mourning for thirty days. And B. J. Wiley heareth a voice and was well pleased; and the fifteenth year of his age, the eighth month of the year, and the sixth day of the month, and the fourth hour of the day, Wiley retired from his labor. And on the same day all his labors were completed.

"On the seventh day of the same month of the same year he rested from all his labors. Such is the generation of the first born."

Thus is the story of one of Randolph County's first officials, told in a unique way by someone who knew Mr. Wiley well and desired to make a matter of public record the activities of one who did much to help get the wheels of the infant county in an infant state rolling smoothly.

James P. Ingram

In the list of leading men in the history of Randolph County the name of James P. Ingram figures prominently, as does that of his son, J. W. (Blind Bill). The elder Ingram settled near the present Ingram cemetery, between Maynard and Supply, in 1824, and for exactly one-half a century he was one of the leading men of the county. He was county judge from 1854 to 1860, was justice of the peace and deputy sheriff for over twenty years, and possibly was the administrator of more estates than any man in the county's history. The official records show where he was guardian of many orphan children, was road commissioner and other local activities.

In the family history section of this book will be found a more detailed story of these two men. Uncle "Blind" Bill followed in the footsteps of his father, except he held no county office for many years and the one of the great characters of the county. Both men were sociable, yet unassuming men. While well fixed in this world's goods, they avoided display and show. The story goes that during the time James P. was county judge, one day a prominent attorney of this time desired to see the judge on official business. Not knowing Judge Ingram personally, he rode up to the judge's home and inquired for "Squire Ingram." Mrs. Ingram told him he would possibly find him down on the creek. The visitor rode down to the creek and found "a fellow attired in a long shirt, plowing corn with a yoke of oxen." He asked the fellow where he could find the judge. Thereupon the "fellow in the long shirt" told him he was the judge, much to the surprise of the attorney.

Many descendants of James P. Ingram reside in the county today. My wife's great grandfather.

Edward McDonald

The name of Edward McDonald in the history of Randolph County has an interesting angle. So far as we know, no one knows where he came from. He was a prominent figure in the county, especially in the Fourche de Thomas settlement during the early days. He was old Lawrence County's representative at the Territorial Legislature in 1820 at Arkansas Post. Richard Searcy and Joseph Hardin also served with him. McDonald was elected President of the Council.

He married Milly Drenold at the home of Jarrett Robinson at Fourche de Thomas (then called Columbia) March 21, 1842, although he had figured prominently in the affairs of this section for many years previous. This was possibly his second marriage.

The records show where he purchased lots thirteen and fourteen in the town of Davidsonville, February 6, 1817, from William Drope, a cotton merchant of New Orleans who was also a land speculator who owned several tracts of land in this section at that time.

On date of July 29, 1822, Jacob Miller sold Joseph Looney and Edward McDonald the farm known as the Hix plantation on Current River.

He was also justice of the peace for a number of years and is listed as witness and executor of several wills, but his name seems to fade from the written records and memory of men during the forties, and oblivion has swallowed up his final destiny. Possibly someone who is a descendant of this early man of old Lawrence and Randolph County will tell us where the family now resides.

Joseph J. Anthony

After the organization of Randolph County, her first Representative in the lower house of the Arkansas state legislature was Joseph J. Anthony.

At the time of his election, Anthony lived in section 20, township 21, north range, 3 east. His farm was the southeast quarter of the section named above. This place is east of the present town of Supply and is now in Clay County. For several years after the formation of the county, Randolph extended over into what is now Clay County for some distance.

During the first term of the legislature in 1937 Anthony was murdered in the old statehouse by John Wilson, who was the Speaker of the House at that time. Thus Randolph County's first representative is remembered chiefly as losing his life while at the post of duty for his people.

Trouble came up over Anthony's stand against the rechartering of the Real Estate banks of which Wilson was president at the time. An argument ensued after Anthony had offered an amendment and the two met in the aisles in bodily conflict. Anthony was stabbed and died instantly. Wilson was arrested and charged with first degree murder. The case was taken to Saline County where he was acquitted, a verdict which caused intense indignation throughout the state. Wilson was a brother to the wife of James Campbell, the first sheriff of Lawrence County. After the crime Wilson was expelled from the legislature, Grandison D. Royston taking his place as Speaker, and he moved to Pike County (he then represented Clark County) where five years later he again was elected to the same office, and again caused trouble in the body, this time with Dr. Lorenzo Gibson, who reminded Wilson of his previous crime here when he showed a disposition to start a fight.

The records of the county show that on date of January 1, 1838, one Samuel Anthony appeared in court and asked to be appointed administrator of the estate of Joseph J. Anthony, stating that "so far as is known he left no will and no known relative or representative nearer than myself." He does not state his relationship, which was possibly a cousin. He was appointed.

Robert N. Hamil

One of the best known merchants who has lived in Randolph County was R. N. Hamil. He is a son of William A. Hamil and Sarah Elizabeth Crepps, natives of Indiana but who came to the county in 1848 when R. N. was one year of age. For over one-half a century "Uncle Bob" sold merchandise in Pocahontas.

The author's maternal grandfather once told us many years ago that in 1882, the year following the serious drouth, that he and many of his neighbors traded with Mr. Hamil on credit from March until "gathering time" to enable them to make a crop after the complete failure of the year before.

He said he and the others living around him (He lived out east of Attica at that time.) would hitch up early in the spring and drive into Pocahontas, where they would go to the store of Uncle Bob and "lay in the summer's provisions." It was not a case of going to town every few days as we are accustomed to doing at this time.

The story goes that a certain resident of the county approached Mr. Hamil and asked to be furnished through the summer. After the necessary papers had been made, Mr. Hamil asked the man what he wanted to buy that day. The reply was, first on the list, a complete outfit of fish hooks, gun powder, shot and several kinds of "twist and flat" tobacco. Upon hearing this, the story goes, Uncle Bob tore up the papers and told the man he just couldn't see his way clear to credit him.

An advertisement of forty-six years ago listed him as "The Pioneer Merchant of Pocahontas."

R. N. Hamil was a half-brother of Uncle Bill (William H.) Waddle and Isabelle Waddle, the first wife of John P. Black, another early merchant of Pocahontas. Mrs. Kate Henderson was an own sister to Mr. Hamil.

His son, Dr. W. E. Hamil, lives in Pocahontas at present.

Elder Isaac H. Witt

One of the pioneer preachers of Randolph County was Isaac Witt, better known among the older citizens as "Parson Witt." Parson Witt came to Randolph County from Gibson County, Tennessee, in 1868. He was the son of Charles Homer Witt of the above-named county.

The wife of Parson Witt was Mary Christiana Shelton, daughter of Jeremiah Shelton, also a Tennesseean. Both Eld. Witt and his father-in-law were Missionary Baptist ministers. Jeremiah Shelton is of the same Shelton family as the noted Revolutionary soldier, John Shelton, who built the well known "Old Rock House" which has been a landmark since about 1790 on the road between Dixon Springs and Hartsville, Tennessee.

The author's paternal grandmother, Christiana Everett Dalton, was also a member of this same Shelton family, which was also related to the Johnson family (John, "Muxy" Jim and others).

The children of Parson Witt were Almus J., who was sheriff and collector and judge of Randolph County, postmaster at Pocahontas and a noted attorney here for many years; Christiana, who married P. W. Kidd; Cora, who first married James W. Shaver and later Wm. L. Johnson; Dr. Caleb, who married Genevieve Maynard; Isora, who married James Williams; William, who married Naomi Hatley, and Lula, who first married Paul Lewis and later Carroll Odom, and later Wm. L. Johnson.

Isaac Witt was a typical pioneer preacher and did much and lasting good in the communities where he labored.

Eli Abbott

One of the leading men of the county around the close of the past century was Eli Abbott. For many years he was one of the most progressive citizens the county has had. Starting out in young manhood with no special financial or educational advantages, through shrewd business management he became one of the largest landholders in the county around the turn of the century. Many citizens of the central part of Randolph County were assisted in a financial way by Mr. Abbott.

Possibly the most valuable and best known act of Eli Abbott was his building of the school known as Abbott Institute in 1893. Seeing the need for a local school of higher learning, he built the school and for several years was patronized by a large number of young men and women who had finished the lower grades elsewhere and who came to Maynard to board and take training for teaching and other professions. More is said about this school in another chapter.

Mr. Abbott owned several good farms along Fourche and developed a large tract of bottom land in Current River bottoms near the present Reece Ridge schoolhouse.

Mr. Abbott was married twice, the last time to Lula Austin. Joe Abbott of Maynard, Lehman of Little Rock and Mrs. Paul Maynard are children of the last marriage.

B. F. BIGGER

B. F. Bigger (Frank), for whom the town of Biggers is named, is a native of the county, having been born here in 1851, the son of J. G. and Catherine Lewis Bigger. He married Ida May Simington, a daughter of Col. T. S. Simington. Mr. Bigger is known as having been the proprietor of the Bigger's Hotel in Pocahontas from 1881 until his death.

This hotel was known far and wide as one of the most popular stopping places in north Arkansas, especially for the commercial traveller, usually called "drummers" in that day.

During the years in which Mr. Bigger operated the hotel he acquired a large tract of land on Current River, where the town of Biggers now stands, and established a ferry and operated a still. When the Frisco railroad came through in 1902-03 it ran through his land and he and others laid off the town. Three of the children of Frank and Ida Bigger reside in Randolph County at this time. They are: Tom, Mrs. R. O. Smith and Mrs. Kate Harrison.

LEWIS DALTON
Born October 25, 1835 — Died November 14, 1929

One of the leading farmers and stockmen of the county was Lewis Dalton, who came from Ripley County, Missouri, to Elevenpoint River valley in 1860.

In this year he married Sarah A. Stubblefield, a daughter of Fielding Stubblefield, who had been living on this stream almost a half century at this time. Here Lewis Dalton opened up a farm near his wife's relatives and began farming, a vocation which he followed the rest of his life, very successfully. In 1874, after the death of his brother, William, he became postmaster and operated a store. He also owned a mill and cotton gin. This was the beginning of the village of Dalton. For fifty years and possibly longer Lewis Dalton was personally active in the job of building up one of the finest farms and some of the finest livestock which the county has ever had. He was a strong believer in the job of taking good care of his livestock. He often said that he personally enjoyed seeing big hogs eat yellow corn. The story goes that once while showing a visitor one of his fine brood sows, the visitor asked him if the hogs' ancestors hadn't been of pretty good blood, thereupon Mr. Dalton walked over to the corn crib and opened the door which showed a great pile of ear corn, remarking, "Here is her grandmother."

Mr. Dalton was also interested in some property and business interests in Pocahontas. He was the father of the late E. Dalton, a long-time resident of Pocahontas, and Mrs. Ascenith Dalton, now of Imboden.

Dennis W. Reynolds

Dennis W. Reynolds was born in Jackson County, Illinois, in 1840. He was a son of James M. Reynolds, a North Carolinian who settled in Illinois soon after the War of 1812.

Dennis Reynolds was married three times, first to Nancy Luttrell, second to Mrs. Mary Kelsey and last to Mattie Wilkes. He and his last wife both died in April, 1924.

He came to Cherokee Bay in 1857 where he began for himself in the mercantile business, which he continued until the outbreak of the Civil War. After serving in the war he returned home and operated stores at Corning and at Old Reyno many years. He was the first business man in the town of Old Reyno, which was named for him.

After several years at this place the Frisco railroad came through Cherokee Bay, missing that town, and, as has been told in this book before, the town was moved to the railroad and the present town of Reyno sprang up. It was also named as the old town.

For many years Mr. Reynolds was sponsor of the Old Settlers' Reunion which was held in different communities of the county.

He was one of the outstanding men of the county in his day, being a large landowner and benefactor to many people.

He was the father of Mrs. Annie Martin of Pocahontas, Mrs. Leota Seymour of Reyno, Mrs. Pearl Freeman of Thayer, Missouri, and other children.

John Wilson Meeks

Possibly no other man who has lived in Randolph County as few years as Judge J. W. Meeks ever became so thoroughly "one of us" as he did. Coming here from Mammoth Spring in 1914, he immediately became a leading citizen of the town and county.

J. W. Meeks served the Sixteenth Judicial District as judge for twelve years. He was one of the men responsible for the removal of the remains of Thomas S. Drew, Randolph County's only Governor, from an unmarked grave in Hood County, Texas, to the Masonic cemetery in Pocahontas.

Judge Meeks was a great friend of the late W. Jeff McColgan, who was a native of the same section of Illinois as was Judge Meeks. As is related in the article about Mr. McColgan in this book, Judge Meeks, Uncle Jeff and the late Senator Wm. E. Borah (of Idaho) were all schoolmates in the vicinity of Barnhill and Taylorville, Illinois, in the days following the Civil War.

The judge and Uncle Jeff were Democrats but Mr. Borah was a Republican. During the days of the Hoover administration when conditions were bad and the party in power unpopular (especially with Democrats), the author had several occasions of being associated with Mr. Meeks and Mr. McColgan, and we remember the two discussing national politics and any time Borah's name was mentioned they agreed that "Bill Borah was the best Republican alive."

Judge Meeks died in 1938. His widow and two daughters reside in the county at the present time. His only son, Charles C., was killed while in service during World War I.

Captain J. N. Bolen

Captain Bolen was a native of Pennsylvania where he was born in 1831. He came to Randolph County in 1865 and is known as the editor of the old *Randolph Herald,* which he published for many years.

Bolen was a staunch Democrat. Being a Confederate soldier, he attained the rank of captain, a title which he wore the remainder of his life.

He is remembered as being one of the old school weekly paper editors who "feared no man" when it came to "publishing all the news that is fit to print." He is possibly the best known editor of a newspaper who has lived in Randolph County, except L. F. Blankenship who followed him in the publication of the *Herald* which has become the *Star-Herald,* the only newspaper printed in the county today (1946).

Grandfather told us that one time a fellow who had made it a habit of dropping into the *Herald* office each time he was in town, in order "to get his name in the paper," during the time of Captain Bolen, dropped in the office as usual, thereupon the captain wrote in his "locals" that "John Doe made his usual visit to the *Herald* office while in town Tuesday."

Captain Bolen married Mary Caroline Albitten in 1858. She lived until 1940, dying at the age of 103. She lived in Pocahontas with her daughter, Mrs. Ella Schoonover, the last wife of Jacob Schoonover.

Mrs. Schoonover, the daughter, died in 1941 at the age of 82.

Mrs. Bolen was a cousin of Mary Todd, the wife of Abraham Lincoln.

Patrick Henry Crenshaw

Patrick Henry Crenshaw was named for his great grandfather on his mother's side, the renowned Revolutionary orator, Patrick Henry, who the histories tell us was the original coiner of the statement, "Give me Liberty or give me Death."

He was one of the most noted lawyers of his time. He was born in Alabama in 1849 and came with his family to Randolph County in 1856. The first Randolph County home was on Elevenpoint River, near where it flows into Spring River. He was a Confederate soldier. His first occupation was as clerk in a store but later he studied law in the office of Baber and Henderson in Pocahontas and was admitted to the bar in 1872. He was a very able lawyer and is remembered today for his witty sayings. In one session of court he is said to have become irritated with the circuit judge and called the judge "Judge Necessity." When called upon by an opposing attorney to explain his statement, he replied, "Don't you know, why 'Necessity knows no law'."

Mr. Crenshaw married a daughter of Atty. L. L. Mack of Greene County.

He was an ardent fox hunter, an eloquent speaker and a member of the Catholic church.

A. W. W. Brooks

The list of early prominent men should include that of A. W. W. Brooks. Mr. Brooks was born in 1832 in Davidson County, Tennessee, near Nashville, the son of Richard P. and Mary Brooks. His father was an official of that county many years. A. W. W. joined the Confederacy and after the close of the war came to Arkansas, first settling in Lawrence County, but in 1867 moved into Randolph, in the vicinity of the present-day Sharum community. He landed here penniless and rented some fresh new ground the first year and started farming. He was very successful in this occupation. At one time he owned eight thousand acres of the best land in Black River bottoms.

He first married Julia Richmond, also a native of Tennessee, in 1855. The children of this union were William P. (Billy,), who is remembered by many persons at this time; Ellen, who married J. P. Rogers; Alice, who married Robert Surridge, and Maggie, who married David Fender. After the death of the first wife, Mr. Brooks married a widow, McIlroy, and to this union was born one child which we remember. Her name was Fannie. Later descendants of A. W. W. Brooks are well known to the public, as the family, for many years, was the best known family in the Black River bottoms section of Randolph County.

William P. Brooks, known as Billy, followed in the footsteps of his father and for many years was one of the leading farmers in this section and owned one of the most prosperous plantations in upper Black River bottoms. The Brooks plantation was for many years a landmark for this section. Descendants of the family still reside in the county.

Purkins-Skinner-Esselman

In the list of noted persons of early Randolph County there is a "family combination" which deserves mention. The parties of which I refer are Judge James H. Purkins, Dr. J. C. Esselman and Will H. Skinner.

J. H. Purkins came to Randolph County from Virginia in 1856. He settled on a farm on Current River along the river in the vicinity of what is now known as the old Downey farm. Prior to coming to this section he was a merchant in the "Old Dominion." He married Clementina Singleton and they were the parents of three children, Clement, Rena and Eliza, who married Dr. J. C. Esselman. After the death of his first wife he married Ava Payne and they had one son, James, who was killed in the Civil War at Glasgow, Missouri.

J. H. Purkins was a representative in the state legislature from 1860 to 1862 and was state senator from this district in 1866. He was elected county judge of Randolph County in 1877.

For many years the Purkins plantation was a noted landmark on Current River. This was possibly the first farm improved on the west side of this stream, in the lowland section.

Dr. J. C. Esselman, who married Eliza, the daughter of Judge Purkins, came to Randolph County in 1866 from Tennessee. He was a soldier in the Confederate army and was in many battles. He was with General Price in his raid through Missouri. He married Miss Purkins in 1864. To this union was born E. P., Tam O., Mazie, who married Mir. N. Carter, and Kate, who married Will H. Skinner.

Dr. Esselman was one of the best known physicians who has lived in Pocahontas. During his lifetime he had a wide range of practice and was considered to be one of the best in his profession in the state.

Will H. Skinner, who married Kate Esselman, came to Randolph County from Ohio in 1885. He is remembered by many of the older citizens as being a good druggist, leading banker and a very public spirited man. He was one of the men instrumental in securing the first power plant for the city of Pocahontas besides other civic activities.

His widow, Mrs. Kate Skinner, still lives in the old home near the new Randolph County courthouse, and although advanced in years, is very active and takes an interest in all public matters. She is a genuine friend to many and this author makes grateful acknowledgment for some valuable assistance from Mrs. Skinner in the job of getting together information regarding the city of Pocahontas before the turn of the century. Her sister, Mrs. Carter, is also still living. She occupies the old Carter home on Thomasville with her daughter, Lucille.

A. Z. SCHNABAUM

A. Z. Schnabaum's name should be included in any list of leading men which have lived in Randolph County.

Mr. Schnabaum came to the United States from Austria in 1881. Like many others who came to this section from the countries of Europe during that period, he came to take advantage of the opportunities of the new country, and to avoid the oppression and crowded conditions in the older country.

Abe Schnabaum is remembered by the older citizens as "Abe Snowtree" as he was called during the first years that the lived in the county.

He was a successful merchant of Pocahontas and Biggers for many years. For a long period of time during the close of the last century and the period of the present century through the time of the first World War, Abe Schnabaum owned and operated the two stores, cotton gins and many acres of farm land. He built his wealth up by careful and consistent dealings with the people of his adopted county and was one of the best-fixed men of his day. He was a good businessman and also a valuable citizen. Many persons living today recall instances where Abe Schnabaum helped them over rough spots. Although a "foreigner" he was a heavy investor in war bonds of the first World War and did many other deeds which helped his adopted nation and local community. His widow and two sons and one daughter reside in the county at this time.

ELIAS C. MOCK

E. C. Mock was a merchant at Maynard for many years. He helped a lot of people during this period. He was always an unassuming "common man" although during his lifetime he accumulated what would be rated a fair-sized estate. Uncle Elias was a son of Isham and Polly Jarrett Mock, both members of very early families of the county. He had a lot of relatives and friends in Randolph County and during his many years as merchant and small town banker he did many acts which were beneficial to the town and county and helped many of his friends and neighbors over spots which were tough during the days of the depression of the early 30's.

His widow still lives in Maynard. They rered two daughters, Mrs. Robert Vann and Mrs. Alene Smith.

Mr. Mock passed away about 10 years ago, a well known, highly respected native son of the section of the county where he spent his entire lifetime. J. B. Weaver, a lifelong neighbor of Mr. Mock, wrote in 1934 that Mr. Mock had been a substantial and valuable citizen of the town of Maynard for a half a century, at that time.

RANDOLPH COUNTY POLITICS

Randolph County is said to be "the banner Democratic county" of the state. Just how true this is is not definitely known. So far as we know, only two Republicans have been elected to office in the county in the last sixty-five years. Just how many have been in office prior to that time is not known. No other political party has figured in the county since the death of the old Whig party.

Two townships in the county have a strong Republican population. These are Little Black and Roanoke.

Randolph County has had a lot of good and efficient officials, and, of course, some who were not so good or efficient.

Randolph County folks take their politics pretty seriously. One characteristic of the citizenry of the county is that they are not very strong on the idea of continuation in office. During the past fifty-eight years only five men have served over four years in succession in the same office, and only one of these served eight, the balance six each.

Prior to fifty-eight year ago only four men served over six years, and these for only eight years each. No man has served over eight years successively in the same office in the one hundred and eleven years of the county's existence. This is quite a contrast from some counties of the state which have perpetuated the same group in office, some for as high as thirty years in one place.

It cannot be denied that too long in office tends to breed corruption and builds up "machines." True, democracy almost demands that the "pie" be passed around as one Randolph County aspirant once stated.

Some families have figured in county politics all down through the years while other have not. One family, the Johnston, has had three generations in one family in office.

Rev. L. F., his son, William Henry, and W. H.'s son, Ben. Mont Armstrong, served in four different offices of the county—judge, circuit clerk, county clerk and sheriff. Ben F. Spikes was sheriff, treasurer and county clerk. Rufe Baker was representative, circuit clerk and county clerk. A. J. was judge, sheriff and representative.

A number of men have served in two different offices. W. H. Phipps and A. H. Kibler are the only two men since the Civil War who have served over six years in the same office. Mr. Phipps was county clerk and Mr. Kibler treasurer, eight years each.

Only three men in the county's history have served fourteen years altogether. They were Joe T. Robinson, who was county and circuit clerk for that length of time, and B. J. Wiley was county judge and county clerk, and Mont Armstrong was judge, county clerk, circuit clerk and sheriff for the same time.

Ben F. Spikes was county clerk, sheriff and treasurer for a total of twelve years. A few men served ten years altogether, and on down the line.

The county has been fortunate in the fact that there has not been a lot of organized machine politics in her history. A few townships acquired reputations of being controlled by a "clique," or in a few remote cases, by one man. This condition did not last, though, and although some good men who ran for office during the time suffered as a result of these remote spots, generally the parties involved were "small fry" in so far as the county as a whole was concerned.

We have, as a whole, a pretty clean political set-up, and it is with pride that we say that a majority of our folks vote their own sentiments without listening to those who would dictate to them if allowed.

So far as we can learn, no man has lost his life during an election day fight, and no very great number of actual personal encounters have resulted from political differences.

MISCELLANEOUS

A few men have been defeated for their second terms; a few have been accused of "selling out," but in a majority of cases the officials have asked for and received the "customary" second term.

A small number of Randolph County officials have "gotten in bad" while in office, especially in the collector's and treasurer's offices; a few have made bad records, but mostly the men who have served us down through the years have been good men and carried on their work efficiently.

No woman has been elected to office in the county. Only four have been candidates up to the present time, and they suffered defeat.

At the present date (July 31, 1946) there are nine former county judges living. They are: H. M. Bishop, S. M. White, Ben A. Brown, Dee Mock, George W. Million, Joe S. Decker, Joe Snodgrass, C. H. Brooks, and Oscar Prince.

Eleven representatives are living. They are: T. W. Campbell, Horace E. Ruff, W. L. Pope, E. N. Ellis, J. J. Lewis, E. G. DuBoios, J. E. Smith, H. H. Price, R. K. Baker, Alvin Burrow and Walter Jackson.

Nine circuit clerks survive. They are: Ben A. Brown, J. J. Lewis, Dee Mock, Ed. R. Hicks, Joe Snodgrass, R. K. Baker, Jeff Lawhon Jack Thomas and Carl Brown.

Eight county clerks are still living. They are: Ben Johnston, Ernest T. Harrison, W. H. Phipps, R. K. Baker, Myrt Waldron, Jim Shivley, Harry Talbott, and Wesley Nibert.

Six sheriffs are still alive. They are: R. H. Gullett, J. P. Spikes, C. H. Brooks, J. T. Thompson, Roland Morris and Guy Amos.

Nine treasurers survive to the present. They are: S. M. White, J. D. Gossett, H. L. Haynes, Clarence Abbott, Will S. White, John J. Moore, Jeff Lawhon, Edgar Poe and Lawrence Dalton, author of this book.

*Those above underlined, are now deceased (1972)

Seven tax assessors are living at this time. They are: R. I Higginbotham, H. H. Hollowell, W. E. Tiner, Wesley Brown, Luther Harnden, Walter Jackson, and Earle Tilley.

The last named man in the above lists is the present incumbent.

A small per cent of the voters of the county are influenced through the use of liquor in the election. This is regrettable and an undesirable situation. It breeds corruption and is an uncertain problem within itself. It is generally known that a man who will sell his vote for a drink does not rate his great American privilege very highly, and a lot of times will vote for the fellow who gives him the biggest or last drink.

But an all-over look at the political set-up in Randolph County through the years will cause one to see that we have a pretty good county at last, and one which would rate with the very best in the state.

HISTORIC SITES

The author has for a number of years advocated that the county and state should work together and take the necessary steps to mark the more historic spots within Randolph County.

Why we say the state should be interested in this is the fact that several of these spots are "firsts" in the state's history.

We think that a small state park should be set aside and supported by the state at Old Davidsonville because of the fact that this is the site of the first courthouse, first postoffice and first land office in Arkansas.

The site of the first court held in the state is also in our county, not far from Davidsonville. This place should be marked by the state.

We hope that some day when a future reader peruses these pages and comes to this article he will say, "Well, they finally did this."

Below we list a few of the places which should be marked besides the two sites named above. They are:

The old Lindseyville site and cemetery, which has the grave of John Gould Fletcher and other early settlers of Arkansas.

The old Salem church site (First Baptist church in Arkansas, at the present day Jarrett schoolhouse).

Old Pitman Ferry site across Current River in northeast Randolph County, the first ferry in the state and site of two Civil War battles.

Bettis home site in Pocahontas, founder of Pocahontas.

De Munn mill site near Pocahontas, first in the state.

John Janes first home, considered by some as the first settler of the county. Also the site of the first home of Dr. William Jarrett and Matthias Mock in the county, both very early settlers.

Old Mount Pisgah church site, first Methodist church in the county.

Siloam church, oldest existing Methodist church in the county.

Glaze Creek Church of Christ, oldest existing church of that faith in the county.

Old Military road which runs across the county, the first road in the nation west of the Mississippi River to receive Federal recognition.

Hite cemetery, site of first church in Cherokee Bay.

There are many other places which should be marked. This list is possibly the major ones. The North and East have long ago marked many places in their section of far lesser importance.

Communities

Part Three

ATTICA

This village and community is located in one of the early settled spots of the county, although the village itself was not established until around 1890. Miss Clara Hill was the first postmistress. Other merchants and postmasters have been the following, and possibly others whose names we do not have. The list is as follows: Tobe Chastian, Jasper Pace, Sular McNabb, John Johnson, Curtis Williams, Raymond Elkins, Witt Waddell and Hulitt Haulcroft.

Possibly the first settlers attended their first religious services at the old Fourche de Thomas "Salem" church which was not so far away. Some of the first residents of the community, especially on the north side, may have gone to church at old Mount Pisgah on Tennessee creek, but the first church in this immediate community is said to have been an early Methodist church built sometime before 1880 at Noblin Springs, near the present home of Joseph Thomas. The cemetery was started about the same time, or possibly a little earlier. Before the cemetery was begun here the Gross cemetery was used by all the settlers for several miles around.

The author's great grandfather, Epps Marlette, and wife are buried in the Gross cemetery. They moved to this community from the Wabash valley of southern Indiana in 1879. Most all the early families are represented in the old cemeteries.

The church named above was moved from Noblin Spring to Attica soon after 1880 and has remained here since. The church is known as Oak Grove.

The Missionary Baptist church, on the hill south of the village, was built soon after the Oak Grove church. Both churches are active today.

As stated in the beginning, this is an old community. In this community settled the Biggers, Sweaza, Russell, Garrett,

McDaniel, Simington, Johnson, Thomas and other families before the Civil War. As has been mentioned in connection with other articles in this book, James G. Russell settled where Mack Riggs now lives, south of Attica, about 1825. He and other members of his family lie buried in the family cemetery near the Riggs home. Here was held the first Randolph County court, April 3, 1836.

In this community lived Isaac L. Garrett, who was the first county surveyor of the county. The late Wiley R. Russell, who was sheriff of the county and a grandson of James G. Russell, was reared here also. His father, Marion Russell, was killed in the Civil War. William Russell, who was appointed justice of the peace for "the settlement of Fourche de Thomas," May 27, 1815, may have been a relative of this family.

At the first term of Randolph County court, John C. Johnson, who was a resident of this community, was appointed road overseer for that portion of the old Military road from the present-day Foster bridge on Fourche to the Roanoke township line.

James F. Shaver stated in his family history in 1889 that his father, John Shaver, once told him that he hauled wheat to Russell's flour mill to have it ground into flour in 1838. He states that this was the only flour mill in this part of the country at that time. This old mill was in this community.

Col. Thomas Simington settled in this community before the War Between the States. His wife was a daughter of James G. Russell. He was the father of the late F. L. Simington and Mrs. Frank Bigger and other children.

The Bigger family settled in this community about 1840.

The Holderby family also lived in this community during the first half of the nineteenth century.

The first settlers of the Attica community came into the county over the old Military road, which ran through the community. They were intermarried with the settlers in the other early communities of Columbia, Pocahontas, Warm Springs and those on Elevenpoint, which makes the recordings of the early settlers in this and other communities read much alike.

ALBERTHA COMMUNITY

This community is that section of the county lying between Maynard and Brockett. This community and its environs is sometimes referred to as 'Flatlick' or "Stringtown" at the present time, but the old Albertha was located on the Pocahontas-Maynard road just west of the present home of R. L. Baker. The first postoffice in the community was farther down the road and a short distance west of the present "Sago's Store," and was called "Columbia." This office is not to be confused with the Columbia which the old settlement of "Fourche de Thomas" was later called. However, this is all in Columbia township, and the fact is that this was all just about referred to in the early records as "Columbia." Sam Sago, Sr., was the postmaster at Columbia before the office was moved to Albertha. John Autrey was the first postmaster at the new location, and he named it Albertha.

Among the merchants who were in business here during the existence of the town were Joseph Marshall, G. W. Stump and Hiram Smith. Hiram Smith was the father of Aunt Mary Spencer, Aunt Amelia Phipps and Uncle Wash Smith, now living at Maynard, and the late James Smith. His wife was Betty McGregor, daughter of William McGregor, another early settler of this section.

Early settlers in this community were the Sagos, McNabbs, Stumps, Buxtons, Ryburns, Carrolls, Martins, Lambs, James Johnston, Marshalls, Davis, Kerleys, Overbys, and others whose names are listed in the nearby communities of Jarrett, Attica, Engleberg and Maynard.

On the hill just south of the old Albertha town site was formerly located the old Thorny Thicket or Pleasant Grove church building. This was one of the pioneer churches of this section. For many years this church was the central assembling place for the wide section of country between Brockett and Maynard, and from Fourche to Current River.

On the day of the big hailstorm, which occurred July 25, 1895, lightning struck this old building and it burned. It was not rebuilt.

The story of this hailstorm, which was heaviest in the vicinity of Middlebrook, is told in this book in the "Miscellaneous Happenings" chapter.

The Washington and Stokes schoolhouses and also two Churches of Christ of the same name are located in this section. In this community live several old families. Two of the oldest citizens of the county who live almost in the same spot where they were born are Uncle Lewis Johnston and Uncle Sam Sago, of this community. Uncle Will Luter, a member of an old family of the county and who for years was known far and wide as the "Sweet Potato King" of the county, lived at the site of this now dead town until his wife died a few years ago. He now resides at Doniphan.

BIGGERS

The town of Biggers came into existence as a town about 1900 when the St. Louis-San Francisco railroad was built through Cherokee Bay.

B. F. Bigger bought a tract of land here about 1889 and established a distillery and ferry. When the railroad came his way, he and others laid out a town and called it Biggers.

It was early known as a mill town. Several lumber and stave mills were located here and ran several years, until the timber became exhausted.

COMMUNITIES

Some of the first residents of Biggers were the Shavers, Brumleys, Rileys, Shores, Blounts, Brooks, Hites, Fords, Robinsons, Tiptons, Johnstons, Estes and Johnsons. Some of these still live here.

Some of the long-time residents who live in Biggers at present are E. C. Whittington, H. I. Johnson, H. A. Nicks, Joe H. Johnson, Dr. R. O. Smith, Myrt Bennett, George F. Johnston, J. C. Graham, Harry Hite, the Tipton and Luter families and others.

The town at present has a population of about four hundred fifty. There are four stores, four churches and a good ten-teacher high and grade school.

The country surrounding the town is good farming country.

Contrary to the story that is generally true of the communities in the lowland section of the county, Biggers is located in an early settled community.

The land where the town is located is a part of the plantation of Governor Thomas S. Drew. Drew and his family lived here around 1840.

Henry Slavens, Daniel Duckworth, the early Shavers and Luttrells were here around 1815 to 1830. Other early settlers in this community were the Bounts, Sims, Sparkman, Brimmage, and Shoemaker families.

Others who came later were the Hite, McCrary, Hatley, McIlroy, Arnold, Ford, Crawley and Brumley families.

Shaver's Eddy on Black River south of Biggers is an early landmark on Black River. Shumaker and Duckworth ferries on Current River and Sims Landing, also in this river, are early river points in the Biggers community.

The first church in this section was built by B. J. R. Hite, grandfather of Harry Hite, now living in Biggers. The old church was built at the Hite cemetery and was used both as a church and school. Hite was a Methodist minister, but the building was used by all who cared to worship therein.

Joe H. Johnson (Big 4), now almost eighty years of age, recently told the author that he attended church here March 7, 1882, with his parents. The preacher was Parson James, an early Church of Christ preacher. This was almost sixty-five years ago. The old building has been rebuilt, but the same huge cypress logs used in the original building built around eighty years ago were used and are in good condition. A photo of this building is in this book.

Another old church near Biggers was the old Yellow Hall, located just north of the present site of the Mississippi River

FIRST CHURCH AND SCHOOL IN CHEROKEE BAY
Located in Hite Cemetery.
Mr. and Mrs. Harry Hite in picture.

Fuel Corporation pumping station. It was so named because yellow paint was used to paint the building. This may have been the building originally sponsored by Daniel Duckworth who died before a building was built, and which he had been instrumental in getting built, according to early church records. It was a Baptist church. Duckworth operated a ferry near by.

Just south of Biggers was the old Peru postoffice. This old office was the first in this section. It was first near the Hite cemetery and then moved to near the site of the present-day Current River Beach. Daniel McIlroy was the postmaster here in 1883, and the river crossing where the present-day Highway 67 bridge is located was called McIlroy's Ferry. Later the office was moved back up near Riley's cotton gin.

"Squire" Riley, father of the late Sid (J. S.) Riley, lived just east of the present pumping station referred to above.

Drewry S. Ford, one of the men who helped hold the first county election in the county in 1837, lived near here. In his will, on record in the vault at Pocahontas, among other things, he stated that he was holding out five hundred dollars "to be used to catch and prosecute the culprit in case I am murdered by one of my enemies."

Another resident of the lower end of Cherokee Bay was Daniel Lieb, whose name is listed in the Tennessee records of officers of the War of 1812. He came here at the close of the war. His relatives moved to Greene County after his death.

The Luttrell family lived near the present farm home of John Luttrell before the Civil War. The Luttrell cemetery near by is the oldest burying ground in Cherokee Bay.

Hugh McCrary was an early settler near here.

The communities and towns of Reyno and Biggers have a lot of history in common. Many of the names listed in this article were also identified with the establishment of Reyno. Some of these are the Sparkman, Shaver, Luttrell and other families. In fact, the combined histories of Reyno and Biggers is just a history of Cherokee Bay.

BLACK RIVER BOTTOMS

That portion of Randolph County commonly known as "Black River Bottoms" is the part of the county south and east of Black River and north of Lawrence County and west of Clay and Greene counties.

In this territory are the communities and towns of O'Kean in the extreme southeast corner, Surridge in the east, and Elnora, Lesterville, Manson and Shannon on the Frisco railroad. There are several other lesser communities within the general outline as given above. Some of these are Skaggs, Sharum, Holmes (the old James Mill), and farther south, Fender, Gum Stump and Meredith.

Most of these places are no longer in existence save for a school or church. There are still trading points at Fender, Manson, James and other points adjacent to the older settlements.

Just who the first settler in Black River bottoms was is not known. The French settled at Peach Orchard on Black River, just over in Clay County, before 1800 but did not remain permanently. The first settlers at Pocahontas laid claim to most of the land near the town across the river, but most of this section was a vast, unbroken, swampy wilderness which held no inducement at that time. This was not true of all the land, as there were high ridges of very fertile land, but mostly inaccessible because of swamps around it.

The section was a hunter's paradise. The woods abounded with bear, deer, turkey and all the smaller fur-bearing animals. It is likely that the first permanent settler was a hunter who was attracted by the fertile soil which he found on the higher ground during some hunting trip.

After a few had cleared land and built homes, roads were built, and this led others to move in. Some settlement was made here about 1840, but the coming of the Civil War found very few families as yet in Black River bottoms, except on the high ridges.

The Dean family settled near where some members of the family still reside about 1860. A. W. James settled on the farm, which is still owned by later members of his family, about 1855. The old James Mill was an early mill and for years a landmark for this section of the country. It was first a horsepower mill but in 1868 was changed to a steampower.

Near the close of the Civil War A. W. W. Brooks came to Randolph County and settled near the present site of the Sharum church and cemetery. For many years the Brooks plantation was one of the most extensive and proseprous farms in the county. The maternal grandfather of this author came to this farm from Gibson County, Indiana, in 1879, and he stated that there was quite a settlement here at that time.

The Brooks family intermarried with the Rogers, Surridge, Fender and other families, and for many years these associated families formed a "settlement" of their own. The Surridge school is named for that family, and for several years the store, gin and farm of David Fender was a thriving community within itself.

One of the first roads laid out in the county ran from the ferry at Pocahontas in a southeasterly direction into Greene County by way of the present town of O'Kean. For miles it ran through the lowlands and was cross-laid with poles. For many years this was the only route of travel from old Greensboro and Gainesville to Pocahontas and the northwest.

Another old road was the road which in later years became to be known as the Pocahontas-Jacksonport road. This road was first called the old Litchfield road, as it ran from Pocahontas to Litchfield, an early county seat of Jackson County. This road ran down the east side of Black River through what is now the Richwoods community.

The Armstrong and Shoffit families were early settlers in the eastern side of this section. Armstrong bend and Skaggs Ferry were well known points along the river during the early days, and the Shoffit family lived near the present Dean community before the Civil War. Another early family here was the Williams and Sanders families, who were also related to the Deans. The Holmes and Perkins families were residents of this section. The Duty family has resided in the community near where Elijah Duty now resides for over three quarters of a century. The Mays and Luttrell families have been here many years. The Luttrell family is one of the first in the county, one branch of which settled in Cherokee Bay before 1830. The Mays family came here from the Oconee community on Elevenpoint River many years ago. A son of B. J. Wiley (who was the first clerk of Randolph County and the third judge), Henry H. Wiley, married a daughter of A. W. James. Wiley township in Black River bottoms was named for this family.

After the St. Louis, Iron Mountain (Missouri Pacific) Railroad was built in the seventies an outlet was opened to the outside markets and a heavy timber trade sprang up. The town of O'Kean came into existence with the coming of the railroad and flourished as a mill town for a number of years.

State Highway No. 90 now runs from Pocahontas to O'Kean, and one of the most highly developed farming sections of the state lies along this road.

Besides Pocahontas, the first trade outlet for this section was the river traffic on Black River. Hoover's Landing, west of Manson, was an early steamboat landing, and western Black River bottoms received its first heavy merchandise from this point.

The old Skaggs ferry on Black River, just above the mouth of Current River, was established many years ago. It served as a crossing place for the traffic from Cherokee Bay to Black River bottoms and farther south. The road followed to reach this old river crossing. It left what is now Highway 67, just above the bridge across Current River, and ran down through what is now the Little Brown Schoolhouse community to the ferry. After crossing over on the south side, it ran down across the bottoms in a southwesterly direction toward Walnut Ridge.

At the point where Henry Higginbotham now lives and has a cotton gin David Fender operated a large store, gin, etc., for many years.

Before the levee on Black River below Skaggs was built the river broke over during high water and flowed down across this section toward Walnut Ridge and did not run back into the river for many miles. This low "trough" which crosses this section is said to have been the actual river bed centuries ago, before the alluvial plain was built up by the steady deposits of soil carried from the uplands by Current, Fourche and Black, which caused the latter to cut a channel along the foothills.

The schools of Black River bottoms are O'Kean, Sanders, Gum Stump, Lesterville, Manson, Shannon, Carter, Meredith and the consolidated school at Surridge.

Some of the best farms in Randolph County are located in this section.

There are six cotton gins in this section of the county and the farmers here grow a lot of beans for the market, and there is also several herds of good stock cattle.

THE VILLAGE OF DALTON

The village of Dalton had its actual beginning in 1850 when Dr. John W. Bryan established a store and postoffice northeast of the present village, across Elevenpoint River. This postoffice was called Spring Creek.

William Dalton, who lived in the community, bought the business and moved across the river. Here he secured an office which he called Dalton. This was about 1870. He was the father of James L. Dalton whose history sketch is included in this book.

Lewis Dalton, a brother of William, had already located in this vicinity, where he had married Sarah A., daughter of Fielding Stubblefield, one of the first settlers on Elevenpoint River, coming here with his parents about 1812.

After the death of William in 1870, Lewis became postmaster. He held the office several years and was succeeded by his son, Elijah. After operating the store and office several years, Elijah sold out to A. N. Kirkpatrick, who was a merchant and postmaster here many years. After the latter's death the office has been operated by his daughter, Mrs. Basil Barnett, and at present by Earl James.

A. N. and H. T. Kirkpatrick operated stores here and at Elm Store many years.

During the early days of the town Lewis Dalton operated a saw and grist mill, and also a cotton gin, which caused the town to become an important inland trading point from the close of the Civil War for many years.

The cotton gin was discontinued in a few years, due to the fact that the farmers in this section saw the advantage of stock-raising over cotton farming.

As has been stated in another section of this book, this is one of the oldest settled communities in the county. Members of the Wells, Looney, Garrett, McIlroy, Vandergriff and Stubblefield families settled here soon after 1800. Others who came here soon after were the Davis, Baker, Rice, Brown, White, Nettles families. Coleman Stubblefield, from this community, was a member of the old Lawrence County legislature in 1829. William Stubblefield was a juror of the first term of court held in Lawrence County, in 1815.

Dr. J. W. Dalton came to this community from Missouri about 1875 and married Ascenith, the daughter of Lewis Dalton, and for many years was one of the leading physicians of this section.

There has been a number of persons in the mercantile business here during the years. Among them have been William T. McIlroy, members of the Stubblefield and Looney families, besides those named above. Others later are John Whittenberg, Rufe Woolridge, Joe T. Wilson, Earl James and others.

This is one of the most substantial communities in the hill section of the county.

DAVIDSONVILLE

To write the story of the ancient town of Davidsonville is like writing the life story of someone long since departed and who, although he lived a brilliant life, it was of short duration.

As is generally known, Davidsonville was first known as "the town of Lawrence." Just who nemed it such must have been the same individual who named the county for the noted Capt. James Lawrence, a hero of the War of 1812. This name did not last. About 1815, or sooner, John Davidson settled here and is credited with founding a town out of "a few scattered cabins which were located on the site of an ancient Indian village." John Davidson was the son of General William Lee Davidson of North Carolina, who was murdered by a British Tory. The story goes that young Davidson pursued the murderer into the wilds of the west and avenged his father's death at New Madrid in 1805 by killing the Tory. After this John Davidson, hearing of the settlements farther to the southwest, came to Davidsonville and founded the town, as described above. A postoffice was established here June 28, 1817, becoming the first postoffice in the state of Arkansas. Adam Ritchie was the first postmaster.

The land upon which the town of Davidsonville was located was purchased by Lewis DeMunn & Co. from John Fagas, John Jones, Carl LeCombe, Augustus Rowlett and Jerome Watts, who jointly owned the land. This list varies somewhat as given by different historians. The actual record in book "A," page 38, states that this land was situated "about three miles up Big Black River, above the mouth of Spring River," and made up a settlement by Joseph Janis, John Fagas, Cola LeCombe, Jerome Mattix and Augustus

OLD DAVIDSONVILLE
On this site was located the first postoffice and first courthouse in Arkansas.

Revitt. The similarity of the names and spelling shows that the list as originally copied from the record is in error in some respects.

Lewis DeMunn transferred this land to the county (Lawrence County, Territory of Missouri) for a price of two hundred fifty-five dollars. DeMunn purchased the land from the original owners October 16, 1815, and turned it over to the county December 16, 1815.

The original town was made up of "forty-eight lots, a public square, streets, and the commons between the town and Big Black River."

The general layout of the town can still be seen today. The town well, the old streets and the commons, together with the public square, is located on the eastern side of the original plot of the town. This land slopes gently down toward the river and was a splendid location for a river town.

At one time the town of Davidsonville was the most important town in the whole territory of Arkansas. The population of the town has been estimated at from four thousand down to a few hundred. The fact is, there is little likelihood that the population was ever over a few hundred. But even at that it was a very important trading post during the days of the first settlement. Some of the older families now residing in this section of the state first lived in the vicinity of Davidsonville.

Among these early settlers were those named above—the Crabtrees, the Chamberlain family, John Lewis and son, Jacob Jarrett, Benjamin Porter, James Taylor, William Cox and others. In the spring of 1814 Colonel John Miller and Colonel Robert Smith jointly engaged in the mercantile business at Davidsonville. Others identified with the early town were William Robinson, Andrew Criswell, the Kelly family, Solomon Hewitt, James Kuykendall, James Campbell, William Hix and Richard Searcy.

The population of Davidson township in 1820 was four hundred sixty-one. This included the town of Davidsonville, so the estimate made above showed decisively that the town was small, as the township evidently covered a lot of additional territory. There is little chance that the town grew a lot more before its decline in 1829. John Davidson, for whom the town was named, is reputed to have built a nice two-story home, the finest in the town. He operated a jewelry store. Davidson represented old Lawrence County in the Missouri Territorial Legislature in 1816. Dr. John R. Hume, who lived in Ripley County, Missouri, just over the state line from Randolph County, was a nephew of Davidson. He died at Doniphan in 1943. The early Lindsey family was represented here for awhile. Caleb Lindsey, who is reputed to have been the first school teacher in the county, was a resident both here and at Fourche de Thomas (Columbia). His son, John Young Lindsey, was the first Baptist minister in this section.

Besides being the first postoffice in the state, Davidsonville saw the first courthouse in Arkansas built. The mound of crumbled yellow brick can still be seen in the center of the old town. The building is supposed to have been a two-story 40x40 foot brick building. All the whole bricks have been carried away by souvenir hunters. A scene in court at that early courthouse would undoubtedly present a very different picture from the courts of today. The officials, lawyers and jurors came from widely scattered homes. Court lasted sometimes for two or three weeks. "Court week" was the social and business bright spot of the year. People came to the county seat and put up at the taverns and left their horses in the livery stables, and after court hours much gayety and revelry was often the case. But the early court, while sometimes crude and unlearned, dealt out decisions which meant justice for all and was often the Waterloo for many early day desperados who ran afoul of the early men of law.

Besides being the site of the first courthouse and post-office in Arkansas, Davidsonville had the first United States Land Office in the state. This office was established in 1820. Hartwell Boswell was appointed registrar and John Trimble, receiver. The United States Land Office was first established in 1812 as a bureau in the U. S. Treasury Department, and was under that department when the first portoffice was established in Arkansas. In 1849 this bureau was transferred to the Department of the Interior This office played a very important part in the disposition of public lands until the Homestead Law was passed in 1862. Some work was done by the land office direct from Washington before the establishment of the local office. The first land survey in the state was made by the Federal Government in 1815 between the Arkansas and St. Francis rivers.

In many of the state and local histories and magazine articles of the past there has appeared the picture of a log house which was supposed to have been the courthouse at Davidsonville. This is an error that should be corrected here. The house pictured is the house where the first county court of Lawrence County was held in 1815. It was the home of Solomon Hewitt. Solomon Hewitt sold this place to Benjamin Crowley, from whom Crowley's Ridge was named, October 12, 1819. It was located three miles up Spring River, above the mouth of Elevenpoint, on the east side, where he operated a ferry.

Historically, Davidsonville is the most important spot in Arkansas. The old town not only represented the "first" in everything political in the state and counties of both Lawrence and Randolph, it was a very important industrial center, at least from its beginning until 1829.

Many stories have been told about the decline of this, our first town. It will never be known just why Davidsonville passed out of existence in such a short time after the zenith of its career. The fact is, the most logical reason appears to be that when the old Southwest Trail (now known as the old Military road) was permanently marked and improved, it missed the town a few miles, and Jackson sprang up and grew rapidly at the expense of Davidsonville. The first road, as explained elsewhere in this book, ran by Davidsonville, but it was a mere trail and only ran this way because the town had already been established and necessity demanded it. But when a permanent road was marked out, the bad location of the old town in regards to river crossings and flood lands caused the surveyors to by-pass the town, going across the country from Pitman via Columbia to cross Elevenpoint near the present town of Imboden. The town of Jackson was located about three miles northeast of Imboden. Paul Starling now (1946) resides on the site of the old town. When the county seat was moved here in 1829, Davidsonville lost its importance.

The story of a dreadful epidemic of cholera wiping out the population is undoubtedly exaggerated. The true story probably is that it was on a serious decline and when the cholera or yellow fever was brought in by rivermen from the south, and many of the citizens died of the disease, the rest decided to move to the now town of Jackson and elsewhere.

It is interesting to note that, while Jackson caused the downfall of Davidsonville, it too was short-lived. There is very little on record to denote the existence of Jackson after 1835. At this date the county of Randolph was set aside from the mother county of Lawrence. The county seat of Lawrence being Jackson and Jackson being in that part given to Randolph County, Lawrence County was, for the third time in its twenty years of existence, required to seek a new town for the county seat. This was done, and Smithville was the town chosen. Randolph did not choose Jackson as its county seat but held an election (more will be said of this in another chapter) to decide whether it would be located at Columbia or Pocahontas, and Pocahontas won.

Such is a summary of the brief existence of Davidsonville, Arkansas, first county seat town and the first place in the state to be designated officially by Uncle Sam's Postoffice Department for the receiving and dispatch of mail. Five generations of people have lived since their ancestors settled in this frontier town, but tradition and legends handed down to use will always keep alive the story of our first "settlement" within the bounds of Randolph County, even though the town has been buried in oblivion a century and a quarter at this time, in so far as visible existence is concerned.

THE SETTLEMENT OF FOURCHE DE THOMAS

The exact location of the community which was originally called Fourche de Maux is the community which at this date is that part of the country, to state it roughly, from the "Foster ford," sometimes called the "Decker bridge," along the road going northeast toward Maynard to about where William Bridges now lives.

This has been a much-named community in the century and almost one half of its existence. Dr. Englemann, noted German scientist and physician who travelled down the old Military road in March, 1837, states that at that time it was known as "Fourche du Mas," which, he says, was a corruption of the French name, de Maux. He says that the name came from a French trapper who was the first white man in this section. The early records of the county called it "Fourche de Thomas," presumably after some early settler named Thomas. The next name applied to this community was "Columbia." Columbia township, in which this community is located, was named from this settlement. Sometime during this period the east end of this vicinity became known as "Lindseyville." The first merchant here was David Plott, who ran a store here in the early thirties. Years later, and the best known merchant here (at Lindseyville) was the late

Joe Gamel. Since the decline of the above names, the community was called "Foster," and a postoffice west of the river was of that name. Since the decline and passing of the Foster store and office, Uncle Joe Jarrett, a grandson of Dr. William Jarrett, opened a small store on almost the exact site of the old Fourche de Thomas site, and the community is now called "Jarrett." The school building nearby is officially listed on the school records of Randolph County as "Jarrett School District Number 9."

Just who the first permanent settler in this community was is not known. William Jarrett, brother of the above-named Uncle Joe Jarrett who died in Little Rock in 1944, contended that his grandfather, Dr. William Jarrett bought land from Richard Fletcher at Fourche de Thomas in 1801. This Richard Fletcher was the father of John Gould Fletcher who settled here in 1815. Miss Mary Fletcher, now residing in Little Rock, a descendant of Richard Fletcher, states that he never lived in Arkansas. He was one of the original patentees who located in the first settlement of Tennessee on th Watauga River in that state in 1775. There seems to be a possibility that he at one time came to this section and entered land and then went back to Tennessee to spend the remainder of his life, but his son, John Gould, came here in 1815 to make his permanent home. He died here in 1825 and lies buried in the old Lindseyville burying ground.

Some members of the Fletcher family, together with the Lindsey and Davis families, removed to Saline (now in Pulaski) County soon after the death of John Gould Fletcher. The family has been prominent in that section since that date. The Lindsey family, which was much intermarried with the Fletchers, located here about the same time. The first Lindseys to come here were James, Eli and Caleb, who came from Christian County, Kentucky. The first record book of old Lawrence County shows that Caleb Lindsey was administrator of the will of Martin Miller, which was dated November 22, 1819. In this will Miller stated that he had already given his older children their share, among which was a pre-emption claim "on the waters of Fourche de Thomas" which he bequeathed to his daughter, Hannah, who at that time was the wife of Dr. William Jarrett. She had been previously married to Gabriel Seavers, who is reputed to have been wounded at the battle of New Orleans. Caleb Lindsey is reputed to have taught the first school in Arkansas, in a cave in western Randolph County, while he lived here. He died in Pulaski County in 1826. Eli Lindsey was the first Methodist preacher in Arkansas. He preached on a circuit on Spring River in 1815. Eli and Caleb are said to be the sons of James Lindsey, and John Young Lindsey, one of the first Baptist preachers in Arkansas, was a son of

OLD COLUMBIA OR FOURCHE DE THOMAS CHURCH SITE
Site of the first Baptist Church in Arkansas

Caleb. He is said to have been one of the organizers of the church at Columbia (Fourche de Thomas at that time), which was the first Baptist church in Arkansas. Houck's History of Southwest Missouri states that one Rev. J. M.

Peck preached at this church in 1817. The actual date of the organization was probably in 1815. This old church stood on what is now Uncle Joe Jarrett's land, just up the hill a short distance south of his home and store building. After a few years John Young Lindsey moved to Saline County, where he established another "Salem" church. This was the name given the first Columbia church.

Other early settlers here were the Kellys, Robinsons, Davis, Martins, Plotts, Bollingers, Carrolls, Mocks, Shavers, Russells, Morris and others, including Thomas Foster, who settled here in 1820. Roy Foster and his brothers, grandsons of Thomas Foster, now own land of which they have a deed made to John Murray and signed by President Van Buren. This deed and also some owned by Mr. Jarrett are written in long-hand on sheepskin.

The old Fourche de Thomas postoffice was discontinued about 1857. Henry Schoolcraft visited this frontier settlement in 1818 and spoke favorably of it. Dr. Englemann, in his account of spending the night of March 12, 1837, at the home of David Plott here, states that the future reader of his notes refrain from thinking that he was in the midst of a settlement of ignorant backwoodsmen. But contrary to this, he wrote in his record that they were well informed and intelligent, industrious people.

On July 4, 1821, the settlers around Fourche de Thomas celebrated the forty-fifth anniversary of the signing of the Declaration of Independence with a big barbecue. The day was royally celebrated, according to information handed down to us. A liberty pole, taller than the trees, was erected. This pole stood for many years and became a noted landmark. A military parade was staged with Jacob Shaver as grand marshal. He was mounted upon a fine Kentucky stallion and put the menfolks through a series of marches. Daniel Plott read the Declaration of Independence with great fervor. Matthias Mock presided over the feast and was ably assisted by Dr. P. R. Pitman and Dr. William Jarrett.

COMMUNITIES

When Randolph County was organized and the time came to choose a site for the county seat, Fourche de Thomas (although it was called Columbia then) was a strong contender for the place. The proposition was left to a vote of the people of the county as a whole. The story goes that Ransom S. Bettis and his son-in-law, Thomas S. Drew, owned the land where the town of Pocahontas was located and on election day they advertised a free barbecue and picnic, where eats were plentiful and liquor flowed freely. At this time a citizen could vote anywhere in the county he desired. With a majority of the citizens of the county in attendance, and with spirits running high as a result of the free drinks, the majority voted in favor of Pocahontas instead of Columbia. If this story is true, this is why the county seat was located at Pocahontas instead of Columbia.

An old settler of Columbia was asked later why the town of Pocahontas was thus named. He replied that it was supposed to have been named for the Indian princess who saved the life of Captain John Smith, but that he had a different story. He said the unfair tactics used against Columbia to land the county seat at Pocahontas justified naming it "Poke-it-on-to-us" instead of the regular way of spelling it.

So with this we close the story of the "Settlement of Fourche de Thomas." For almost one hundred and fifty years this ancient settlement has lived on in its place in the history of Randolph County. A traveller who passed along this way today, not knowing the history of this region, would move over soil which felt the footsteps of the Frenchmen De Maux, David Crockett, Stephen F. Austin, James Woodson Bates, Washington Irving and all the hosts who went southwest over the old Military road trail to become the pioneers and forefathers of the millions who now inhabit Arkansas, Texas and Oklahoma unawares. If the old cedars at old Lindseyville could speak they would tell us stories of long dead men who once lived and had their homes in this community, whose stories we will never know.

GLAZE CREEK CHURCH

This old church is named for the creek near which it is located. In the early records of old Lawrence County the creek was called "Glaze Kenon" creek. The legal description of the church is: "Fractional part of the north part of the south one-half of the northeast quarter of the southeast quarter of section eight, township twenty-one north, range two east."

There is something about a legal land description, while explicit, yet is vague and far away sounding. This old church is located near the eastern boundary line of Siloam township, about two miles northwest of Supply.

It was founded as a Church of Christ in 1845 by William Torrence Johnson (who was the father of the late John A. Johnson), Asa Taylor (the grandfather of Ben F. and Albert Taylor), James Tibb Johnson (father of the late William and Randolph Johnson), William McNatt and others who had formerly been members of the old Knob Creek church near Dukedom, Wheatley County, Tennessee, before migrating to Randolph County, Arkansas.

The first building was a small log house, used for both church and school. Later a hewed log house was built, about one-half mile southwest of the first one. The site was deeded to the church by William T. Johnson, one of the members spoken of above. This was before the Civil War. This same building was used until 1894, when a nice frame building was erected. This building was blown down by a cyclone June 5, 1915, and the present building was erected soon afterwards.

Some of the first ministers to preach here were Elders Lemmons, James, Rush, Hollowell, Peter Shaver, Curry and Uncle Zera Allen who lived only a short distance over the hills to the northeast. Many other leading ministers of the church have preached at this place in later years.

Some of the first members of the Glaze Creek Church of Christ were the McNatts, Woodalls, Parishs, Rings, Jacksons, Johnsons, Cox, Wilsons, Taylors, Athys, and others who lived in this section during this time.

Uncle Ben F. Taylor of St. Louis and his brother Albert, now of Doniphan, have been members of this church over sixty years.

Two sisters, Mary Ann and Evaline McNatt, were two of the most faithful members of this old church during its first days. They helped organize it. They were both over fifty years of age before they married, and neither had ever cooked on a cookstove until after her wedding.

Descendants of all the above families still live in this section.

GRAVESVILLE AND SURROUNDING COMMUNITY

That section of Randolph County east of Elevenpoint River, north of the Imboden-Pocahontas road and southwest of Hamil and Elevenpoint neighborhoods, is a long-settled section, however, lacking one definite community center or town.

On the Pocahontas-Dalton road is located the old Gravesville community. Here settled some of the Tylers, Weatherfords, Hibbards, Johnsons, Thompsons and others during the first half of the past century.

The father of Vincent Segraves, also named Vincent, settled in this community in 1833, coming here from North Carolina. The school and community gets its name from this family. Just why the first two letters (Se) were dropped is not known. Segraves opened a store here about 1880 and was later joined by W. E. Hibbard, and later by J. W. Weatherford. These families are still represented here. The Presley family also lived near here.

A few miles northwest of Gravesville is the Elevenpoint old postoffice location which was first called Lima. Daniel McIlroy ran a store and was postmaster here around 1870. He later moved from here to Cherokee Bay, where he was postmaster at Peru, reference of which is made elsewhere in this book.

The Ross, Tyler, Vandergriff, Looney, Wyatt, Jackson, Stubblefield and other families settled here during the early thirties. Some of the oldest existing buildings in the country are in this section. The old Pocahontas-Elm Store road ran through this community.

South of the Elevenpoint and Gravesville communities is the New Chapel school district and its environs. The old McIlroy ford (now bridged), the Layl ford and the Black's ferry bridge are crossing on Elevenpoint west of these communities.

In the New Chapel community settled the Hawkins, Hulvey, Bly, Graham, Cravens, Burke, Pierce, Cavenar, Tolliver, Camp, Kirk, Farrow, Lee and other families during the early days of settlement.

The present New Chapel school is a consolidation of the original New Home and Lee's Chapel schools. The old Pocahontas-Black's Ferry road ran through this community. Some of the oldest settled farms on Elevenpoint River are in this section.

"Five Mile" Spring or Shiloh community is just east of here. This community had a postoffice for several years called Lorine. J. C. Mondy and others operated stores here around the turn of the century.

THE HAMIL COMMUNITY

This section of Randolph County is located on the "headwaters of Tennessee creek," between the Warm Springs-Pocahontas road and Elevenpoint River.

The town had its beginning about 1890 when J. D. Jackson opened a store and secured a postoffice which he named for the Hamil family.

George W. Brown was also a merchant here many years.

The Waldron, Massey, Hurn, Spikes, Johnson, Roach, Presley, Jackson, Brown, Davis, Tyler and Whitrock families are early residents of this community. Some of them came here as early as 1830.

The old Antioch church is located in this community. It is one of the oldest Baptist churches in the county. There was also at one time a church at the old Roach cemetery, the land having been given to the church by William Roach.

Just east of here is the site of the old Mount Pisgah church, which was first started by William Spikes and others about 1830.

Just east of Hamil is also the site of the old Swarts postoffice. Ben F. Spikes, Tom Tiner and others operated stores here many years ago.

The story goes that Mr. Spikes desired that the office be named for his wife and sent in the name "Neatie" or "Neetie" and that the authorities in the Postoffice Department at Washington misread the word and sent Uncle Ben a stamp with the word "Necktie" on it and a commission as postmaster at "Necktie." The name was changed to Swarts after that.

Waddells, Roaches, Cooks and others have operated stores at Hamil since the days of Jackson and Brown.

This community has always been very civic minded. They take a very active part in the affairs of the county.

It is possible that this township (Jackson) has furnished more county officials than any other small township in the county.

There are a number of good farms along the creek, and this section is a good livestock growing community. There is also some rough land in this section with some of the highest hills in the county.

The schools nearest to Hamil are the Hamil and Pleasant Hill schools.

A number of substantial farm families live in this community and most of them are descendants of the very first settlers who came here.

JOHNSTONTOWN, ON CURRENT RIVER

This, now dead, river town was located on Current River about one mile west of the present town of Reyno. Just when the town was first established is not known. It is possibly one of the oldest river steamboat landings in north Arkansas. In the old cemetery near the site of the old town lie buried some of the first settlers of the county, especially Cherokee Bay. The Winninham family, which is one of the first names known in this section, resided near here, and several members are buried in the cemetery near the center where the large cedar trees stand.

As is recorded elsewhere, Sherrod Winningham was ordained to preach in this community, June 7, 1834. William Macon and Henry McElmurry were also citizens of this community at the time. The Blount family was also early residents here, as were the Watsons and other families already referred to.

COMMUNITIES

The place gets its name from James Johnston, who was the son of W. P. G. (Green) Johnston, who came to the village from Little Black township during the latter part of the last century and became the leading citizen and business man. He owned a lot of land in the vicinity and was a stock-raiser and cotton ginner. He died at Reyno in 1924.

The following article about Johnstontown was written by J. C. Renie of Reyno, which we publish below. It is a very good article about this place and also portrays the story which was true of the fate of so many of the old river towns of this period. It is as follows:

"Prior to the building of the Frisco railroad from Pocahontas to Cape Girardeau, in 1902, the eastern portion of Randolph County which lies east of Current River was almost completely isolated from Pocahontas on account of overflow lands and bad roads. The only dependable means of transportation to the outside world was by river boats. Numerous points along Current River became noted as boat landings. Among these was Sim's Landings, McIlroy's Ferry (now Current River Beach), Bigger's Ferry, Shumaker's Ferry, Box House Landing and Johnstontown.

From about 1880 until 1904 Johnstontown was the leading river town between Pocahontas and Doniphan. It would be impossible to enumerate all the business establishments which were located during that period at this town. There were several sawmills, one distillery, grist mills, cotton gins. One of these gins was the only cotton gin ever operated in Randolph County which produced round bales. There was also a brick and tile manufacturing plant, a heading and stave factory, shops and stores too numerous to mention.

The railroad missed Johnstontown about a mile. A spur switch was built from the main line to the town and river. Quite a lot was done by the enterprising citizens of the town to hold the trade at Johnstontown, but most everyone wanted to see the cars go by, so other sites were secured along the railroad.

The towns of Reyno and Biggers, on each side of this ancient town, sprang up, and old Johnstontown began to go down. The slow steamboat gave way to the train which was so much faster.

All this was the death knell of Johnstontown. All that is left of the old town at this day is a memory of former glory. Nobody ever goes there or is interested in this, one of the county's first towns, except to fish. This is a good place for fishing and is now known only as "Johnstontown's Eddy on Current River."

HIGH POINT SCHOOL

The subject of this article is a little one-room school, tucked back on a common country road in western Siloam township. There is nothing unusual or spectacular about the place in the least, except it happens to be the spot where the author of this book attended his first day of school in July, 1906. The first building was about a mile east of the present one. It was in the old building that this writer began his upward climb on the ladder of education. (We did not climb high enough.)

Mrs. Joe Perry Spikes, now living in Pocahontas was my first teacher. She was then "Miss Dora" King. Other teachers that we can remember at this time were Lindsey and Myrtle Miller, Martha Acree Grissom, Ed. Buxton, Lora Poynor Wilson and Mara Stubblefield Crews. We believe that these were all the persons whom we had the pleasure of studying under at this place. Also Eric Smith and Gene Purdy.

This old school was established sometime between 1885 and 1890. Before it was established the children in this community attended school at an old house which Uncle Bert Grissom built on his farm near the state line. Those who did not go there were sent to old New Hope, on Mud creek near the old Mock farm, or down "in the Jarrett Settlement."

We can see the old building today through the eye of memory. It was about eighteen by thirty feet in size. Two windows on each side and a double door made up the openings. It was ceiled on the inside with pine lumber at least twelve inches wide. The outside was "boxed and stripped." It stood in a grove of virgin white oak trees which grew acorns by the bushels, the long shiny brown ones which look like machinegun bullets. At the rear of the house, on the east, was our ball ground. "Home base" was about thirty yards down the road from the school building, and it was definitely a mark of distinction to anyone who could bat a ball that "hit the schoolhouse."

OLD MASONIC HALL—IN SILOAM TOWNSHIP
One of the first Masonic meeting places in the state. Now the home of Mrs. Molly Marlette and daughter.

The seats were home-made. A wide desk was built on the back of the seat, which was too heavy in proportion to the seat front. They were easily overturned, often a whole row falling over at one time. A "good" blackboard was nailed to the wall at the back of the room and a black strip about three feet wide was painted along the wall on both sides to provide extra writing surface when needed. The painted part was slick and the chalk did not adhere to it very well. A long varnished veneered Rand-McNally map case was hung on the wall near the blackboard, on the south side of the room, but was seldom used.

The inside of the building was never painted, and during all the years which we attended the school the smell of pine rosin was in the room. A cistern was dug at the southeastern corner of the building, but it soon caved in, leaving the corner of the house suspended in the air. After that water was carried from a small spring about three-fourths of a mile northeast of the school in "Turkey Pen" hollow, near Fourche Dumas creek.

During the days of heaviest population in the district there were around forty-five pupils. While there was never over one teacher, there has been some of the best teachers that the county ever produced who taught here.

During the days when the school fairs were popular, and one was held each October at Pocahontas, this little backwoods school carried away several top honors. From about 1910 to 1918 this was considered the champion school of the county for good "spellers."

On Friday afternoon "between recess and turning-out time" there was usually held a spelling and ciphering match. Sometimes neighboring schools would visit there and hold contests. When there was no spelling or ciphering match there was usually a "program." Poems were recited, dialogues were rendered and sometimes debates were held.

The last day of school was always a gala affair. The teacher always brought a "treat" of candy for the children and several of the patrons attended. Prizes were awarded for those who "got the most headmarks." Such was a picture of

High Point school during the first years of this century. The district now has a nice, new building, built on modern lines, and, like all other rural schools of the county, has a lot of advantages over the old-time ones.

While this school district has not produced any Henry Fords, Abraham Lincolns or John D. Rockefellers that we know about, yet it has turned out many good and useful citizens who have made their mark in life.

MIDDLEBROOK

First name "Siloam". Dr. William Carrens was first P.M.

The town, or village, of Middlebrook is located about one mile south of the early trading post called Cedarville. Old Cedarville was a trading center a hundred years ago. A mile and one-half southeast of Middlebrook is located the old Siloam church which was also built about a hundred years ago. Two miles west of Middlebrook is located the "Old Hall" place. This old two-story log residence is reputed to have been the site of the first, or one of the first, Masonic lodges in Arkansas. Three miles east of this village is located the old Glaze Creek church which is also a century old. Thus the town of Middlebrook is located in the midst of a very old section of Randolph County.

The town of Middlebrook proper came into existence about 1878. The late Charles G. Johnston and Ruben Wilson opened up a small store here in that year. The name of the town was taken from the creek which runs just south of the village and is supposed to be half way or the "middle brook," between Doniphan, Missouri, and Pocahontas.

Johnston and Wilson built a large store building about two years later and in 1885 Lewis B. Johnston became a partner with his son in the store. A few years later they sold the business to Eli Abbott and J. M. C. Lehman. In 1889 G. H. "Dock" Ingram built a cotton gin at Middlebrook and for many years it has been a good inland trading post. W. M. Hogan, ex-sheriff of the county, who was a well known timber dealer, opened another store to supply his trade, and later sold out to Rev. J. A. Spence, who operated the store and postoffice for over twenty years. Other merchants who have been in business at Middlebrook are S. I. D. Smith, Bob Cox, S. M. Johnson, M. J. Pace, Jess Burrow, and of late Ellis Wright, Clifford Phipps, Barkley and Son, J. T. Jones, and at present J. G. Jones and Son. Tom Phipps operated a store a long time just west of Middlebrook at his mill, now the home of his son, Claud, and family.

Middlebrook has always had a good one-room country school.

The physicians who have served this community during the years were Dr. W. T. Swindle, Dr. Moses Wilson, Dr. William Carrens, who lived here, and Dr. J. R. Loftis, Dr. C. Finnie and others from Maynard and other nearby communities.

Some of the early families in this community were the Luters, Raperts, Jones, Odoms, Spencers, Lindseys, Spences, Parkers, Wilsons, Phipps, Johnsons, Toys, Wrights, Johnstons, Browns and others too numerous to list here.

MAYNARD

In the foothills of the Ozark Mountains, eleven miles north of Pocahontas, nestles the little town of Maynard.

Maynard is at the crossing of the old Military road and the Doniphan-Pocahontas road, also the old road which ran from the old Columbia settlement to the old Perkins (later the Downey and other) Ferry.

Captain John Maynard settled here in 1872 and established a mercantile business. This store was located on the hill where the old Maynard home now stands. He called the place "New Prospect."

Captain Maynard also owned an old-time treadwheel cotton gin.

In 1885 a postoffice was established here and called Maynard for the Maynard family. Claiborne Tipton was the first postmaster.

J. M. C. Lehman had the first drug store in Maynard.

James Brockett came to Maynard in 1884 and installed a flour, saw and grist mill. He later moved down the road to the present steel bridge across Fourche and built another mill, secured a postoffice and put in a store, and the place was named Brockett.

Albert Hatley built a cotton gin in Maynard in 1888.

The town has three churches, a Missionary Baptist, Methodist and Church of Christ. All three churches have held regular services for many years.

Prof. R. L. Williford and S. O. Penick established the first newspaper in Maynard in 1895. The paper was moved to Pocahontas but later W. R. Lindsey secured full ownership and moved it back to Maynard and named it the *Northeast Arkansas Enterprise*. A "Boom Edition" of the paper which Mr. Lindsey published a short time before his death was a notable issue and several copies of it are still in existence.

In 1884 E. C. Mock opened up a store in Maynard and for over one-half a century was one of the leading merchants of Randolph County.

The town of Maynard has three fine springs which have never failed. These are the Abbott, the School and the Big Spring. They furnish cold, healthful mountain water for many people.

In 1899 the Bank of Maynard was organized by E. C. Mock, Eli Abbott, J. M. C. Lehman and others, and for almost forty years was a thriving institution, until it was moved to Pocahontas and merged with the bank there a few years ago.

Eli Abbott built a school of higher learning in Maynard in 1894. A more complete story of this institution is recorded in a special chapter, *Maynard Schools*.

The town and community has always been strong for education.

Prof. John and "Miss Eliza" Hogan were the town's most noted educators. Other educators, most of whom were college graduates (even during the days when educational requirements were low), were the Hogans, Rorex, Shaw, Downs, Orr, Myrick, Johnson, Wyatt, Hamil, Peters, Cummins, Freeman, Goodgame, Phipps, Williford and others whose influence will never die.

Many persons who have become noted were educated at Maynard.

The story of the town's schools, including the Abbott Institute, Ouachita Maynard Academy and the present-day school is recorded in a separate article.

The brothers of Captain John Maynard, Thomas and Stith, were also early residents of the town as were many others including A. J. Weaver, father of J. B. Weaver of Maynard at present.

J. B. Weaver should be included as one of the builders of the town. A resident of the town said a few years ago that when they needed something done, instead of applying the old familier saying of "Let George do it," everybody would say "Tell J. B. Weaver, he will do it."

The writer is indebted to Mr. Weaver and Mrs. Clifford Price for the following list of other early residents of Maynard. Mrs. Price is a daughter of Stith Maynard. The list is as follows:

COMMUNITIES

J. C. Phipps, S. R. Phipps, the Templetons, the Hogans, the Richardsons, Dick Beemis, Uncle Hiram Smith, William Bradford, David Culver, J. S. Anderson, Uncle William Lewis, C. H. Carter, Rev. Downey, Dr. Slaughter, J. D. Poynor, W. H. Tipton, J. R. Acree, W. A. Hurley, Rev. M. D. Bowers, Jeff Woodall, W. H. Johnston, John Vester, R. A. Lentz, Rev. E. T. Lincoln, T. J. Redwine, D. H. Hawkins, J. A. Spence, W. D. and C. M. C. Spencer, H. M. Crockett, Dr. J. B. McClure, W. R. Bolen, W. E. Navy, J. Q. Pond, T. W. Campbell, H. R. King, Adam and John Anspach, W. M. Crismon, Joe Lomax, H. M. Bishop, Doss Pratt, Dr. W. T. Swindle, Marshall Weaver, J. L. and Don Robinson, O. H. L. Cunningham, H. S. Burton, John Spikes, Bud Brooks, C. L. Cate, Dennis Downey, Uncle Jim Chester, R. E. Anderson, Milton McNabb, R. J. M. Wyatt, B. Short, A. S. Johnson, Tom Johnson, the Pattersons, Willis Hufstedler, and others not remembered at this time.

J. R. Acree and J. D. Poynor were the "Village Blacksmiths" of Maynard for many years. Mr. Acree and Jim Lindsey were possibly the best known "hack line operators" during the days when the mail was carried to Pocahontas by horse-drawn vehicles.

Among the physicians of the town were Slaughter, Hogan, Swindle, McClure, Finney, Carrens, and Loftis.

Dr. J. R. Loftis lived here many years before moving to Pocahontas.

The names which are associated with the life of the town of Maynard during the three-quarters of a century of its existence is a roster of the names of the early settlers of the northeastern part of Randolph county.

The town is a wideawake high type town of around three hundred people.

MAYNAD'S SCHOOLS

Abbott Institute—Ouachita Academy—High School

The village of Maynard has long been known as a town which worked for and appreciated it's schools. As is true of the other communities of the county, Maynard's first school was a one-room school with limited advantages.

About 1893, Eli Abbott, wealth citizen of the town, seeing the need for a school for higher grades, built what was to become known as the Abbott Institute. The first school taught here was in 1894, beginning in the fall of that year. Prof. R. L. Williford was principal and John Q. Pond and L. F. Maynard were assistants. Miss Jessie Lehman (now Mrs. Ben A. Brown) taught the primary grades.

The school proved highly successful and in a few months young folks were coming to Maynard to attend school from a radius of many miles. Several out-of-the-county pupils attended.

In the fall of 1895 Prof. S. O. Penick from Tennessee came to assist Prof. Williford in the upper grades. By 1896 several from Missouri were enrolled here. In that year Prof. Johnson, also from Tennessee, came to assist Prof. Williford. His wife taught elocution. Mrs. Lizzie Maynard was the music teacher. The fall of 1898 found Prof. Tom W. Campbell and H. W. Roberts at the head of the school. William Henry Johnston was a teacher in the grades. Roberts and Campbell also taught in 1899, but Mr. Campbell's health failed and he resigned. At the close of this term of school Prof. Roberts conducted a normal. In the years previous to 1899 the following had conducted normals here after the regular term had closed, they were Jordon, Gardner and Paisley. When the fall term began in 1899, Prof. Hugh Bishop and a Prof. Haggard from Tennessee were in charge. When school closed for Christmas that year Prof. Haggard did not return to finish his term. Prof. Rorex was also a teacher in the Abbott Institute.

Early in 1900 the Baptist church of Arkansas was establishing schools around over the state, known as "mountain schools." Maynard looked like a good place to establish a school, so they bought the Abbott Institute and opened a school known as the Maynard Baptist Academy.

Under this plan and leadership the school continued to grow and the town of Maynard became known far and wide as one of the best "school towns" of the state. We remember an advertisement of the school about 1910 which stated, "Maynard Ouachita Academy is located in the foothills of the Ozarks, far away from the death-lurking swamps of the South, and the dangers associated with the metropolitan areas of the North and East."

For a period of twenty-eight years, from 1900 to 1928, this school flourished. In 1928, the Maynard school district purchased the building and equipment of the Ouachita Academy and after that date the plant was used by the Maynard public school.

During the lifetime of the Abbott Institute and the Ouachita Maynard Academy, many young men and women received their education there. Several hundreds of good citizens, now scattered over the nation, owe their success in life to the training which they received in these two pioneer seats of learning. Many of these people are now holding responsible positions of trust and honor.

After the establishment of the various high schools in the towns, the Academy ceased to prove profitable to the Baptist Church, which had established several of these "preparatory" schools around over the state. Due to this fact they offered the Maynard plant to the school district at an attractive price and the latter purchased it.

The old Academy building was used as a high and grade school until 1937-38 when a public works program was secured and the present new building was erected.

The new building is a credit to any town much larger than Maynard. The school now employs ten teachers and has recently annexed several adjoining rural districts and operates buses to transport the pupils from their homes to Maynard each day.

This is one of the best schools in Randolph County today.

NOLAND

The village of Noland is located a short distance north of the site of old Davidsonville, the first town of the county. Some of the families still living in this community are descendants of some of the people who settled here when Davidsonville was a town.

Among these families are the names of Cox, Hardin, Davis, Sloan, Pyland Leathers, Ragan, Gwin, Slayton, Penn, Level, Van Hoosiers, Sissons, Hufstedlers, Lemmons, Pace, and possibly others which should be listed here, which are not available to the author at this time.

The actual first settlers here are the ones listed in the article on old Davidsonville, but the list above also includes others who have come to this community at later dates. This community also includes the Cedar Ridge community, and which is made up of the same families.

The village of Noland was first known as Cherry Hill. On the old Jim Slayton farm are still to be seen a few scrubby old apple trees which are said to have been brought here during the early days from Tennessee, in a pair of saddle bags.

COMMUNITIES

B. A. Pyland was the first postmaster at Noland. The office is said to be named for his wife, Nova Pyland, using the first and last part of her whole name. Some have thought that the name originated with Charles Fenton Mercer Noland, early resident of Davidsonville and Batesville, who was at one time U. S. land agent here. The first postoffice was established here about 1890. The first school building was an old log house on Gwin creek.

For many years the Clark brothers, J. C. and J. E., were merchants here, until bad health forced them to retire. Mack Hufstedler has been the postmaster many years and is now the merchant of the town.

Old Scott's Ferry on Black river is at the old Davidsonville site, and for many years afforded a crossing from this ancient community to the bottom country around Manson. The Scott family is also an early family here.

The old Burn's Ferry is across Spring river between this community and Black Rock, in Lawrence County.

On the east side of the Noland community is Black river. On the river was an early boat landing known as "Hoover's Landing." A postoffice was established here about 1890. A Mr. Mercer was the first postmaster and he kept the office in his residence.

This office gave way to the village of Manson which came into existence when the railroad was built from Hoxie to Pocahontas. The name came from a village of the same name in Clinton county, Indiana, where a number of settlers in this community had formerly lived. Mrs. W. J. Matthews was the first pastmaster.

In the Noland section of the county we also find the location of one of the county's oldest churches. This is the Hubble Creek church, which was first established by John M. Lemmons and others in 1852, as a local congregation, but did not own the site of its church building until 1868 when A. J. and Helen Pace deeded the site to the Church of Christ, on September 1 of that year.

There are three school houses in this community. They are Hubble Creek, Noland and Cedar Ridge.

A number of the leading families of Pocahontas at the present time are natives of the Noland community and some of the best citizens of the county still live in this section.

WATER VALLEY COMMUNITY

This community is that section of Elevenpoint river valley around what has been Black's Ferry ever since David Black settled here in 1815.

The next settler of which he have actual record was James Taylor Haas who came here not long after Black and settled west of the river when only two tracts of land was cleared in what is now Water Valley township.

The first postmaster at Water Valley is said to have been D. C. Black, who lived on the old Mattix farm at the time. Later it was moved farther west to the old McMillen place and D. B. McMillen became the postmaster.

The Haas family is still represented in that section. Uncle Jim Haas of Ravenden Springs is a son of the James T. Haas named above.

The first schoolhouse was built by Newt Williams in 1870, with the help of colored hired man, Kit Shockley. The first schoolmaster was Dr. A. G. Henderson, who is still living at Imboden in 1946.

The first mail route ran through this community to Kingsville, later called Walnut Hill, just below the town of Ravenden Springs.

COMMUNITIES

W. M. Clark was postmaster about twenty-five years, prior to his death in 1944. Mrs. Deward Helms is the present postmistress.

There are a number of good and substantial families living in this community. The McMillen family is still represented here. One of Lawrence county's pioneer families is represented here in the person of Ray Pickett and family. The Picketts moved here about sixteen years ago from Lawrence county, where foreparents of the family have lived over a century.

It is in this community that the proposed Water Valley dam site is located. If built, it will dam up Elevenpoint river a distance of many miles, and will cover up some of the best farm land in the United States.

Millions of dollars in farm revenue will be lost to the county for all time. Since the dawn of Randolph county's first settlement, Elevenpoint river has contributed financially to the upbuilding of Randolph county in a major degree. We hope that if the dam is built that it will bring in the advantages its sponsors claim, to offset this loss. November, 1973, twenty seven years later, the dam has not yet been built; November, 1981, dam never built.

One of the oldest inland communities of Randolph county is the community now known as Oconee. Being situated in Dry Creek valley, it is the site of some of the first homesteads in Elevenpoint river valley.

Among the first families to settle here were the Rices, John Wells, Rodney Crawford, the Selbys, Barbers, Howell White, some of the McIlroys, some of the Stubblefields, Davis and Jacksons.

Ezekiel Rice was one of the first Justices of the Peace in Davidson township, in which this community is located. Isham Alcorn was also an early settler here.

The first school house is reputed to have been built on the north bank of Dry creek near the present Oconee ford, about 1874. It is possible that an earlier "meeting house" had been built in the community at an earlier date, but nothing definite is known of this. The house built in 1874 was used both as a school and church until 1894.

Near this date both the Baptists and Church of Christ built churches here.

Oconee was first known as Ricetown. William C. Rice was the first postmaster after the office was established in 1894. He gave it the name Oconee. The following have been among those who have been merchants at this place: H. M. Rice, J. A. Rice, Thomas White, Harve Boling, Avery Nuckles, Charles Casey, Freeman Owens, M. A. Baker, and Ora Sullenger.

Dry Creek, while not a large stream, flows down out of the dividing brakes between Janes Creek and Elevenpoint River and possesses a nice fertile "bottom" which was taken up by the early settlers and made into a number of nice farms. The old Crawford house is one of the oldest existing buildings in the county.

Near this community were also found the Bellahs, Moores, Rickmans, McLains, James, Taylor and other families during the very first days of settlement.

PITMAN'S FERRY AND COMMUNITY

The country around the present-day villages of **Pitman** and **Supply** in Little Black township, is one of the earliest settlements in north Arkansas. As we also have said about the old Fourche de Thomas (Columbia) settlement, the historian who states that Pitman was the first, or next to the first settlements in Randolph county, would have a lot of evidence to support his claim. At this place the old Natchitoches Trail, later known as the old Military road, crossed Current river. A ferry was established here about 1803. William Hix was the first owner of the old ferry and the place is marked on the first maps and records as Hix ferry. The noted German scientist and physician, Dr. Englemann, made a trip from St. Louis to Little Rock in March, 1837. He states in his report that Dr. Peyton R. Pitman lived here at this time and had been here over twenty-five years at that time. This would make him a resident here in 1812. It is known that William Hix operated the ferry many years, so it must have been opened not later than 1803. Dr. Englemann states in his notes that, "On March 12, a gloomy rainy day, we passed the boundary of Arkansas. The border is marked by scores hewn into the trees. A quarter of a mile south we crossed the Current river, a beautiful clear stream, which, though larger than the Black, which we passed two days before, empties into the latter a short distance from here. On the south bank of the Current is situated a beautiful plantation, with a handsome dwelling surrounded by a veranda, many outhouses and extensive fields on both sides of the river. Dr. Pitman, the owner, has lived here for twenty-five years."

Jess Cheek and Bernard Rogan laid out a town just south of Pitman in 1820 and called it "Currenton." It did not last and the residents and owners really became a part of Pitman. At one time the village of Pitman was a hustling trading port. Some of the first settlers here were the **Kellys**,

OLD PITMAN FERRY SITE

First ferry in Arkansas, opened about 1803 across Current River. Author's son, Herman Dalton, in picture.

Daniel Ashabranner, Eli Lindsey, John Pierce, Looneys, Berrys, Bells, Tom and John Gambill, and also William Hix and Dr. Pitman. The Hanover brothers, Jews, were among the first merchants. Michael Looney, Erasmus Pitman and others, were also early merchants.

A plat of the town of Pitman was entered on the deed record of Randolph county in 1853 and showed a town of considerable proportions. It contained twelve blocks. The names of the streets were, Sunny, Second, Third, Center, Mill and First. Front street was located 99 feet from the river front. E. D. Pitman and Michael Looney gave a mortgage to Clark, Renfrew and Co. of St. Louis, in 1853, on the following property: "Situated in the town of Pitman, Arkansas, one steam, saw and grist mill, and distillery, with all fixtures, also the ground upon which this is located, bounded on the north and east by Mill and Second streets, on the south and west by Current river, containing nine acres." Edward McDonald, who represented old Lawrence county in the Territorial (First) Legislature of Arkansas at Arkansas Post in 1820, lived near Pitman. Joseph J. Anthony, who was Randolph county's first representative in the State Legislature, and who was murdered in this first term by John Wilson from Clark county in 1837, was also a resident near here.

The old town of Pitman was located on the river quite a distance northeast of the present postoffice of Pitman. It was located near the state line and at the edge of what is now Clay county. The first deed record of Lawrence county shows that James Smith sold to William Linn his "improvement on Glaze Kenon creek, a branch of Current river," for $100, November 15, 1818. A neighbor, Alexander Dunin, was a witness to the deal and stated that he knew that Smith had cultivated the place in 1812. This was near Pitman. The first election in Randolph county which was held in 1836, named Dr. P. R. Pitman as county judge. Jess Driskill, James P. Ingram and Thomas Hinton were

OLD PITMAN FERRY CEMETERY AND CIVIL WAR BATTLEGROUND

the election officials for Little Black township and the election was held at Pitman. The Cockrum and Pierce families have long been represented in this community. James Cockrum and Levina Pierce were married December 19, 1822. Henry Cockrum was county judge from 1862 to 1868. The Randolph county tax book for the year 1854 only listed seven merchants in the county. There were a lot more than this, but they evidently were overlooked by the assessor. Four of these were in Little Black township. They were J. W. Crossen, H. Frederick, Michael Looney and J. C. Whitesides. Dr. Englemann stated that in 1837 he found several pretty, but old, peach and apple orchards in this section. Henry Schoolcraft, who passed down the old Military road and who stopped for awhile at both Fourche and Pitman, stated that there were many nice improved farms along the road in 1819. William Hix, the first owner of Pitman, evidently invested in the closeby proposed town of Currenton, as the records show that on March

15, 1821, he sold lot 3, in block 1, and lot 38 in block 7 of Currenton, to William Rogers of Tennessee.

Mount Pleasant Baptist church at Pitman is one of the oldest churches in Arkansas, and possibly is the oldest in continuous existence. It was established in 1826 by Tom and John Gambill, John and William Berry, William Bell and others whose names are not available.

The old Antioch Methodist church was organized at Pitman in 1850. The organizers are not known. Some of the early preachers were Philemon Wright, Larkin F. Johnston, W. H. Phipps, W. A. Downing, Jesse Robinson and Willis H. Hall. This church no longer exists.

Here at the old town of Pitman, besides being the oldest ferry in Arkansas is the site of one of the major battles of the Civil War in Arkansas, and one of the oldest cemeteries in the state.

In the old cemetery which is now abandoned and neglected, lie buried some of the leading citizens of early south Missouri and north Arkansas.

This old townsite is now owned by a Mr. Clark and son. A previous owner, a few years ago built a house in the old cemetery and it is said that he used monuments from the graves for a foundation. At any rate, very few stones are in order today. Many have fallen. On the face of one, this writer recently read the following inscription: "Sarah Kelley, wife of J. Kelley, born in 1799 and died in 1861." The stone had been erected by a daughter, Susan "Hanauer." The latter spelling was either the original Jewish way of spelling "Hanover" or the last "A" had been actually an "O" and the "U" was an "N," making it Hanover instead of Hanauer.

The Hanover family were early residents here, and as stated elsewhere in this book, were Jews, who operated stores here and later at Lindseyville and finally in Pocahontas.

It is a melancholy sight to look across this old cemetery which was begun before our grandfathers were born, and see how it has been abused by those who thoughtlessly and carelessly wrecked and spoiled the last resting place of those who came here during the misty morning hours of the nineteenth century to build a home and civilization for we who live now.

There is a long sunken trench, plainly seen today which is the grave of many men who died in battle here, and were later removed to other places.

The old battle ground is adjacent to the cemetery and many "minnie" balls can be picked up today. Down next to the river is an old well which was dug during the time the Confederate army was encamped here. The river became polluted after battle and continual occupation of the area and the leaders fearing an epidemic as a result, dug this well as a source of pure drinking water.

Possibly some day in the future, some descendant of the Kelleys, the Hanovers, the Pitmans or somebody else who lies smouldering in this old burying ground, will come forward and restore the spot as best as is possible and erect a marble shaft in honor of the legion of unknown, who are sleeping here, forgotten, unhonored and unsung.

It is difficult for the historian to record a true and unbroken story of a community like Pitman. The early importance of this gateway to th egreat southwest is recorded in legal documents and old stories, tradition, etc. With the further settlement of the county as a whole and the center of population shifting to other places, naturally causes a decline in such places of very early importance. There likewise follows a period of unrecorded time and incidents. Later the place again assumes some importance and there is a gap for the writer to bridge. The very earliest history of Hix's Ferry and Pitman is well known, but it is left to the families of the early settlers to preserve the history of that

COMMUNITIES

period from about 1850 to 1880, except for the stories of the wartime sixties.

Many families well known today came into this community during this "middle period." The Ruffs, Shemwells, Legates, Wrights, Halls, Lewis, Reeves, Cunninghams, Jollys, Ingrams, Allens, Dismangs, Taylors, Fowlers, Redwines, Hawkins, Pringles, and many others, have taken up residence in the Pitman community of Little Black township since the days of Hix, Dr. Pitman, Ashabranner and Cheek and Rogan.

It is said that this community has produced more physicians and ministers than any other community in north Arkansas.

The Ruff, Shemwell, Reeves and Hawkins families have been the merchants the greater portion of the past three-quartrs of a century, with a sprinkling of the other names along in between.

Another characteristic of this community is, that it has had a large group of Republicans in their political setup, possibly more than any other community in the county. But even with Randolph with a heavy Democratic majority, this community has furnished several county officials during the years since the county was organized.

PALESTINE CHURCH AND THE INGRAM COMMUNITY

The postoffice now named Ingram, which is located on the Warm Springs-Pocahontas road is several miles from the spot where the first postoffice of that name was located.

The first Ingram postoffice was located at the "Dock Ingram Ford" on Mud creek, which is now known as the Price farm. Here G. H. "Dock" Ingram operated a cotton gin and mill during the last quarter of the past century. There was also a still house and other businesses there, including a blacksmith shop. Power to operate the machinery came from a dam which was built on the creek.

The first postoffice was established in the store of Rufe Roberts and a Mr. Keith, about 1890. Henry Ator operated a store there about this time and the office may have been in his store part of the time.

Later Roberts moved his store and the postoffice over to his farm southwest of the first location. Here it remained until about 1910, when he was succeeded by Jeff Morris, who moved the office to what was generally known as "Henpeck." Peter Ator and Rob Morris were already in business there. This location was about one-half mile south of the presentday Palestine church building. Prior to this, since about 1885, Bart Long operated a store over on the Belview road east of the church. The postoffice remained at the Henpeck location until about 1924 when it was moved to the present location. During this time a number of parties were in business there, among these were Joe Price, J. D. Driskill, W. E. Tiner, Dock Condict and others at the old location, and several others later at the present site.

The first school house in this community is said to have been about one-fourth mile east of the present home of Ran Shaver. It was an old log house and was used for both school and church. The next schoolhouse was west of this location near the Beasley spring. The first house served from about 1880 until 1892 and the second until a house was built on the present locatio nabout 1900 and called Palestine, the name that had previously been applied to the church building.

The first church building was the one referred to above as being the schoolhouse and also a church. This old building was called "Gooberhull." This was actually the first church that was the forerunner of the presentday Palestine, however church had been held for many years at homes in the neighborhood. Chief of these was the home of Uncle Isham Mock. He had a large two-story log house and the upper story was used by the neighbors for a church building.

The present building was built about 1890 through the efforts of Isham Mock, Jake Waddle, the Shaver families and others living nearby.

This community has always been made up principally of families whose religious affiliation was with the Church of Christ. The first Mocks, Shavers and others were of that belief and their influence spread.

The above is the "modern" history of the Ingram-Palestine community. Many years before the above places came into existence, there was a postoffice up the creek a short distance from Palestine called "Mud Creek," and Mathis Mock was postmaster in 1836. This is probably the first trading place in this section. He had been living there twenty-one years at that time.

John Shaver settled in this community in 1823, coming here from Georgia

Henry Waddle settled there in 1832. The Fletcher and Morris families were early settlers there as were the Davis and Carter families. Levy Fletcher married Elizabeth Shaver in 1823. Matthias Mock married Leah Shaver there about

1817, as this union was the parents of four children before the mother died about 1827. He married Margaret Hill Mansker in 1828. Other early families were Condicts, Wallaces, Longs, Tiners, Spikes and Shocklees. The census of 1820 gave John Shaver as being over eighty years of age.

His son, John Shaver, was appointed by the first court of Randolph county "to serve as road overseer for the Belview road, from Ransom Eldridges on Fourche creek to the state line to Jumping Springs." Just where the latter place was located is not known, but was possibly somewhere near where the Military road crossed the old Belview road.

Michael Shaver, Minatree Carter and James G. Russell were appointed by this same court to mark out a road from Duckworth's Ferry on Current river to this community.

The old New Hope church school and church which is mentioned in connection with the article about Warm Springs was only a short distance north of this community and was possibly used at an early day as a place of worship by the folks who lived in this section as well as those at Warm Springs, next community northwest of here.

Some of the first Church of Christ preachers of Arkansas lived in this community. Among these were William and Peter Shaver, Newton George, Eld. Norwood, Parson James and Brother Zera Allen who lived near Supply but who helped establish the church here.

Besides the Ingram postoffice, there was another postoffice in this community called Mock. It was established by the late W. L. (Fayette) Mock and was at the store which he and his father, General Mock, had previously established on Mud creek about a mile north of the first Ingram office. Near here settled Parson Isaac Witt, Bias Russell and others soon after the close of the Civil War. Some of the folks living in this community are the seventh generation since their forefathers landed in Randolph county.

POCAHONTAS

The city of Pocahontas had its beginning not as Pocahontas, but as a trading post known as Bettis Bluff. Even before it was called Bettis Bluff, there was a French trading post here.

Spot where first house was built in Pocahontas.

Tradition tells us that early Frenchmen came down the Mississippi from the north and hunted and traded with the Indians, possibly as early as 1765. It has even been said that a descendant of one of the ten men left here by De Tonti in 1686, who had evidently married an Indian girl, lived in this section, possibly on the site of Pocahontas. His name may have been De Maux, from which, in a corrupted form, the Fourche de Mas got its name.

Anyway, the first traders followed the water courses for different reasons, and this being a choice site, with its foothills extending its toes out into the alluvial river bottoms, "forcing Black river to flow around them," possibly afforded the choice site from which to travel out through the forsets. The trader, paddling his canoe up the river may have tied his dugout to a willow tree which grew where the limestone ledge projects out into the river just below the railroad bridge today. On the hillside where the Pocahontas Lumber Company and McFall's used car lot is now located, may have been the wigwams of the Indians and the cabins of the French trader. This is possibly the first modern history of Pocahontas.

Tradition tells us that the Indians chose the site of Pocahontas for an ancient village because of its natural location being a protection against storms. It is a fact that during the one hundred and fifty years of its known existence the town has never been visited by a destructive storm. However, a few years ago, one did dip down as close as a section of the city in the vicinity of Barthel's home and hatchery.

The French called Pocahontas *Encore de Flueve Noir* in their language.

But back to Bettis Bluff, which was named for Ransom S. Bettis.

Bettis came to this section about 1815 from North Carolina. He is said to have been a pioneer trader and physician. The early records of southeast Missouri show the route of an old mail route from Harrisonville, Illinois by way of St. Genevieve, Hix's Ferry and "Dock" Bettis, Davidsonville to Polk Bayou (Batesville) on White river. This was in operation as early as 1818 and possibly succeeded the old original route "from Monroe, Louisiana, to St. Louis, by way of Davidsonville and Arkansas Post." So we infer from this that Bettis had a postoffice here at that time.

Very little is known of the Bettis family. We know that he had one daughter, Cinderella, who married Thomas Stephenson Drew. It is by this that we learn what we know of this, possibly the first white family to make the site of Pocahontas their home.

The Bettis home was located on the hill, near the present site of the old Hamil home and the present home of Dr. W. E. Hamil, which is nearby. This site originally overlooked the river front and was an ideal spot for a pioneer home. In recent years the front has become the "back" as the two Hamil homes face the west and Highway 67, wherein the Bettis home faced the east. The old family cemetery was also located here. Members of this early family were buried here during the days when the "town" consisted only of the Bettis home and the trading post and surrounding buildings. Many years later the remains were taken up and re-interred in the Masonic cemetery, near the grave of Governor Drew. (These graves were made in the cemetery before Drew was re-interred here in 1923).

After Thomas Drew married Cinderella Bettis, Drew had been an itinerant peddler who lived in Clark county, they also made their home in Pocahontas near her father's home for some time. Later Bettis gave his daughter a large tract of land in Cherokee Bay where the town of Biggers now stands, and Thomas and Cinderella Drew moved to it. Here they lived several years.

While living in Pocahontas, Drew and Bettis conceived the idea of establishing a real town. They could see the country being opened up, the possibility of the county being cut off from Lawrence and a demand for a new county seat for the new county, if this did happen. They busied themselves about the job of founding a town. When the county was organized in October, 1835, they had already "started a town." Lots were being advertised for sale and invitations were being sent out to the merchants and other shop keepers to come to the new town, as it was destined to become the "Metropolis of the West."

The story has already been told in the Fourche de Thomas article in this book about how the free barbecue and picnic was the trick which pulled the voters to Pocahontas when election day came around to decide whether Columbia or Pocahontas was to become the county seat of the new county. Bettis and Drew were the sponsors of this proposition and they each donated land and cash to the new town. A street in the town is named for Bettis and that part of the city which is located between Highway 67 and the Fisco railroad at this time was originally the "Drew Reserve" or Drew Addition to the town.

Thomas O. Marr was another early settler of the town and we have Marr street and Marr's creek to remember him by. He built the first courthouse.

Lewis De Munn and his brothers, Frenchmen, had already built a water mill on the creek just south of the town, below what is now known as the Cypress Springs, on Mill creek. A few years ago the old cast "arm" of the power wheel of this old mill was unearthed on the bank of this creek. What a story this old piece of metal could tell if it could speak! On one side it is marked "Made in France." Just picture the journey this mill machinery must have traveled in that day (about 1820) to come from France to Pocahontas! The first lap of the journey was the long boat ride across the stormy Atlantic, possibly landing in New York and later transferred to a vessel going down the coast to New Orleans. Here it was loaded on a boat for the long slow ride up the Mississippi to the mouth of White river; thence up White river to the mouth of Black and from there up Black to Pocahontas. It was probably hauled on a wooden

COMMUNITIES

POCAHONTAS' SIX CHURCHES

Upper left, St. Paul's Catholic; upper right, Church of Christ; middle left, Freewill Baptist; middle right, Missionary Baptist; lower left, Methodist; lower right, Pentecostal.

wheeled oxcart from the river across the bottom to the mill site. The location of the old dam can still be seen.

One of the first settlers in the vicinity of Pocahontas was Casper Schmick, who settled two miles down the river from the present town. He was one of the active persons in the various movements which started the town.

On the north side of Pocahontas was George Mansker, His family was related to Thomas S. Drew, the two families coming to Arkansas from adjoining counties of Tennessee. Soon after the establishment of the town of Pocahontas, one of the first families to move here was William L. Rice, who had already become the first citizen of the village of Warm Springs. The first map of the town of Pocahontas, made soon after the town was plotted, showed the following as owners of some of the lots and blocks: White, Hanover, Looney, Hunter, Rice, David Fine, Mitchell, Black, Imboden.

Thomas S. Drew sold William Looney the land where the Sallee handle mill is now located "in the fork between Marr's creek and Black river" in 1846.

The first map referred to above showed that William Looney owned the whole block on the south side of the old courtsquare, the space from the bank to Johnston's drug store at present. Hanover brothers at that time owned the block which was later to be known as the Biggers Hotel block.

The Marr and Drew families owned most of the present site of the town during the period of its establishment.

Blacks moved to Pocahontas from what is now known as Black's Ferry on Elevenpoint river soon after the town was started. The father of William, John and Rufe Black settled at that place about 1815.

COMMUNITIES

John Imboden (for whom the town of Imboden, in Lawrence county was named) was also an early resident of Pocahontas.

The list is too long to mention all the first residents of the town. Many of the first families are still represented in the city at the present time. A list of family histories from all these families would be a history of the town within itself, but this is impossible.

Anyway the town got off to a good start from the very beginning.

The December 26, 1838, edition of the Arkansas Gazette carried the following statement concerning Pocahontas: "The new town of Pocahontas, county seat of Randolph county, is said to have become, within eighteen months of its existence, one of the most flourishing places within the state. Lots in the town had increased in value from 100 to 500 per cent. The farm lands in the county, which had lately sold for $1.25 per acre, was now much in demand at $20. Transportation in and out of the town and county is principally by steamboats on Black river and business of every kind is lively with the people saying little about hard times." This was the rosy picture of the first years of Pocahontas, as recorded by the state's leading newspaper of the time.

The Arkansas Gazette also carried an item from its Pocahontas correspondent in July, 1846, which told of the Fourth of July celebration as follows:

"At twelve o'clock a procession was formed and we marched, preceeded by the Committee on Arrangements and a band of music, to a beautiful grove near the spring on the bank of the river, where Mr. C. R. Landers, after a few appropriate remarks, read in a clear impressive manner, the Declaration of Independence."

Thus we have a picture of a Fourth of July a century ago here in Pocahontas. The Gazette correspondent from Pocahontas is not known.

The early roads of the county had been opened generally between the communities of Davidsonville, Pitman Ferry and Columbia (Fourche de Thomas). After the rise of Pocahontas, the routes of travel were changed. The roads were opened in the direction of Pocahontas, instead of the other places. A branch of the old Military road was cut into Pocahontas from the Russell or Foster farm where Mack Riggs now resides. After a few years the travel came by Pocahontas, even when headed southwest, which had previously gone through directly to the crossing on Elevenpoint. A road was built from Pitman direct to Pocahontas which is now the Pocahontas-Maynard road.

The old town of Albertha grew up on this road. Robert M. Frier, early settler of Madison county, Missouri, opened a stage line, which ran down this road from St. Genevieve, on the Mississippi below St. Louis to Pocahontas, sometime between 1825 and 1840. He later extended this route to Little Rock. This was after the decline of Davidsonville and routes of travel had changed. He is said to have become a wealthy man from his income from this stage line.

In the paragraph above which told of the actual plotting and establishment of the town, we should have mentioned the fact that Drew donated $3,000; Bettis $1,000 and Thomas Marr $200 cash to be used toward the erection of public building, etc., in the new town, provided that it remained the county seat.

In the list of first businesses of the town of Pocahontas we find the names of Hunter and Rayburn, Oakes and Truly as merchants, McCleary, a tanner; William Hubble, harness maker. The county court of 1837 granted Bird M. Simpson the first license issued in Randolph county, "to keep and sell all kinds of groceries, for a term of one year." Simpson was the first county treasurer. At this same term of court John L. Glasscock was given license to sell groceries and all kinds of liquor for one year. He was charged ten dollars for the license. The amount of Simpson's license is not given.

The property tax for the whole county that year was $430.53 and the peddlers and merchants licenses amounted to $170.

Green R. Jones was an early merchant of Pocahontas. We wish it were possible to tell you just what years each party began in, or at least the time they were in business here but this is not obtainable. William Allaire was an architect during the first days of the city and we find that at least some of the physicians were Drs. Payne, Doughtitt, Beashoars and Harrison. John and William McDowell were merchants here in 1854.

Thomas O. Marr made a bond to Wash R. Hunter, February 6, 1947 to guarantee that he would "ferry all of Hunter's employes and all those who had business with Hunter," across the river on Marr's ferry. The bond was $500. By this early date Hunter who became the largest land owner who has lived in Pocahontas, had acquired large holdings and employed several men in the improving of a lot of rough property. He is said to have been the first postmaster.

The tax record of 1854 lists a William Evans as a merchant of Pocahontas. He was the only merchant charged with tax in that year from Demun township. Just why no others were, is not known.

James Martin was postmaster at Pocahontas in 1838.

The first ferry was located a short distance down the river below the present railroad bridge. This was near the end of Broadway street, where the street ran down the hill to the river. After the old original buildings of the "Bettis

Bluff" trading post were abandoned, the next business street in the town was up this street from the ferry and steamboat landing.

The name of Hanover is associated with the early history of the town and county. There were three brothers, of Jewish nationality. The eldest was named Lewis. They were in business first at the old town of Pitman. Later we find them at old Lindseyville where the old Doniphan-Pocahontas road crossed the old Military road. Later they came to Pocahontas. It is possible that they owned stores at more than one location at the same time.

They were also large land holders and for many years were prominently identified with the political and business life of the county.

Other merchants of Pocahontas in the period from the close of the Civil War until about 1900 were, Levi Hecht, R. N. Hamil, R. Nicholas, Isaac Hurst, John P. Black, Jacob Schoonover and many others whose names we do not know. Black's store was located on the present site of the post-office and was used also as temporary quarters for a "part" of the courthouse records and equipment around 1870. Hamil had his store in different locations in the town before 1893. In that year he built the building which is now the King store.

Of the early hotels of the town the St. Charles and the Biggers hotels were possibly the best known. The old St. Charles was located on the north end of the block now occupied by Baltz Hardware and Lewallen Hotel building.

Eli Heavener owned the Biggers Hotel before it became the property of B. F. Bigger. On date of February 11, 1882, Heaverner sold it to Bigger, together with the land adjacent, which was lots three and five in block nine and all of block ten. From that date forward for a period of forty years it became known far and wide as a popular stopping place. A livery stable was nearby and customers of the hotels who had business out of town hired "rigs' 'to drive out sometimes as far as Poplar Bluff and Mammoth Spring.

When the large group of European immigrants arrived in Pocahontas in 1880, a number of them secured lodging in the old Heavener Hotel and it was here that many of these folks experienced their first close-up association with the Western world.

The Hecht Hotel, located on the block north of the present postoffice building, was also in operation during this period. There have been other hotels through the years, possibly good ones before the ones listed above, and some since the priod described.

The first millman other than the De Munn brothers was David Jones, who operated a saw mill on the present site of the Sallee mill. He was here before the Civil War and operated many years. He is said to have been a high type citizen who did much for the frontier town.

Following the period of the war other people came to Pocahontas. Among these were several doctors. Among these were Dr. Esselman, Dr. Tom Hall, Dr. Putnam, Dr. Silverberg and Dr. Means.

Every old town has its ancient burying grounds. Pocahontas has hers. Just beyond Mansker creek on the Maynard road is the old cemetery which is said to have been started during the War Between the States. On Catholic Hill near the church is an old cemetery, almost forgotten, which was used during the early days. One of the graves in it is that of Col. Marvin, who was related to the Miller and Crenshaw families. As stated above the first cemetery was near the Bettis home, near the present site of Dr. Hamil's home.

There are some graves near the present home of N. E. Pace, in the north part of town and it is said that there were several hundred graves of Confederate soldiers buried in the woods near the old De Munn mill site on Mill creek south of town. We know little about either of these old cemeteries.

The Catholic and Masonic cemeteries are the present-day cemeteries used. Many of the families of Randolph county are represented in these cemeteries.

Little is known of the early schools of the city of Pocahontas. It is known that there was some kind of school for the children of the early town, but just who the teachers were is lost to us.

B. J. Wiley and C. C. Elder are supposed to have taught here and other officials, preachers and laymen, did their part in seeing that some educational advantages were offered.

Around 1880, Prof. John Hogan, whose biography is printed in this book, together with his wife, Miss Eliza, taught in Pocahontas. Their work was in an old lodge hall near the present school building. They were highly educated for their day and did a lot of good in the town and county.

Another teacher during this period was Mrs. Surridge. She taught at her home which was located on the site of the present home of J. M. Dunn.

Since that period we have seen many talented educators come and go.

In the chapter about the early churches of the county will be found the history of the first churches of Pocahontas.

The history of Randolph county's part in the Civil War has already been related in this book, and since much of it happened in the vicinity of Pocahontas, there is not much to add. Old Camp Shaver was located on Mill creek south of the town and several thousand men passed through here at different times during the war. Among the notables who were at Pocahontas for a time during the conflict were

COMMUNITIES

General Hardee, Gen. Hindman, Colonel Robert G. Shaver, General Earl Van Dorn, besides all the local officers.

Henry M. Stanley, the noted African explorer, joined the Confederate army at Pocahontas in 1862. He served under Col. Shaver and was in the battle of Shiloh. He later became a big game hunter and explorer. Finally returning to England, where he is said to have renounced his American citizenship, married into British royalty and thus spent the rest of his life far from the land of his youth.

General Steele of the Federal army occupied Pocahontas a short time toward the last of the war. Very little damage was done in this section.

After the close of the war the country in general saw a period of stagnation and decline. Reconstruction days were hard days. Pocahontas, which had been a hustling frontier town, slowed down during this period.

There were other reasons besides the aftermath of war. The seventies saw the building of the old Iron Mountain railroad, which crossed a corner of the county at O'Kean, and soon after this the main line of the Frisco was built up Spring river to the west. Since the river division of the Frisco which now passes Pocahontas was yet unbuilt, the trade naturally turned to the railroads. Steamboating was on the decline. No good roads had been built. This caused Pocahontas to enter a passive state which she did not awaken from until around 1900.

However, with the coming of the branch line from Hoxie to Pocahontas in the late nineties and the extension to Cape Girardeau in 1902-03, the town started growing. Since that date it has seen a steady improvement.

On another page in this history is a photograph of the business houses on the south side of the court square about 1885. The picture is that of a typical inland frontier town. The only brick buildings in town at that time was the courthouse, which was completed in 1873, and the Biggers Hotel, which was built near the same time.

Most of the modern improvements have come to the town since 1900. First was the railroad. Then in 1911 a light and power plant was built and electricity replaced the old kerosene street lights, and a maporily of the homes and business places were wired for electricity.

Ben A. Brown, local abstractor and long-time resident of Pocahontas, has the distinction of being the first individual who ever turned on an electric light in the city. The drop and shade which hangs over the front desk in his office on the southwest corner of the old court square is the original light which he turned on in 1911.

Next came the water system in 1915. This was one of the greatest advantages any town ever has. The water hauler who supplied the town, those who had no wells and cisterns, went out of business, and much illness caused by the use of untreated Black river water subsided. The original old metal storage tank is still used as an auxiliary storage vessel but a new concrete reservoir was built this year out on the Dalton road, to replace the old tank.

Highway 67 was built through the town in 1928. Today we are only two and one-half hours from Little Rock, a little over an hour from Memphis, and less than five hours from St. Louis, by highway travel.

It would possibly be appropriate to add here that in the not far distant day the above time will be cut at least in half by air travel.

The first hard-surfaced streets to be built in Pocahontas, other than gravel, was in 1928, when Thomasville and Highway 67 were concreted through town. In 1940 and 1941 several miles of streets were black-topped.

The Arkansas-Missouri Power Corporation built a highline through this section. The line ran through Pocahontas.

At this time the local power plant was taken over by the corporation and the electric power for the city had been supplied by the latter concern.

During the early days of World War II a section of land across the river east of Pocahontas, adjacent to the city limits was taken over by the Federal government for use as an auxiliary airfield. There is a possibility that this may later be used as a municipal airport.

Between this area and the highway bridge there has been opened a new addition to the city and it is being improved rapidly, principally as an industrial addition. Another addition has been opened just north of the Dalton Addition and is being sold in lots and blocks by A. J. Baltz and

This is the block in Pocahontas from the Bank of Pocahontas to Johnston's Drug Store.

others. It is known as the "Lakeview Addition." In the northwest section of the city, Ray Bowlin has recently opened an addition and is now opening streets and selling lots. Joe S. Decker and W. T. Crismon have opened up an addition on the west side and others have improved and offered lots for sale in various sections of the city. There has already been a lot of new buildings constructed, but due to the present shortage of materials and restrictions on buildings, the building program is handicapped. There will be at least two hundred new residences and around twenty-five new business buildings of different kinds erected as soon as conditions permit.

The Brown Shoe Company of St. Louis is now building a $200,000 shoe factory in Pocahontas and other industries are likely to enter the city soon.

This is a fair summary of the history of the town of Pocahontas from around 1815, as Bettis Bluff, and from 1835 to the present as Pocahontas:

The city has a number of civic organiaztions, among these are the Chamber of Commerce and the Rotary Club.

The City Council is composed of the following: A. L. Wright, mayor; J. M. Dunn, John V. Baltz, Clifford McNabb and Edward Promberger, aldermen.

The Pocahontas School Board is composed of the following members: Robert P. Sallee, George M. Booth, A. F. Million, E. C. Cox and Lawrence Dalton.

Plans are under way to build a modern high school building on the ground just north of the present building. The present building will be re-conditioned and used for the lower grades. Approximately twenty-four teachers will be employed this year. The Catholics maintain a separate school, both high and lower grades.

RAVENDEN SPRINGS

The village of Ravenden Springs is known throughout north Arkansas as the "Dream Town." It is located in the vicinity of one of the oldest settlements in this section of the state. John Janes, a Revolutionary soldier, settled near here on the creek which bears his name about 1809. The first records of Lawrence county, of which this was a part until 1835, mentions the names of many families who still reside in this vicinity. One of the oldest mail routes in Randolph county ran from southeast Missouri "by way of Dry Springs on the state line, Janes store and Batesville." Later there grew up, just south of the present-day Ravenden Springs, a village called Walnut Hill and also Kingsville. Both passed out of existence and the "dream town" came into existence about 1880.

About the same time, or soon after John Janes located here, there came the Wells, Wyatts, Davis, and later the Baileys, Guntharps, Hendersons and Deckers, Lands, Picketts, Tanners, and others.

The establishment of the town of Ravenden Springs came about from a dream which Rev. William Bailey, Methodist minister, had. He had suffered from a stomach ailment for many years. All remedies used had brought no relief. One night he dreamed that there was a spring deep down in the canyon on Hall's creek on which he lived, and that he climbed down in the steep canyon wall and drank of its water and was cured. He dreamed this three times in succession. The next day he did as he dreamed he did and continued to drink of this water and was soon completely cured.

The story of Rev. Bailey's dream and cure became widely known. It was told to the late Capt. R. D. Welsh, who at that time was a conductor on a passenger train of the old Iron Mountain railroad between Little Rock and St. Louis.

Capt. Welsh visited the spring and was so impressed that he resigned his position and went to St. Louis where he organized a stock company, returned to the spring and laid out a town and built a forty-room hotel just south of the spring and built steps from the hotel down into the canyon to the spring. Captain Welsh succeeded in getting a stage line established from the new town to Walnut Ridge, a distance of about 35 miles. Soon after this the Kansas City, Fort Scott and Memphis railroad was built up Spring river valley and missed Ravenden Springs six miles. Captain Welsh succeeded in getting the nearest station on the line named Ravenden Junction. The mail was carried from Ravenden Springs through Walnut Hill to Ravenden Junction. In 1906 a high school was built and in 1907 a bank was established. Only three persons have owned the spring and surrounding land. Rev. Bailey obtained the land from the Government and deeded it to Capt. Welsh, in 1880. Welsh deeded it to Joe S. Decker in 1919.

The following were early builders of Ravenden Springs: Dr. Lambert, J. C. Parnell, Dr. Montgomery, A. G. Henderson and Bob Blackshear.

Bob Blackshear opened the first general store in the town and John Guntharp opened the first drug store. Prof. Dave Hays taught the first school in the town after it was established. Cal Moffit and Jake Lane were the first blacksmiths. George Pace, father of Roy and Troy Pace of Hoxie, was the constable of the town in 1880 and also the first mail carrier after the postoffice was established. Others who have figured in the history and progress of Ravenden Springs are: J. B. DuVall, Will McKinley, Charles Shelton, Webb and Childs, Capt. Mockabee, W. T. Fry, J. B. Elkins, J. B. Reynolds, John W. Cruse, Eaves brothers, C. A. Dixon, W. W. Rogers, S. L. Davis, C. C. and L. G. Hogan, W. F. Blackwell, Frank Davis and sons, William Marriott, and later R. L. Higginbotham and sons, W. A. Davis and sons,

J. J. Eaton and at present Lonnie Smith, O. B. Rickman, Arthur Stinnett, Cecil Crain and B. J. Simmons.

George Shelton and Josh Kellett, aged 88 and 87 respectively, are the two oldest citizens of the Ravenden Springs community. They were residents here when the town was established. Dr. A. G. Henderson, aged 94, at present, was a resident of this place in 1880, but now resides at Imboden. Dr. Henderson is the author of the following concerning Ravenden Springs and the origin of the name:

"The raven den was actually a raven's nest, high up in a hole in one of the immense boulders of the canyon. Tradition tells us that the ravens were building their nests in this place as early as 1820. George and Sam Henderson visited the place in 1860 and the birds were here as they had been for years, but the next year, in 1861, they left and never returned. Just why they left and where they went will always remain a mystery. I visited the canyon and inspected the raven den in 1865 and it was an awe-inspiring sight, due to the rugged unique grandeur of the place. The "Lone Rock," the "Needle's Eye," and other parts of the canyon was, and still is, a deep, mighty mass of rock.

"At the time Rev. Bailey dreamed of, and discovered the spring he was suffering from an arid type of stomach trouble (dyspepsia), more recently called the 'American stomach.' People suffering this way, have an active imagination and the psychology of the mind adds to this activity and makes dreams more or less visual. Rev. Bailey's dream impressed him very much. He drank the water four or five days and his condition showed such an improvement that he sent for me. I was practicing medicine at Walnut Hill at that time and he wanted me to investigate the water. I sent aspecimen of the water to the Health Department at Little Rock. The chemical analysis showed it to be pure water with a trace of alkali. I then began to investigate the physical properties of the water and found that it is permeated, saturated with free oxygen. It is buoyant, animative, light and volative. Upon these qualities it's healing powers depend. I can give only a few names of those cured by this water. They were W. W. Bailey, Bob Blackshear, Clay Sloan, Josh Holder and Dona Bloodworth. There were scores of others. Eighteen months after the discovery of the spring the population of the town was around 1,500. This was in 1880. In 1893 the management of the spring built a concrete reservoir around the spring.

"The analysis of the medical spring water is given below:

" 'On analysis of the water of Ravenden Springs, Ark., we find temperature 52 degrees, specific gravity 1.0012. Total solids per gallon, 20.92 grains composed of—

	Grammes	Grains		Grammes	Grains
Carbonate of Lithia	.082		Sulphate of Lime	Trace	
Carbonate of Lime	.299	4.61	Soluable Silica	.054	.83
Carbonate of Magnesia	.293	4.48	Iodine and Iron, each	Trace	
Chloride of Lime	.081	2.19	Organic Matter	.21	.86
Chloride of Magnesia	.136	2.35	Gas. Carbonic Acid	21.5 cubic in.	
Chloride of Sodium	.142		Atmospheric Air	13.3 cubic in.	
Sulphate of Aluminia	.153				

Respectfully, Wrights & Merrill, Chemists, St. Louis, Missouri.'

"In 1874 there were a number of prosperous farmers living in the country around Ravenden Springs. Some of these were: Sol and Mich Davis, Elrod Poteet, Kinson Land, J. E. Pickett, John Griffith, John, Henderson and Josh Wrenfro, Rufus Bowen, George Bloodworth, M. B. and Jimmy Janes, Frank and Abe Decker, George and Dudley Wells, Wm. Lomax, John Guntharp, Rhodes and W. W. Bailey, S. Woodyard, George Shelton and Josh Holder.

"The doctors have contributed much to the progress and permanency of Ravenden Springs. Dr. J. R. Jones came first, in 1881. Then Dr. B. E. Pickett, Dr. H. B. Hull, Dr. Nixon, Dr. Ellis and at present Dr. Alvarez.

"The public school has been a material factor in the progress of the town. The high school building was erected in 1907. Prof. Watkins was the first principal of this school.

"In 1914 County Judge Joe S. Decker went before the Arkansas Legislature and secured the formation of a road improvement district, for the purpose of building a gravel road from Ravenden Springs to Ravenden Junction. This was the first road improvement district in north Arkansas. The road was built in 1915 and today stands as a monument to the foresight and business sagicity of Judge Decker.

"The churches of the town at present are: Methodist, first built in 1885, present membership 89; Presbyterian, organized in 1882, present membership 40; Baptist, organized in 1911, membership now 90; the Church of Christ building was built in 1909, present membership 40. The present population of Ravenden Springs is 425, and 259 of these are members of some church. This makes this the most religious town in Randolph county. The town has no mayor, no aldermen, no marshal. The people are religious, peaceful, tranquil, industrious and moral." Such is the "raven den" story from the pen of Dr. A. G. Henderson.

REYNO

The present town of Reyno is an outgrowth of the original town of the name which was located two miles southwest of the present town. When the Frisco railroad was built through this section in 1901, the old town was abandoned and the business houses and most of the residents moved to the location on the railroad.

The site of the present town was called Esselwood at the time. The original town of Reyno was a settlement several years before the Civil War. Dennis W. Reynolds is credited with building the first residence and hotel on the actual site of the town, in 1857. Stephen C. McCrary built the first cotton gin and saw mill at the town. The first church was built about 1888 and was actually the old Antioch or Cherokee Bay church that was moved to the town. Among the first preachers were Henry Slavens and Sherrod Winningham of the old church and the following in later years: Hiram Kirkpatrick, W. P. King, F. C. Neely, Bob Carroll, Oscar Cunningham and Elder Watson.

The first merchants of the town were D. W. Reynolds, Martin Brothers, John P. Dunklin and possibly others. Some of the first families to settle in the vicinity of Old Reyno were Joseph Herron, Ben Bowden, John C. Wisner, the Watson, Winningham, Womack, Jones, Nelson and Owens families. The first physicians are said to have been Dr. Pringle, Dr. Hill and possibly others. During the days in which the old town of Reyno was prosperous, before the coming of the railroad, it was the only trading point in Cherokee Bay, in Randolph county, except Peru and later Johnstontown.

It has often been stated that if the railroad had been built by way of Old Reyno that a large town would have grown up instead of the two smaller towns of new Reyno and Biggers, only a few miles apart.

The present New Reyno is built upon what is known on early land records as the Francis Surget lands. During the early days this Frenchman bought up thousands of acres of Randolph county land in its wild state with an idea of improvement for speculation. This land was later sold to many different individuals by heirs of the original owner and the title was a matter of much litigation for years. D. Hopson was the owner of Esselwood when the town of Reyno was established and he sold the town site to the various citizens of old Reyno who were the first citizezns of the new town. The sites of the three churches of the town and the town park and school ground was donated for the respective purposes by Mr. Hopson.

W. M. Shrader, a native of Bavaria, was the first settler on the site of Reyno. Some of the first settlers after the new town was established were D. W. and A. M. Reynolds, J. L. Jones, Sam Conner, H. L. Sparkman, John W. Shaver, John Chorice, and several others. The first school board was H. L. Sparkman, John Chorice and W. C. Glasco. Sparkman was the first postmaster of the new town, and also the last one at Old Reyno. Some of the early merchants were J. M. Hawk, D. W. Reynolds, J. L. Jones, H. L. Sparkman, J. M. Smith, Logan Whittington and others, and later H. L. Richardson, E. G. Richardson, Tezzie Smith, L. P. Smith, John B. Shaver, Bland Brothers, John Lamb, John T. Robinson, and others, some of which are still in business there today.

The first school was taught in the old Masonic Hall over J. W. Shaver's store. The teacher was a Miss Owens.

After seven years as an unincorporated community, the town was incorporated by Elder John L. Fry, F. W. Cox, and twenty-four others, August 19, 1908. The first officials of the town were as follows: W. C. Glasco, mayor; J. T. Glasco, recorder; John Lamb, John Chorice, H. L. Sparkman, D. W. Reynolds and J. L. Jones as aldermen.

The physicians of the town during the first thirty years of its existence were Dr. Hill, Dr. Cox, Dr. Roberts, Dr. R. O. Smith, Dr. J. E. Smith, and possibly others.

Other long-time residents of the town, not named above, were C. T. McClure, T. H. Robinson, T. R. Robinson, Myrtle Ladd, Leota Seymour, J. R. Reynolds, L. P. Smith, W. R. Jackson, Ed Jackson, Peter Cockrum, C. T. Poteet, N. P. Simmons, Jesse Redwine, F. E. Belford, the Richardson family, the Lamb family, J. W. Franklin, P. H. Bundren, H. D. Parker, and many others, including the writer's family, which lived here twenty-two years. The writer operated a store in Reyno several years and five members of the family served in various capacities as town officials, our father being a member of the town council at the time of his death in 1945. One of our brothers, Acel E., was a teacher in the school there several years.

Reyno is at present a town of about 350 inhabitants. It has three churches, four stores, a four-room grade school and the usual number of other business places and professional people. It is situated in a good farming section and there are a number of attractive farm homes in the vicinity.

THE SUPPLY COMMUNITY

The communities of Supply and Pitman have much in common. Being close together, they have been populated by the same families of people. This causes much of the history of the communities to be the same. As you have already read the names of many of the first settlers in this section, you will see that the above is true.

The first store located at what is now Supply, was opened by William H. Fowler sometime about 1850. He was the great-grandfather of Tom A. Fowler and others now living in this community. The family came originally to this section from Pike county, Indiana. It is an interesting fact that during the almost a century since the first trading post was opened at Supply there has been a merchant of Fowler name or blood continually during that time, at this place. Among these have been William H. Fowler, son of the above and William H. Fowler, son of the latter, Dan Fowler, Tom A. Fowler, Charles Ennis, Jollys, Will Allen, Rex Fowler and others who were related to the above. Other merchants which have been in business here are, Haywood Hawkins, William Ainley, Dismangs, Redwines, Ruffs and others unknown to the author.

Supply was a stagecoach "terminal" on the old Military road during the Civil War period and even before this time. Stables and an inn was located here for the accommodation of the stage driver and his passengers. An extra team was kept here, ready at all times to replace the tired and worn out team which came in from the last division of the road.

The next station to the north was at Ironton, Missouri, and to the south, somewhere near Batesville.

Many a dusty, tired traveler on the old stage, and hot and wornout team drank the cooling water of the old "Fowler well," which is now in the center of the village. The first telegraph line in the state ran down this old road.

The first schoolhouse in this community is reputed to have been built by Zera Allen, one mile northwest of Supply about 1840. Mr. Allen, who was the grandfather of "all the Allens in Randolph county," as one of the family stated it, was a minister of the Church of Christ. He is said to have built this house for the purpose of providing a suitable meeting place for church purposes, as well as a school. This places this church in the list of the first half dozen churches established in the county.

The first Baptist church built in this community was located near the present home of Uncle Sam Stout, south of Supply. It was a United Baptist church and called "Little Vine." This church was later moved to a spot just west of the present Church of Christ building and became a Missionary Baptist church, which was later moved to the present New Home site.

The Free Will Baptist church at Pleasantview, or Dilbeck, was built a few years later.

Among the first families which settled around Supply, other than those named above, were the Crossens, Knowltons, Dilbecks, Ballards, Reeves, Taylors, Pringles, Winninghams, Pierce, Shemwells, Brown, Wallace, Vester, Ainley, Jones, Cockrum and many others whose descendants still live in this section.

The early marriage records show that James Cockrum married Levina Pierce, Dec. 19, 1822, and Nellie Cockrum married James Jordon, Dec. 28, 1824. From 1822 on, there is recorded many marriages between members of all the families named above.

Another old family of this community is the Ingram family. James P. Ingram, a Virginian by birth, came to this community in 1824. Here he married Rebecca Mansker, daughter of George Mansker, one of the first settlers of Demun township, April 12, 1825. Ingram was the fourth county judge of Randolph county and an influential man in his day. They were the parents of several children, a number of which died in childhood. Those which grew to adulthood and are remembered by older citizens are G. H., always known as "Dock;" Lurana, who married W. P. Green Johnston; J. W., known as "Uncle Blind Bill," and Leddie B., who married Henderson Hatley. The latter coupe were the parents of this author's mother-in-law.

This community has been noted since early days as the location of more cotton gins than any community in the county, although in the hill section and not actually in "the land of cotton." Among those who have operated gins in this immediate section were the Duff, Jolly, Johnston, Ingram, Ruff and Allen families. Green Johnston built the second cotton gin in eastern Randolph county. The author remembers, as a small boy, going with our father from western Siloam township, to the gin of Uncle Bill Ingram. This gin was located some distance southeast of Supply, and afforded the best cotton market in this section for many years.

This community has furnished six county judges since the county was formed. Twenty-nine years of the one hundred and ten years of the county's existence has seen a man from Little Black township in the judge's office. They were P. R. Pittman, James P. Ingram, Henry Cockrum, Henry Richardson, J. H. Perkins, and Rex Jolly.

This community is crossed by two of the oldest roads in this section of the state. As has been mentioned a number of times, the old Military road crosses this section from northeast to southwest and was an important reason for the early settlement of the Supply community. The other road is the old Warm Springs-Corning road which crosses the old Military road just south of Supply. This old road was an early route from the hill section of northern Randolph county to the lowlands of Clay county and the "bootheel" of southeast Missouri.

SILOAM CHURCH

About one and one-half miles southeast of Middlebrook is located one of the oldest Methodist churches in north Arkansas. It is the old Siloam church. Siloam township in which it is located, was named for the old church. The first church building was erected here in 1845. It was an unhewed log building, built without nails. The gables were of logs and the roof was made of long boards weighted down with poles. About fifteen years later a hewed log building twenty-four by eighteen was built and the only nails used in it were made locally in a blacksmith shop. This building served the congregation until about 1884. At this time the local F. and A. M. Lodge and the members of the Methodist church built a two-story building. The second story to be used as a lodge hall and the ground floor as the church. This building stood until June 5, 1915, when a cyclone blew it away. (This was the same storm which destroyed the Glaze creek church only a few miles northeast of Siloam).

At the time the latter church was built there developed some opposition to the building of the building because of the fact that the church did not own the land upon which the house had stood all these years. To remedy this situation Jasper Newton Rapert and his brothers and sisters, as heirs of Daniel M. Rapert, who had entered the land, made a deed for four acres for church and cemetery purposes. The deed was made to C. G. Johnston, D. M. Robinson, C. M. C. Spencer, W. P. G. Johnston and Joseph Burton.

After this building was destroyed in 1916, another building was erected on the same site, a single story structure.

In the early spring of 1945, another storm blew this house off the foundation and across the ground some thirty or forty feet, but the building was not seriously damaged it was raised, placed on a substantial foundation and repaired, and is again in good condtion at this time.

Those who were instrumental in the building of the first church here are among the first settlers in this section. Some of them were: Benjamin and Joseph Wilson, Gregory Johnston, Carroll Thompson, George Murphy, George Mansker, John Chandler, J. D. Cross and Judge J. P. Ingram.

Some of those instrumental in the building of the church and lodge hall were, C. G. Johnston, L. F. Johnston, Jesse Robinson, the Raperts, Spencers, Swindles, and others.

About 1878 a large brush arbor was built just west of the present house, near the spring, and during the summer months church services were held under it. About 1870 a cemetery was started here. The first person buried was John Hawkins. The cemetery was first fenced with rails, which were destroyed by fire in a few years and no other fence was built until 1886, when it was enclosed with a wire fence.

The story goes that one night during the Civil War a bunch of Federal soldiers surprised the congregation at Siloam church and took several prisoners. Some of these were Daniel Rapert, Daniel Spence, L. F. Johnston and others. William Swindle was wounded and several of the younger men ran away and were not captured. L. F. Johnston was preaching.

The Rapert, Wilson and Johnston families have had a continued membership in this old church since it was established. The Johnston family has furnished this and other churches a number of preachers. Rev. Jesse Robinson, Rev. L. F. Johnston, and Rev. S. L. Johnston, who is still living at this date, were among the older ministers in the family and at the present time, Rev. Sam Pulliam, Rev. J. W. Johnston, Rev. Liston Johnston, and Elder Calvin Cox are all members of the Johnston family of Randolph county.

Among the first preachers to preach at Siloam were Rev. Robinson, L. F. Johnston, Philemon Wright, Ankrum Hilburn, Calvin Paddy and earlier than these were possibly Jonathan Wayland, Philip Davis and Eli Lindsey. As these were last named old-time circuit riders were living in this section even before this church was established. The names of very few of the first ministers are available at this time, which, if they could be found, would add an interesting item to the history of this ancient church.

As stated in the beginning, the first church at Siloam was also used as a schoolhouse. This was true of most of the earliest church buildings.

Just who the early teachers were is not known. The only name handed down to us is that of Prof. Nimmo, who taught here before the Civil War. He is said to have been a good scribe, a fair reader, but a little shy on the subject of mathematics. No pupil was ever allowed to go beyond the "double rule of three," which we now call long division. Siloam church may be the first Methodist church established in the county.

UNION TOWNSHIP

The most distant point in Randolph county, from Pocahontas, is the northwest corner of Union township, yet in business and politics this township is closer associated with the affairs of the county seat than many closer communities.

The folks in this section have always taken a lot of interest in county politics and related subjects.

The first settlers who came to this section settled along the banks of upper Janes creek. The country is generally broken but there are a number of good farms along the creek. This section originally was covered with a heavy growth of good timber and all down through the years this has been a leading industry. Another leading industry has been sheep raising. This broken unland is especially well adapted to this animal. Some good cattle are also raised in this section.

Just who the first settler of this immediate community was is not known. The first land record of Lawrence county shows that Lot Davis was living here in 1818. On September 24, 1818, Richard Woods sold to Joseph Janes a claim on Janes creek "adjoining Lot Davis." Stephen F. Austin, later to become the "Father of Texas," signed the document as a witness. It is entirely possible that this man for whom the capital city of Texas was named, may have been a resident of this community before he ever saw the Lone Star state. J. H. McIlvain was also a witness, so we infer that he also lived here.

Some of the very first settlers of a little later date were the Rogers, Taylor, Bellah, James and English families. These were soon followed by Baileys, Marriotts, Honeycutt, Fry, Wells and other names well known in this section. The Allison, Poteet, Wyatt, McFann and DuBois families have been here a long time too.

At one time there were two postoffices in this section. They were Ring and Yadkin. At Yadkin, William Davis and sons operated a store many years before moving to Ravenden Springs. The old Ring office was near the present-day school of the same name and I. F. James was one of the merchants of thirty-five years and more ago. Just who the first merchants were is not known.

This section was first supplied with a trading point from Elm Store, Mammoth Spring and Myrtle, Missouri, in the days before the beginning of the present century. Of course the lower end of the township came to Ravenden Springs or Pocahontas. After the Frisco railroad was built up Spring river this made an outlet for this section. In later years, with the coming of the motor cars and trucks and better roads, the trade which had been going across the hills to Mammoth Spring on that railroad, desiring to do business in this home county, turned to Pocahontas. There is a pretty good road down the creek to Ravenden Springs and this route is followed by a lot of the people to that town and also in coming to Pocahontas. There is another route going east by Taylor's store, which intersects with the Pocahontas-Elm Store road at the Dr. Dalton farm. Most any day, at anytime of the year you will see as many citizens of Union township in Pocahontas as there are from many other sections closer in.

The churches of this section are a Baptist church at Yadkin and the Church of Christ meets at Ring. The latter congregation meets occasionally at English Bluff.

The schools in this township are Cedar Bluff, Cedar Grove, Ring, Campbell (Dial's Creek) and Bluff Springs.

The names listed above in this article were all residents of Janes creek valley and a few may not have lived actually in Union but were close.

ELM STORE

The village and community of Elm Store is one of the older settlements of the county. The Stubblefield, Job, Hudson, Nettles and other families settled here soon after the turn of the past century.

Shadrach Nettles and Obediah Hudson settled on the state line near this community in 1812. Other early settlers were the England, Hall, Chester, Bounds, Doran, Rice, Johnson, Going, Looney, Bryan, and Brown families. The King family also was here during the pioneer days.

One of the first roads opened in the county, after the county seat was moved to Pocahontas was the old Pocahontas-Elm Store road. The old Johnson watermill and the old Stubblefield ford on Elevenpoint river in this community, were two early landmarks.

The Kirkpatrick Brothers were merchants here a half century ago. Just who ran the first store is not known.

From Elm Store south, down Elevenpoint river to Birdell, a distance of some thirty miles, the valley was at one period (about 1850) owned almost entirely by the Looney, Stubblefield, Wells and McIlroy families.

The three schools in the Elm Store vicinity are Elm Store, Gladesville and Baker, across the river east of the village.

There are a number of buildings in this section of the county which have been standing around three-quarters of a century.

A greater portion of the first names to locate in this community are still represented.

COMMUNITIES

WARM SPRINGS

Just what year this village came into actual existence as a town or community center is not known. It is possible that there were people living here as early as 1815 or 1820. William Rice was granted a license to operate a tavern here in 1837. This tavern was a combination hotel, store and dram shop. Rice was one of the associate justices in attendance when the first Randolph county court was held at the home of James G. Russell, April 4, 1836. He was also county treasurer from 1846 to 1852. The story goes that Mr. Rice was a very religious man, and at his home was held the first church services in the town. He had a son who was a bit wayward at times, and "Uncle Billy" would call the boy into his room and after giving him a "good talking to," would punish him and then kneel down and pray. Wm. L. Rice married Rebecca Mansker, February 27, 1842. One of the next store keepers at Warm Springs was Moses Bailey. Soon after this, about 1860, David Allen, William Burrow and a little later, Elijah Dalton were in business here. Mr. Allen and Elijah Dalton, and others operated cotton gins and sawmills here. Later merchants were, Moses and Jerry Burrow, John C. and Rufus Dalton, Tom Thannisch, the Kings, Holts, Stevens and others of later years.

The 40-room Dalton Hotel was built in 1874 by a partnership composed of Lewis Dalton, Dr. Kibler and W. H. Waddle. Prior to this a small hotel, as stated above, had been built, which this one replaced. It was built near the springs and was widely known as a popular stopping place for those who came here to drink the waters of the famous warm springs. Bath houses were also erected, together with bowling alleys and other amusements to entertain the visitors and patients. Two and one-half acres were fenced and inside this enclosure were sixty springs. Three different kinds of water came from the springs, chalybeate, sulphur and carbonate. An advertisement of the springs in 1890 stated that they were "equal to the famous chalybeate Vichy waters of Europe." After the turn of the century the fame of the springs subsided and were allowed to fall into bad repair and are scarcely discernible today. During the time they were advertised and improved, and before the large hotel burned, many people came from the lowlands of eastern Arkansas to take advantage of the healing qualities of the springs. Dr. G. A. Seal was one of the leading physicians of the town at that time. Other early physicians were, Dr. Stone, Dr. Byrd, Dr. Slaughter and later Dr. Hughes, Finney, and Carrens.

Elijah Dalton, who owned a large farm on Dry creek a few miles northeast of Warm Springs, just over the line in Missouri, moved to Warm Springs some time in the early "seventies" and became the first postmaster of the town. He was a brother of the writer's grandfather. Grandfather was one of the early blacksmiths of the town, after he moved there from the old home on Fourche and Dry creek. Grandfather's name was David Dalton, but was always called Tim. Uncle Elijah was the father of a large family, as also was my grandfather. Mrs. W. A. Holt, who still lives at Warm Springs in the old home of her father, was one of Uncle Elijah's children. Mrs. Martha P. Phillips, who resides with a son southeast of Doniphan, Missouri, at the present time, is the eldest child of grandfather David Dalton. She is now eighty-two years of age.

Other early families at Warm Springs were the Wooldridge, Holt, Barrett, Flannigan, Creason, Carter Wrights, Russells, Nettles, Burrow, Yarbrough, Whittenberg, King, Bailey, and others. John Holt, the grandfather of John R. Holt, now living in Pocahontas, settled on the creek below town now known as the old Whittenberg place in 1821, coming here from Washington county, Missouri.

The first school near Warm Springs of which we have any record was old New Hope, located on Mud creek, below the village, near the old Mock farm. All the early schools were subscription schools. This kind of school was supported by a voluntary tuition plan, paid by the pupil directly to the teacher. The late Thomas D. Mock once told the writer that he taught the first public school in Warm Springs school district in 1874. C. C. Elder, who was county and circuit clerk of Randolph county under the Confederacy and until 1868, was one of the first teachers at Warm Springs. The widow of Major Surridge was a teacher here about 1880. Next came a Mrs. Johnson. Dr. Bird built the first school building in Warm Springs on the site where the residence of Mr. Heflin now stands. Soon after this a school building was built by private donation, which served until the present building was erected. The late W. L. (Uncle Dock) Holt and a Mr. Baker built the second house. Soon after 1880, Prof. F. E. Tilford and wife came to Warm Springs and were employed as teachers and their school became known as Tilford's Academy. This was one of the best and most famous schools of northeast Arkansas during the days before 1900. Tilford's Academy saw the zenith of it's career about 1883. The class of 1883 was made up of many persons living at this time. Among these, living and deceased were, Alice Johnson Pulliam, Maggie Nettle Baker, Lively Dalton Wells, Nora McIlroy Dalton, Sarah Dalton Spikes, Mary Dalton McIlroy, Malissie Dalton Holt, Josie McIlroy Johnson, Prof. Tilford's daughters, W. A. Holt, John Y. Tilford, Jerry Burrow, Jim Kenner and John P. Campbell. The writer's father was a student under Prof. Tilford but was younger than the class named above. This school, while possibly not in a class with our present day better class schools, sent out into the world many men and women who made their mark in important places and would be a credit to any school.

The first church in this vicinity was at old New Hope named above which was also the first school. Here church services were held by all who felt disposed to worship regardless of belief or creed. Later it was used principally as a Baptist church before the church was established at Warm Springs proper. The present church building was erected and a Freewill Baptist church organized in 1885. The late Rev. Demps N. King and Rev. G. A. Barrett were the organizers. Among the charter members were Mr. and Mrs. John Holt, Mr. and Mrs. Jasper Carner, Pleasant Carter and Mrs. W. A. Holt. The church is still active and some of the charter members still live nearby.

The first man buried in the cemetery was a soldier who died one night during the Civil War while a company was encamped on the creek just above town. The soldiers left sometime in the night, and buried the man in a very shallow grave in the sands of the creek. They were Federal soldiers. The next morning an old citizen of the town, Uncle Jim Barrett, and some small boys took the body and re-entered it in the present graveyard. There were no able-bodied men at home. All were away in service. The next person buried there was a colored man who, at that time, had been living southeast of town.

Some of the earliest ministers to preach here were, Alonzo Burrow, N. C. Dodson, and others later among whom were John Yarbrough and Demps King.

The town and township of Warm Springs had a reputation during the early days as a rough-and-ready place. A fact which was true of most of our early communities. Many personal encounters of a pugilistic nature were engaged in during these days. There were a few murders and a large number of local citizens who sometimes boasted of being the "best man" in the community. The community has long taken their politics seriously. Several of our county officials came from this section of the county, even from the beginning. But some of this has changed. The town is now a typical inland trading center and is populated by some of the best and highest type of people in the county. It is a nice, peaceful community. A nice place to live.

Family History

Part Four

FAMILY HISTORIES AND BIOGRAPHICAL SKETCHES

The following pages are devoted to the histories of certain families and individuals who have resided in Randolph county.

Those included are by choice of that individual or some member of the family. The author of this history did not say who could or could not be included here. A nominal charge was made for these articles. No one was denied the privilege of having their family represented.

We are happy to state that in the list included here are to be found the names of some of the finest families which have lived in the county or state. Our county has profited much by having folks like these live within her borders.

We are sorry that there are a number of families within our county whose history is not included, which by reason of past and present prominence in county affairs, should have been. It was their choice that this is the case. This was their perfect right and privilege to take no action in the matter. They are our very good friends and neighbors just the same, but we do feel that they missed a nice opportunity of having their family history recorded for generations of the future to read, including their own children and grandchildren.

We would be very sorry indeed, if there should be found one person who desired to have their family history included who did not know of this opportunity. But we hardly think this possible. We ran several advertisements in the local paper and sent out a lot of form letters, besides scores of personal letters, informing the public of our work. In addition to this, the Star Herald gave our proposition some favorable publicity, of which we are very grateful.

With all this in mind, we desire to once more state that the writing of this book, both the general history and the family articles part, was not written as a money-making proposition. We did it solely to preserve the fast disappearing story of the early days of our home county, while we had the time and opportunity.

THE DANIEL THOMAS ATHY FAMILY

Daniel Thomas Athy and Sarah Cordelia Redwine were married January 1, 1893. Mr. Athy was born September 7, 1870, near Supply. Mrs. Athy was born February 12, 1875, in the same community. Both are living at present.

Daniel T. Athy is a son of Harvey C. and Julia Annie Hall Athy. Harvey Athy was born October 7, 1846, in Illinois and died February 24, 1930, near Pitman, Arkansas. Julia Hall Athy was born in Illinois February 13, 1950, and died near Pitman, February 3, 1901.

The father of Harvey Athy was a native of Ireland. He made two trips from the old country to America. The first time he came, he did not like the country and went back across the Atlantic. Later deciding that he liked the new country better than he thought, he again migrated to America and lived the remainder of his life here.

Harvey and Julia Hall Athy were married April 7, 1867, and were the parents of the following children: Mary Elizabeth, born September 7, 1868, and died July 10, 1911; Daniel T. (our subject); Charles M., born September 18, 1872, died August 8, 1877; Rhoda Cordelia born September 26, 1874, died July 20, 1895; John Alma born February 28, 1877, died October 3, 1938; Edward born February 10, 1879, died February 16, 1902; and Laura Tabitha, born July 1, 1881, still living.

Sarah Cordelia Redwine Athy is a daughter of Lovelace Alexander Redwine and Nancy Jane Bearden Redwine, who were married about 1870.

The father of Lovelace Redwine was Travis Redwine and his mother was Sally Ann Harrison, a relative of the two presidents, William Henry and Benjamin Harrison. This couple came to this section from Massachusetts, via Kentucky, shortly before the Civil War.

The children of Lovelace and Nancy Jane Redwine were: Amanda Magdalene, born August 27, 1871, died July 2, 1908; William Edmond, born March 9, 1873, still living; Sarah Cordelia (Mrs. Athy); Henry Franklin, born March 6, 1877, still living; Thomas Harrison, born March 22, 1880, still living; Iva Jane, born July 27, 1882, still living; Oscar Lee, born June 23, 1884, still living; Amy Myrtle, born April 27, 1888, died July 21, 1889; James Clarence, born February 20, 1892, still living; Ernest Eugene, born March 12, 1894, still living; Anna Mae, born October 18, 1897, still living.

There were 11 children born and nine of these are living today.

Lovelace Redwine was born April 20, 1849, in Kentucky and died October 28, 1937, in Tulsa, Oklahoma. Mrs. Redwine was born December ,5 1854, in Tennessee and died September 6, 1940, in Atwood, Oklahoma.

To the union of Daniel T. Athy and Sarah Cordelia Redwine were born three children: Charles F., born January 10, 1895, still living; Ronald R., born July 7, 1900, still living, and Horace Eugene, born June 13, 1906, also living. All were born near Supply, Arkansas.

Charles F. married Rosa Stoner of Calico Rock. She died in 1935. They were the parents of one child, Charles F., Jr. After the death of his first wife, Charles married Hazel Kirk, daughter of Mr. and Mrs. John F. Kirk of Des Arc.

After completing school Charles located in Little Rock, where he has lived about 30 years. He has been employed in the Democrat Printing and Lithographing Company plant for several years, as a linotypist.

Ronald married Berniece Anderson and they are the parents of four children: Thomas, Calvin (who lost his life in service in World War II, in 1943), Kenneth and Barbra Jean. The family now resides in California. Ronald's wife, Berniece Anderson, is a daughter of R. E. and Martha Richardson Anderson, now living at Reyno.

Horace Eugene married Lora Evans, daughter of William R. and Anna Pond Evans of near Maynard. They are the parents of one son, Doyle.

Ronald has the distinction of being the first Randolph county citizen to operate a motor freight truck line out of Pocahontas. For several years he was owner and operator of the Athy Truck Line between Pocahontas and St. Louis and did a heavy volume of business.

Eugene is a rural mail carrier, out of Maynard. His route lies east of Maynard toward Current River and north via Supply and other points. He has been the carrier on this route since its establishment November 2, 1936.

The subject of our sketch (Mr. and Mrs. Dan Athy) lived many years on the old Maynard-Cherokee Bay road, in the edge of Current river bottoms. They reared their family there. A few years ago they sold the old home and bought one near Maynard, in the hills.

This family has long been one of the substantial families of Richardson township. The family church affiliation is with the Church of Christ.

DR. JOHN WALLACE BRYAN

Dr. John Wallace Bryan was born in Todd county, Kentucky, December 20, 1826, and died February 27, 1880, in Randolph county, Arkansas.

He studied medicine and finished his education in Kentucky. He came to Randolph county in 1853. Prior to coming here he married Isabella Bush, a member of a prominent Kentucky family. She passed away September 3, 1869. July 26, 1871 Dr. Bryan married Jennie Capps, daughter of Nimrod and Synthia Mattix Capps. She died February 20, 1878.

The old records of Lawrence county show where Nimrod Capps and Synthia Mattix were married by Isham Alcorn, justice of the peace, on June 13, 1830. Capps at one time operated the Bay Mill above Doniphan. The Mattix family were early settlers on lower Spring river.

Dr. Bryan was the father of six children. They were, Bush, born March 23, 1857. He married Harriett Fike in 1875; Ben, born March 11, 1860. He married Sarah McClellan in 1881; William, born March 11, 1862. He married Lou Stubblefield in 1890; Richard, born in 1864, and died in 1878; Mary (Mollie), born May 6, 1867. She married John T. Baker in 1884. Mrs. Baker recently passed away; Lelie, born April 14, 1876. She married Gifford Blanchard of Missoula, Montana, in 1903.

The old family homestead has been in the Bryan family for 93 years. Alvin Bryan of Denver, Colorado, and Willard Bryan who lives on the farm have owned it for years, and Willard recently bought his brother's interest and is now sole owner. J. O. Baker, another grandson of Dr. Bryan, lives on an adjoining farm.

The farm on which Dr. Bryan settled is located on the east side of Elevenpoint river, about half way between Dalton and Elm Store, on the old Thomasville road.

When Dr. Bryan came here in 1853, he brought men here from Kentucky with him to build the family home. It was a very modern home for that day, with Negro cabins in the rear. He owned four slaves, a woman and three men, who operated the farm and helped with the home work.

Tobacco barns were built, an ice house was also built for storing ice, a cotton gin for caring for the cotton crop and baling it for shipment, and hogsheads were made and used to ship the tobacco crop to market. A large orchard with many kinds of fruit was planted.

He had equipment for the making of furniture and made many nice pieces from native walnut. A solid walnut stand table is still in existence in the family. He was a progressive farmer of the day.

Dr. Bryan was also known far and wide for his medical practice. His territory which he visited was many miles wide. Rough roads and forest trails were his routes of travel from one remote home to another. During the Civil War his life was constantly in danger from attack from jayhawkers. When the war broke out, he was one of the physicians who were asked to remain in the community to care for the sick, mostly women and children. He made many calls for which he received no pay.

Besides his work as a progressive farmer and physician, Dr. Bryan also was postmaster of the old Spring Creek office from 1857 until 1866. This office was the forerunner of the present-day Dalton postoffice; William Dalton moving it from the original location to the present site of Dalton and changing the name to Dalton in 1871.

Dr. Bryan was a Methodist, being a member of the old New Prospect church which is now called Bakerden.

An interesting story concerning Dr. Bryan is handed down to us from Civil War days. As was stated above, there was grave danger for a doctor or one who possessed money and other property, at the hands of the roving bands of jayhawkers. The story goes:

One evening late, a group of men on horseback, rode up to Dr. Bryan's front gate, which was more than 100 feet from the front portico, and asked if they might obtain supper. The doctor, thinking that they were soldiers, invited them to dismount and come in and wait until the meal was prepared. The Negro woman, Mrs. Bryan and a widowed woman school teacher, who was boarding with the Bryan family, began to prepare the meal.

This school teacher had a 10-year-old daughter who stayed with her. During the time occupied in the preparation of the meal her mother happened to go into the living room. Here she saw the men (who turned out to be jayhawkers) holding Dr. Bryan with a gun pressed to each side of his body, while the rest searched the room for money, etc. After finding the money they forced him to accompany them to the front gate. As they went out the little girl, whose name was Tommie Harris, clung to his arm and would not allow him to go alone, over the protests of the doctor and other members of the family. They all, including the doctor, thought they meant to kill him, as they knew he would follow them. However, at the gate they released him and ever afterwards Dr. Bryan contended that the girl saved his life. Dr. Bryan did follow the men and recovered his horses, which were also taken. They found his money in the small closet under the stairway beside the fireplace.

Dr. Bryan was a loving husband and father, a friend to his neighbors, a valuable citizen of the community and one of the grand old pioneers of our county.

(Contributed by his daughter).

JOHN STONE CAMPBELL
Father of James W., William H., Tom W., and Joseph N. Campbell.

CAMPBELL SISTERS
Arlene, Reland and Roberta, daughters of Mr. and Mrs. Tom W. Campbell

FAMILY HISTORY

THE CAMPBELLS

In 1846 Judge William Claiborne Campbell moved from Coffee county, Tennessee, to Union county, Illinois. He then had four sons: Thomas Leander, James Sevier, William Claiborne and George Washington Campbell. At Anna, Illinois, March 1, 1847, his fifth son, John Stone Campbell, was born. In 1855 Judge Campbell moved to Mountain Grove, Missouri, taking with him his three youngest sons and his several daughters, but leaving in Illinois his two oldest sons, Thomas and James, then grown. In 1861 Judge Campbell and his three youngest sons, with most of their Missouri neighbors, joined the Confederate Army, while his two oldest sons, with most of their Illinois neighbors, joined the Union Army. Judge Campbell was killed during the war. In 1866 his youngest son, John Stone Campbell, brought his widowed mother and his sisters to Randolph county, Arkansas, and settled near where Birdell now is. His four brothers soon followed and settled in the same neighborhood. There the five brothers—the two who had worn the blue and the three who had worn the gray—married, reared big families and died, all of them living to become nonagenarians except the youngest, John, who was drowned at the Adams Ford in Elevenpoint river in 1915, at the age of 68.

John Stone Campbell, youngest of the five sons of Judge William Claiborne Campbell, settled on a farm on the west bank of Elevenpoint between Birdell and Black's Ferry; and there his four sons were born and reared, James W., William H., Tom W. and Joseph N. Campbell. James W. Campbell was superintendent of schools at Pocahontas, and at the same time county examiner of Randolph county, from 1904 to 1909. He died in Los Angeles, California, in 1943. William H. Campbell became a doctor and settled in Oklahoma, where he still lives. Joseph N. Campbell settled at Shreveport, Louisiana, where he was traffic manager for the

TOM W. CAMPBELL

Louisiana Railway — Navigation Company for many years, until his death in 1937.

Tom W. Campbell was born September 7, 1874, the day the present constitution of Arkansas was adopted. He attended Add-Ran College at Thorp Spring, Texas, now Texas Christian University, from 1892 to 1894. He then returned to Randolph county, Arkansas, and married Jenny Roberts in 1895. They have three daughters, Arlene, who married Walter L. Pope and now lives in Washington, D. C.; Reland, who married Henry C. Graham and now lives in Little Rock, and Roberta, who married Joseph Norbury and also lives in Little Rock. All three of these daughters were born in Randolph county. Tom W. Campbell was county examiner of Randolph county from 1896 to 1900, and during that time was also president of Abbot Institute at Maynard. He represented Randolph county in the State Legislature in 1901 and 1903 and was chief clerk of the

MRS. TOM W. CAMPBELL

Lower House of the Legislature in 1905. He was admitted to the bar in 1904 and became immediately law partner of Clarence H. Henderson. In 1914 he organized the law firm of Campbell, Pope & Spikes at Pocahontas. In 1917 Mr. Campbell was appointed first assistant attorney general of the state and moved to Little Rock, where he has lived ever since. In 1919 he became general counsel for Arkansas Corporation Commission. From 1919 to 1923 he was a member of the law firm of Pace, Campbell & Davis at Little Rock. From 1924 to 1926 he was chairman of the Democratic State Central Committee. In 1925 he served as special associate justice of the Arkansas Supreme Court. Since 1925 he has been engaged in the general practice of law in Little Rock. In 1941 Mr. Campbell wrote a dual biography of Matthew Lyon and Andrew Jackson, entitled "Two Fighters and Two Fines," published by Pioneer Publishing Company of Little Rock, the first edition appearing in September, 1941, and the second edition in December, 1941.

THE DALTON FAMILY

The Dalton family of Randolph county, Arkansas, and Ripley county, Missouri, is descended from one John Dalton who is reputed to have been born in Ireland, and came to the United States about 1760, he entered the Colonial Army and fought in the Revolution. After the close of the war he moved to North Carolina, and in a short time moved up into Virginia. After staying there a while he removed to Kentucky and then, about 1809 he moved to Madison county, Missouri. Later he moved down into Ripley county, Missouri. Here he spent the balance of his life.

The place where John Dalton settled about 1812, was at what is now known as the old "Dalton Mill" ford on the south fork of Fourche Dumas creek in Union township, Ripley county, Missouri, where the old Warm Springs-Doniphan road crosses this creek. John Dalton and other members of his family lie buried out in the middle of the bottom field, northwest of the ford.

John Dalton, whose wife's name Susannah Sebastia, was the father of eight children. Their names were: William, John P. (always called Jack), Elijah, David, Lewis, Sally, Maria and Dinah. Of these eight children we know very little except Elijah, Jack, David and Maria.

Elijah married Zillah Gaines, Feb. 9, 1832. They became the parents of seven children, William, James, Lewis, Elijah, Zimriah, Zilpha, and Levi.

The second wife of Elijah Dalton was Elizabeth Stubblefield, whom he married in 1859. They had one child, Joseph. The last wife of Elijah Dalton was Margaret Johnson, whom he married in 1869.

John P. (Jack), wife's name not known, was the father of 10 children. Their names were: Adam, Ferguson (called Forg.), Oliver, Isham, Elijah, John, Zillah, Sally, Lively and Nancy.

Maria married Jim Keel. They reared a family near Greenville, Mo., and one of her sons, Jack, married Martha Johnston, a daughter of Lewis B. Johnston.

David Dalton, son of the original John, was born in Kentucky, as were his brothers Jack and Elijah, and came to Ripley county, Missouri, with his parents about 1812. He married Priscilla Dennis of Greenville, Missouri, in 1826. He died in 1859 and his wife died in 1857. They were the parents of the following children: Elijah, David, Priscilla, who married John Bond, she and David were twins; Sarah, who married George Matney; Susanne, who married William Cross; Nancy, who married Harrison Davis, and Ruth, who married James Parker.

Of the children of the first Elijah named above, the best known in this section were William, Lewis, Levi and Joseph.

William, born May 30, 1834, died September 7, 1878, married Caroline Myatt. They were the parents of the following children: Zilpha, who married Thomas D. Mock; Zillah, who married Jeff Stubbefield; Rufus C.; Zimriah; Mary Elizabeth, who died in infancy; James L. (the inventor of the Dalton adding machine); Sarah P., who married Ben F. Spikes; Lively A., who married Thomas H. Wells; and Ascenith, who died young. William was the first postmaster at Dalton, Arkansas.

Lewis Dalton, who married Sarah A. Stubblefield in 1860, was the father of two children, Elijah who resided in Pocahontas many years, (and who is the father of Mrs. Lucien Sloan, and two sons Mack and Lewis), and one daughter, Ascenith, who married Dr. J. W. Dalton.

Levi Dalton was a resident of Doniphan, Ripley county, many years but later moved to Texas. He also resided at Ponder in the same county a number of years.

The youngest son of Elijah Dalton was Joseph, who first married a Miss Ponder and later married Nora McIlroy (who had formerly married James Dalton who died). He spent his entire life on the old homestead near Ponder, Ripley county, Missouri. This is a brief listing of the descendants of Elijah Dalton the son of the original John Dalton.

Of the children of David Dalton, who was a son of the original John, named above, there were (already named above) the daughters whose families moved to Texas many years ago, except James Parker's family. Two sons of Ruth Dalton Parker are now living, Harrison at Reyno and David at Success. John died during the Civil War. Elijah, who resided at Warm Springs many years was the father of the following children, (he married Grace Jane Head): John C., Nancy, who married William T. Stubblefield; James, who married Nora McIlroy; Mary, who married William T. McIlroy; Malissa, who married William A. Holt, and Rufus and Elijah A.

The other son of David (son of the original John) was named David. David married Christiana Everett and they became the parents of four children. They were William, Susuan, who married Byron Murphy; Martha P., who married Noah Phillips, and Elijah F. (this Elijah Dalton is the father of the writer of this article). David's second marriage was to Rachel Young. Their children, who grew to adulthood were Joseph, Ida, Maud, Myrtle, and Fred. Joseph married Dilla Grissom; Ida married Harry Irvine; Maud married Eld. John H. Harper; Myrtle married James Garrett and Fred married Mary Garrett.

John P. (Jack) Dalton, son of the original John, named above was the father of 10 children, as already stated. Of these 10 children we have the following information: One of the sons, Ferguson, called "Forg", was the father of Dr. J. W. Dalton, who married Ascenith, the daughter of Lewis Dalton. One of Jack Dalton's daughters married Dr. Greenwood. Her name was Zillah. Another daughter, Sally, married Robert Pacton. Jack Dalton had a son, John, who reared a large family. Three of his sons are now living at Patton, Mo. Their names are John, Levi and Albert.

The above is a brief description which touches the high spots of the large Dalton family which came to Ripley county, Missouri, in 1812. The family is very widely scattered at this date. Different "branches" of the family of the original John Dalton are now located in Randolph county, Arkansas, Ripley, and other counties of Missouri, in Oklahoma, Texas and many other states.

As stated above, John Dalton settled on Fourche creek in Union township, Ripley county, Missouri. His son Elijah settled farther north on the north fork of this same creek. This farm is still owned by the grandsons. David, another son, settled a few miles south of his father, near the state line on Dry creek, a tributary of Fourche. The other son, named above, John P. "Jack", lived awhile in this section but reared his family in the vicinity of Fredericktown and Greenville, Missouri, as did his sister, Maria Keel. Possibly several years were spent by both the latter at each location.

The reader will note that there have been many sons and daughters of the Dalton family with the same name. This makes it difficult to present a clear picture of the various branches of the family tree. As is noted there has been Elijahs, Davids, Williams, Zilphias and Johns in almost every individual family for seven generations, to say nothing of the duplications of James, Lewis, Joseph, etc.

This article is a rough summary of the family of the writer. Individual articles are also included in this book which give further details of certain families within this one great family. This is true of the writers' family and others. The articles in this book which include some member of the Dalton family in their family are: Elijah F. Dalton family; James L. Dalton, inventor; the William Tipton Stubblefield-Nancy Dalton Stubblefield family; the John Lamb family; the Spikes family; the Marlette family; the W. L. "Fayette" Mock family; the A. F. Rickman family, and the Holt family.

JAMES L. DALTON—INVENTOR

James L. Dalton was born near Ponder, Ripley county, Missouri, December 28, 1866, and died in Poplar Bluff, Missouri, January 10, 1926.

He married Clara B. Wright of Doniphan, Missouri, sister of the late Thomas and Joseph Wright, Sr.

To this union was born the following children: Charles, who married Ethel Morrison. They had two children, Clara Alice and Mary Jeane. Charles died in 1924. Grover W., who married Francis Burke. They have two children, James L. Dalton, Jr., and Richard; Phoebe, who is not married, and Mary, who married Lincoln Hinrichs.

Grover and his sisters live in Poplar Bluff. He is a well known business man and the state chairman of the Republican party in Missouri at present.

The parents of James L. Dalton were William M. Dalton and Mary Caroline Myatt, natives of Ripley county, Missouri. William Dalton was born May 30, 1934 and died September 7, 1878. His wife was born October 9, 1938 and died April 12, 1890.

William Dalton was a son of Elijah Dalton, who was a son of John Dalton who settled in southern Ripley county, Missouri, about 1812. A complete list of the Dalton family is included in this book.

FAMILY HISTORY

The brothers and sisters of James L. Dalton (our subject) were: Zilpha, who married Thomas D. Mock; Zillah who married Jeff Stubblefield; Rufus C., still living at Doniphan, Missouri; Zimriah, who drowned at age 14; Mary Elizabeth, who also died in infancy; Sarah P., who married Ben F. Spikes; Lively A., who married Thomas H. Wells. Mrs. Spikes and Mrs. Wells are living in Pocahontas at present; Ascenith, who died when 11 years of age, and two half-sisters, Dora Arnold, who married Ervin Reynolds, and Ida Belle Arnold, who married Andrew Conner. Mrs. Reynolds lives near Elm Store.

The life story of James L. Dalton would be appropriate subject matter for a Horatio Alger story. He rose from the position of a practically uneducated backwoods boy to become the owner of the largest department store in the Middle West and the head of one of the world's largest business machine manufacturing plants, devoted to the manufacture of the Dalton Adding and Calculating Machine, of which he was inventor.

When a small child, living with his mother and other children he was constantly engaged in experimenting with machinery. His father died when James L. was 12 years of age. An older member of the family once said that James was "all the time fooling with wheels." His mother bought a sewing machine about this time and the boy made an exact copy of it of wood, and it would sew!

The year he was 18 he decided to go forth into the world and seek his fortune. With $60 which he obtained from a bale of cotton which he grew in the hills of what is now Baker township, Randolph county, he set forth. He first went to St. Louis. Finding no job he went on to Chicago. Finding nothing to his liking he came back to St. Louis where he obtained a job in the old William Barr Dry Goods Company at a salary of $5 per week. This was in 1884. After working there a short time he came back to Doniphan, where he went to work in a hardware store of his future wife's relatives at $12 per month and board. He was soon made a partner and later became sole owner. He built this business up to where he saw greater possibilities in the larger town of Poplar Bluff, to which town he moved. It grew to be the largest department store in the whole Midwest and one year the retail sales reached $765,000.

All the time he was building this great store business he was still thinking about "wheels." Observing that the adding machines of that period were a complicated arrangement of keys and other cumbersome contraptions, James L. Dalton there decided that he would build a better one!

The first machine was perfected in the year 1901. It took a lot of nerve, perseverance and capital to put the deal over.

Mr. Dalton turned the store over to his son and others and devoted his entire time to the adding machine. He once stated that during this time he was "president, general manager, factory manager, timekeeper, paymaster, bookkeeper and chief salesman." The first factory was in a side room and Mr. Dalton said that during that period the three or four mechanics who built the first machines watched him leave on a sales trip with great interest, because, as he said, "if I didn't make a sale they didn't get paid." But after a few years, aided with the capital of friends, and a refusal to become discouraged and quit, success came his way. The machine began to sell on the market and 200 sales offices were ultimately opened up in different parts of the world, and sales ran up to $1,000,000 worth a month. The job had been done.

Besides being a merchant of great success and prominence and an internationally known inventor and manufacturer, he became a brilliant speaker and writer. Hearst's Magazine published a feature article on the life of James L. Dalton many years ago, in which the feature writer stated that,

"Although he was never in his life taught to 'parse' a sentence, he is now a brilliant speaker and writer, the recipient of requests from leading chambers of commerce and other civic clubs throughout the country to address their conventions and banquets."

Mr. Dalton was identified with many civic and fraternal bodies and always took great interest in the affairs of business and the state.

At the age of 22, while living in Doniphan he was elected Master of the Masonic Lodge. At 26 he was District Deputy Grand Master of the State of Missouri.

He was the first Republican ever elected to the State Legislature of Missouri from Ripley county.

James L. Dalton, although not a highly educated man, had a fair education. Some feature writers who "wrote up" his life after he became prominent, seemed to desire to leave the impression that he was unlearned. This was not true. He attended the country schools near his home. Some of these schools were at Bakerden, Warm Springs, Doniphan and at Dalton. He also attended the old La Crosse Institute at La Crosse in Izard county. He and his brothers and sisters would cross Elevenpoint river in a "dugout" canoe when they attended school at Dalton. His teacher at Bakerden was Prof. William Thomas. Later Mr. Dalton taught school for a time at Dalton, Bakerden and seven months at Elm Store, assisted by his sister, Neeta.

All this was before he went forth into the outside world to make a name for himself and to bring honor not only to himself but his homeland as well.

A photograph of the Dalton Adding Machine Factory was carried in a number of national weeklies during the days when Mr. Dalton was actively at its head in Poplar Bluff, and the caption under the picture stated "This is the industry which has carried the name of Poplar Bluff around the Globe."

Such is a condensed story of the life of a typical Ozark mountain lad who hailed from that part of our great nation known as Randolph county, Arkansas and Ripley county, Missouri, to become the best known citizen who has ever called this section home.

James L. Dalton was not only a great business man, he was also a great friend to many and a neighbor to all who lived near him. He was proud of his home, his family and his native country.

In 1913 he came back to the land of his childhood and staged a big family reunion, to be held at the home of his sister, Mrs. Thomas H. Wells, near the town of Dalton. Here assembled at the invitation of James L. Dalton, a total of 257 Daltons who represented his kinsmen in this section. The invitation cards which he sent out stated that "All Daltons, Daltons' relatives and prospective Daltons were invited to attend." Those two days, July 2 and 3, in the year 1913 were happy days in the memory of this family.

(The author of this history remembers with pleasure this occasion which we attended, together with our grandfather, grandmother, father, mother and other members of our family. I was then 12 years of age and took my first auto ride there in a "shiny 1912 model Ford" which belonged to Joseph Wright of Doniphan, the only automobile there those two days!)

THE ELIJAH F. DALTON FAMILY

(The Author's Own Story of His Father's Family)

Elijah F. Dalton was born December 14, 1871, on the bank of Fourche Dumas creek, in Union township, Ripley county, Missouri. The site of his birth later became to be known as "Liebig," on account of a postoffice being established there, years later by his cousin Joseph Dalton. The name Liebig was after a German family of that name which lived nearby.

Elijah F. Dalton departed this life, November 4, 1945, at his home in Reyno, Randolph county, Arkansas. Burial was in the Masonic cemetery in Pocahontas.

He was the author's father. The middle initial of his name stood for "either Francis of Franklin," to use his own words. His mother died a few days after my father's birth and the story goes that grandfather preferred Franklin and she preferred Francis, so upon her death the question was never settled.

My father was a great-grandson of the original John Dalton, who is listed in the special article concerning the Dalton family. A son of John's, David by name, was the father of another David who was my father's father. The last David was always called "Tim." Many older folks remembered "Uncle Tim" well.

This original John was the "Daddy of 'em all," when it came to the Dalton family of Missouri and Arkansas. One of his sons, Elijah, was the father of the late Lewis, William, Levi, and other children of that branch of the family. Another son, Jack (his actual name was John P.) was the father of the branch of the family which still lives in upper southeast Missouri. Dr. J. W. Dalton, who married Ascenith, Lewis Dalton's daughter, was of this family.

MR. AND MRS. ELIJAH F. DALTON
The Author's Parents

Another son of the first John was David, the man referred to above, as the father of the second David, my father's father.

For a more complete list of the various members of the Dalton family, we refere you to the special article.

Anyway, my great-grandfather, David Dalton, married Priscilla Dennis of Greenville, Missouri, in 1826, and opened up a farm about five miles south of his father. This farm was on Dry creek, a tributary to Fourche, and is located one mile east of the old Burr, Missouri, postoffice, and about four miles northwest of Middlebrook, Arkansas.

Here they reared a family. Their names were as follows: Elijah, who married Nancy Jane Head; Sarah, who married George Matney; Susanna, who married William Cross; John, who died in the Civil War; Nancy, who married Harrison Davis; Ruth, who married James Parker; Priscilla, who married John Bond, and David, my grandfather, who was called "Tim." He died in 1859, his wife in 1857. David and Priscilla Dennis Dalton lie buried in the old cemetery, which is located one mile east of the Johnton Chapel Church, in southern Ripley county, Missouri. This old cemetery is on the old Isaac Towell, or Bollenbacher farm. This farm was owned by my father during the years 1921-23.

David Daniel Dalton (Tim) was born on the old home place on Dry creek, March 22, 1844. He died September 16, 1921, and was buried in the Dalton cemetery on the farm where he was born, alongside his brother, Elijah, and other members of the family.

He was first married to Christiana Everett about 1862, during the war. To this union was born William, who was killed in a runaway accident on the farm of Eli Creason near Warm Springs, during young manhood; Martha (Aunt Molly), who married Noah Phillips. She is still living with a son east of Doniphan, aged 83; Susan, who married Byron Murphy. She died in 1923; and Elijah, my father.

Christiana Everett Dalton, my father's mother, died a few days after my father's birth. She was a member of the Shelton, Witt and Johnson families, who came to this section from eastern Tennessee. Her maternal grandfather, Jeremiah Shelton, was a Primitive Baptist preacher of this state during the early days. We might add here that the "original John Dalton" referred to first in this article was also a preacher of this church before coming to this section about 1812. The wife of "Parson Witt," mentioned in this history was also a granddaughter of Jeremiah Shelton.

After the death of grandfather's first wife, he married Rachel Young. To this union was born the following children who are living today: Ida, who married Harry Irving, now of Blountstown, Florida; Joseph, who married Dilla Grissom, now living west of Middlebrook; Maud, who married Eld. John H. Harper, now living at Datto, Clay county; Myrtle, who married James Garrett, now living at Augusta, Arkansas; and Fred, who married Mary Garrett, now living at Corning.

Grandfather, always called "Uncle Tim" in later years, was a very versatile character. He was known principally as a blacksmith, but it was said of him that he could do anything "from pulling teeth to building a chimney" with horseshoeing thrown in. He was a jolly fellow who had many friends. He was a great practical joker. He was a soldier in the Army of the Confederacy, being wounded at the Battle of Prairie Grove. He was shot in the knee and carried the bullet, imbedded there the rest of his life. He spent most of his life in the communities adjoining the place of his birth, but made two trips to Texas with the view of making his home, but did not stay.

On his first trip, when my father was a small lad, the family wagon train camped on the present site of Fort Worth, Texas, then a small backwoods "cow town." A resident of the town owned 40 acres, which is now in the main part of the city. He offered to trade the 40 to grandfather for his team, which was a pair of small horses, worth at that time possibly $150. This was 65 years ago. The property now is worth several million dollars.

The first home of grandfather after he was married was in the vicinity of his birth, but later he lived at Warm Springs, at the Dock Ingram Mill and at Middlebrook. After he reared his family he lived at Biggers a while, just before the two youngest children married. Following this he moved to the vicinity of Brakebill, west of Middlebrook, back near where he was born, and spent the remainder of his days.

Elijah F. Dalton, my father, married Della Florence Marlette, daughter of David J. and Sarah Spore Marlette, November 10, 1897. They were married at Poynor, Missouri, by the late Uncle John Cole, who was a justice of the peace at that time. Their first home was on the farm just east of the old Eldridge Ford on Fourche, near the state line, known for years as the "Nora Dalton farm."

This farm was the home of C. James Dalton (son of my father's Uncle Elijah Dalton), and his wife Nora McIlroy Dalton, until his death, a few years after their marriage. His death was caused by his accidentally cutting his arm.

After his death his widow married Joseph Dalton, son of another Elijah Dalton, an uncle of the other Elijah named here, and my grandfather. She is still living on the old homestead, east of Ponder.

Before Mrs. Dalton married Joseph, my father and mother lived with her, on the place named above. Here my sister, Effie May, was born April 11, 1899. Effie now lives in St. Louis. She married Daniel M. Griggs, a native of Illinois. They have two sons, both married, Paul D., who married Loretta Shellharvey of Troy, Missouri, and Jay Lee, who married Ida May Simhauser in St. Louis. Jay Lee is in the Army, sationed in Colorado at the present time. He is an X-ray photographic technician. Paul D. was recently discharged from three years' service in the Navy in the Pacific area.

The writer, David Lawrence Dalton, is the second child of my father and mother. I was born January 27, 1901, on the farm where Claud Phipps and family now reside. I first saw the light of day out across the bottom field toward Fourche Dumas river, just above the old mill dam at the Phipps Mill, just up the river a short distance above the steel bridge on the Middlebrook-Warm Springs road. (It was then the old Warm Springs-Bridgeport road). I was named "David" in honor of both of my grandfathers, but I have always been called Lawrence. The name Lawrence seems to be a favorite with my people. I have three cousins of the same name, two Lawrence Stubblefields and another Lawrence Dalton. The latter lives at Carthage, Missouri.

My brother next to me, Clarence H., was born at what it now the Ben Choate farm, just across the river and a little below where our sister was born. My father bought this farm about five years after he and our mother were married. After living there a few years he sold it to the late W. L. Johnson and moved farther northwest, where he bought my grandfather's old home place which adjoined Uncle Elijah's old farm where both he and grandfather were born and are now at rest.

While our family lived on the farm which father sold to Uncle Will Johnson, I started to school, at the old High Point schoolhouse, which was nearby. This was in July, 1906. Mrs. Joe Perry Spikes, now my neighbor in Pocahontas, was my first teacher. We called her "Miss Dora." She was then Miss Dora King. After attending school a few days I became very ill. I had a long spell of some kind of fever, which came near taking me away. My doctors were the late Dr. Moses Wilson, the late Dr. William T. Swindle and Dr. J. R. Loftis, who is also my neighbor here in Pocahontas at this time. I owe my life to their untiring efforts in treating me, to make me well, together, of course, with the loving care and long hours of watchful waiting on me, by my father and mother.

After moving to our new home, four more sons were born. The first one was Acel E., who is now living in St. Louis, where he is in the employ of the Federal Government as assistant lay inspector, a Civil Service job. He was formerly a Randolph county teacher, for a period of 16 years. Acel married Tharon Bundren, formerly of Biggers. They have two children, Jean and Wayne.

Clarence, the second son named above, has been in the mercantile business for several years, since he quit farming about 1933. He married Hester Williams, a native of Illinois. They have one child, Donald.

The fourth son of my parents is William Roscoe, who married Adele Gowen, of Datto, Clay county. They live in Memphis where he is also a Federal lay inspector, under Civil Service. He has been in this work 12 years. They have one child, Dickie.

The fifth son is Kermit E., who resides in Pocahontas, where he is a salesman in the local Firestone Store. He married Mary Poteet. They have two children, Charlotte and Frankie. The Poteet family were early residents of Ravenden Springs.

The baby son, Elijah Glenn, married Aldena Jackson of Reyno. They reside in Pocahontas, where they are employed in the Brown Shoe Company's plant. He and our mother recently completed them a nice home. Mother lives with Glenn and his wife.

An interesting fact concerning our family is that of the seven children born to my father and mother, all lived to be grown and married, and are alive today, and all seven were born in Siloam township and the late Dr. William T. Swindle was the attending physician when each was born.

Father was school director at old High Point many years. He was also director at Brakebill school. He was one of the leading men of the township many years.

In 1918 we moved over in the edge of Ripley county, Missouri, to the old Burr postoffice, where we lived three years and father was a merchant and postmaster. He was the last postmaster of the office when the Warm Springs rural route No. 1 replaced the office.

In 1921 father bought a large farm on upper Fourche, referred to before, known as the old Isaac Towell or Bollenbacher farm. Our story was the same as that of countless thousands of that period. We bought high and when the depression came, we sold cheap. 1924 found our family located in Reyno. Here my father and I bought property and for over 20 years this was my father and mother's home, except for one year.

Father passed away last November 4, in his seventy-fourth year. He followed farming and livestock raising, with some merchandising along with it part of the time. He was always interested in the things which make a better community. He was firm in his opinions and decisions but was generally on the right side. He was always interested in the places he lived. He was a member of the Reyno Town Council at the time of his death.

Father and mother reared a large family. The going was not always easy. But father always managed to carry on, to use his own expression, in a way "so that he could look any man in the face." He often said he wanted to live "above board." His word was his bond. He often told we children to never promise anything we couldn't do. During the dark days of the depression when it looked as if too many of our population, when tough sailing came their way, weakened to the point where they lost their self-respect, father would say that he "had rather live on bread and water than betray those who trusted him," and he never did.

He abhored sham and make-believe. He always said he believed in "everyday religion." He had lots of friends.

As his son, I make these statements for the future generations to read, with humble pride and in a spirit of dedication to him who did his job well, as he passed through this uneven journey of life. May he rest in peace. A photograph of father and mother is in this book.

And now just a word about the author himself. Above we have told you briefly about the rest of the family. Now I will begin where I left off farther back in this story, where I had started to school and became very sick. Later on after my recovery, I attended the old High Point school, (there is a short article about this old school elsewhere in this book) several years and later went over to Reyno, after winning a scholarship in spelling at the county fair. I was over there with a case of measles during the big snow in December, 1917. I was boarding with Ben and Effie Wilson, who lived in the residence which is now the home of T. R. Roberson.

Later I attended business college at the old Springfield Business College in Springfield, Missouri. Coming back, I began working in the store of Ben H. Edwards, at Ponder, Missouri. I had previously had some experience in father's store and in the store and postoffice of my uncle Noah Phillips, at old Burr.

Please let me add here that our parents were strong on education. Father used to tell us, "Children I want you to get an education, for that is something that no one can take away from you." We all secured fair educations, four of the family completing high school and two attended business college.

I have always had an inclination toward the mercantile business. I have spent 23 years of my life in that work. I have made a living and maybe a few dollars extra at the job.

I have also made a lot of friends and possibly a few enemies at the game, but I do want to make the statement which is so often disputed, that a man can operate a store and make money and yet deal honestly with his fellow men. I know that some do not. But it CAN be done.

After a long service in the store at Ponder, Biggers, Reyno and Pocahontas, 1943 found me in bad health. I sold my store which was in the building where the Bank of Pocahontas is now located, and moved out to the edge of town where I "took it easy a year and ran for office."

January, 1945, found me back in Pocahontas, located in a modest little home, surrounded with flowers and a big vegetable garden, at the north end of Witt Street. January 1, 1945, I entered the Randolph county treasurer's office, which I still occupy. I have no opponent for my second term, and it looks like I may be here another two years, if the Lord wills.

My family consists of my wife and 17-year-old son, Herman.

My wife likes the store business and so does my son. They plan a big modern store again "some of these days."

My wife was Irene Lamb, daughter of Mrs. Josie Lamb of Biggers, whom I married at Reyno in 1927. Her paternal grandparents were Henderson and Leddie B. Ingram Hatley. Her father was the late John H. Lamb. Both family histories appear elsewhere in this book. This is the rambling story of the author of this book and his family, through six generations, "This August 14, 1946."

FAMILY HISTORY

Since the first printing of this book in 1946, the author's only child, Herman has married. At the printing of the second edition in March 1981, the additional family genealogy was as follows:

Herman Dalton married Eula Mae King on October 1, 1950. Eula Mae's parents are Daniel L. King and Ethel Ann (Hall) King of Elm Store, Arkansas. Herman and Eula Mae have three children, Sandra Lou born May 6, 1952; Daniel David, born April 24, 1953 and John Elijah, born April 2, 1957.

Sandra Lou married Charles Erwin Brewer on June 25, 1971. Charles' parents are Hubert Brewer and Virginia Payne Brewer of Bilmore, Missouri. Sandra and Chuck have one son, Chad Erwin, who was born on January 12, 1978. They are expecting their second child in April, 1981.

Daniel David married Elaine Ruth Jorgensen on December 21, 1974. Elaine's parents are James Harold Jorgensen and Elizabeth Doris (Kovach) Jorgensen of Racine, Wisconsin. Elaine and David have one daughter, Sarah Ruth, who was born on August 28, 1979. They are expecting their second child in June, 1981.

John Elijah married Geraldene Laura Tyler on August 12, 1977. Geraldene's parents are Gerald Cloise Tyler and Loisell (Houseman) Tyler of Noland, Arkansas. John and Geraldene have one son, Jeffery Ellis, who was born on March 2, 1980.

County's Foremost Historian Passes

David Lawrence Dalton, 73, lifelong resident of Randolph County and the county's foremost historian, died in Randolph County Hospital Monday after a long illness.

An author, and a Star Herald columnist for over half a century, Mr. Dalton was a retired merchant, having spent more than 45 years in the retail general store business in this county, operating businesses in Reyno, Biggers and Pocahontas. He owned and operated three general stores in Pocahontas from January, 1941 to September, 1969, when he retired.

Mr. Dalton was author of A History of Randolph County, written in 1946, which is the most accurate and complete history of this county ever compiled, and which has proven to be a much-sought-after publication by Randolph County natives all over the nation. During his lifetime he submitted many historical articles to the Arkansas Gazette and the Arkansas Democrat, and to historical quarterlies.

Born January 27, 1901, he was a son of the late Elijah and Della Marlett Dalton, both members of pioneer Randolph County families.

HAD LONG CAREER WITH STAR HERALD

A writer for the Star Herald for some 50 years, Mr.

Dalton submitted his first article for this newspaper when a lad of 13 years, when he wrote a report of a family get together. Later, his interest in local history grew and his writings for the Star Herald became popular with newspaper readers throughout the nation. In recent years he wrote a column under the heading, "Lawrence Dalton's Column," and his last column in this series was published January 31 of this year.

During his long association with the Star Herald, Mr. Dalton never received recompense for any of his articles, other than the enjoyment he gained writing.

Mr. Dalton was elected president of the Randolph County Historical Society, formed in 1964, and served in that office until his death. He had served on the Pocahontas School Board, the Pocahontas City Council and the Randolph County Library Board. He was elected to the office of Treasurer of Randolph County, serving from 1945 through 1948. Governor Winthrop Rockefeller appointed Mr. Dalton to the Arkansas Historical Commission in 1970, and he served as a member of that group until his death. He was also a member of the Randolph County Committee of the Farmers Home Administration.

He is survived by his wife, Mrs. Irene Lamb Dalton; a son, Herman Dalton of Pocahontas; 2 brothers, Acel Dalton of St. Louis and Glenn Dalton of Pocahontas; a sister, Mrs. Effie Palmer of Doniphan; 3 grandchildren.

Funeral services were held at West Ridge Church of Christ Tuesday at 1 p.m., with Larry Brinkley officiating. Interment was in Masonic Cemetery under direction of McNabb Funeral Home. Pallbearers were his nephews, Don Dalton, Arnold Sullivan, Gail Holder, Paul Griggs, Bob and J. H. Lamb.

FAMILY HISTORY

JOE SHELBY DECKER

The subject of this sketch is a grandson of John Jefferson Decker, who was born in Illinois but who moved to Fulton county, Arkansas, about 1850. He settled on South Fork, about three miles northeast of Salem. He had five sons born in Illinois. Prior to coming to Arkansas he had spent a short time in Kentucky, where two more sons were born.

The maternal grandfather was Kinson Land, who was born and reared in Georgia. The family left Georgia and located in Alabama a few years before the Civil War. Two sons of Kinson Land joined the Confederate Army in Alabama and were both killed in battle. Mary Land, a daughter of Kinson Land, married Abe Decker to become the mother of our subject.

After the close of the war Mr. Land and his brother-in-law, John Bailey moved to Randolph county. Bailey settled on a farm on Janes creek near where Ravenden Springs now stands. Land settled on a farm three miles southeast of Bailey. William W. Bailey, a married son of John Bailey, settled on the site of Ravenden Springs. It was he who dreamed of the healing waters of the springs, the story of which is related in the article about Ravenden Springs. John Bailey's wife was a sister of Kinson Land.

John Jefferson Decker died soon after the family landed in Fulton county, Arkansas. His wife and the seven sons remained on the farm in that county until the boys were all grown. Two of them married in that county. Later the family scattered, some going to different parts of the country. One son, George, joined the Confederate Army in Tennessee and was killed at the Battle of Shiloh. Abe, the father of our subject, and his brothers John, Frank and Jim, joined the Confederate Army at Salem.

Joe S. Decker relates that he has met several ex-Confederate soldiers who served with his father in the army,

JOE S. DECKER
Only Randolph County citizen who has held four commissions as county judge. It was largely through the efforts of Judge Decker that the modern fireproof courthouse was built in 1940.

most of them were from Fulton county. However, he relates that he once heard Uncle Dock Holt, father of John R. Holt of Pocahontas and W. A. of Warm Springs, say that he was with his father in Price's raid through Missouri. His father served under Gen. Joe Shelby and admired him so much that when the war was over and he married, he named one of his sons for Gen. Shelby. This son happens to be our subject.

After the war Abe Decker and three of his brothers came to Randolph county. Bob and John, remaining in Fulton county where John bought the old home place and lived on it many years, selling it to his son, John, who owned it until 1930. One of the first county roads in Fulton county crossed the South Fork river at the Decker ford, which was on this farm. In 1937 the county built a nice steel bridge across the river at this point and it is called the Decker bridge.

After coming to Randolph county the Decker brothers established homes for themselves. Frank married Mary Wells, daughter of Hutcherson Wells, and a sister of the late J. B. (Broadfoot) Wells. Jim married Emely Wells, a sister of the late Turner Wells. Ebb, the youngest son, married Martha Hays, a daughter of the late Dave Hays. She was a niece of the late Tom Blansett.

Abe Decker married Mary Land. This couple became the parents of our subject, and also J. W., Frank C., Evaline (Buchannan), Walter, Homer and Corbett.

Joe S. Decker has the following to say about his father's old home:

"When I was a very small boy my father bought the old Land homestead from grandfather Land. Seven of us children grew to maturity on this old homestead. Long known as the Land farm, it later became to be known as the Decker farm and remained in the Decker family until a few years ago. Father and mother both passed away while living on this old place.

"The records of Randolph county show that the first county road that was granted in the county ran by this old farm. It was known as the Pocahontas and Salem road. My grandfather was living on this farm at the time B. F. (Frank) Bigger carried the mail horseback between the two towns.

The town of Walnut Hill or Kingsville on the creek below Ravenden Springs was the first postoffice on the route going west from Pocahontas. This was long before the Frisco railroad was built up Spring river valley to connect Memphis and Kansas City. This was the same Frank Bigger who became one of the wealthiest men and largest taxpayers of Randolph county at the time of his death.

"Louis Land, the grandfather of my mother and W. W. Bailey was a Revolutionary soldier. He died at the age of 106 years. Grandfather Land died at the age of 90. The Lands and Deckers have fought in five wars."

Joe S. Decker married Oma Pickett, March 11, 1903. Her parents were James E. Pickett and Emily Galbraith Pickett. They have two daughters, Verma, who married Jakie Schoonover, and Wanda Lee, who married Harris Cathey. Joe Decker is at present engaged in the real estate business.

Elsewhere in this book is a photo and short article concerning Mr. Decker's activities concerning the county judge's office and the building of the new courthouse.

MY PIONEER GRANDPARENTS
(Davis and Spikes)

(Written by Mrs. Maud Davis Brown, wife of Dr. J. W. Brown).

"My father, John R. Davis, was born near Atlanta, Georgia, in 1851. He was the son of Elisha and Lucy Burell Davis. His parents came to Randolph county from Georgia in 1870, but they were reared in South Carolina. My grandmother Davis was a granddaughter of Dr. John Burell of Paris, France. Dr. Burell (Burl in French) was a M. D. and skillful surgeon. He came to America with LaFayette in 1777 to help America fight for independence. He married an American girl and never returned to his native land. His wife was of English descent but spoke French as fluently as she did her own language. Dr. Burell never learned to speak our language. Their children were taught to speak both languages.

"My mother, Elizabeth Spikes Davis, was born in Randolph county in 1852. She was a daughter of Jesse and Nancy Copeland Spikes. My mother's grandparents, William and Elizabeth Biddle Spikes, came to Randolph county in 1820.

"My ancestors were all Southerners. My mother was reared near the Mason and Dixon line and my father saw Sherman's march to the sea. They, with their parents, experienced all the suffering and hardships following the Civil War, in which my mother lost three brothers.

"When we think of the courage and the bravery our foreparents had to leave the home of their childhood, their relatives and friends, and make the long, hard, dangerous trip westward, to find homes for themselves and their large families, it makes us wonder if we could have been that brave.

"My people on both sides as far back as I know have been Methodists. My Great-grandfather Spikes helped to build the first Methodist church in Randolph county in 1830. My grandparents did a lot in the early days to establish and carry on the work of the church. With all their work, hardships and sacrifices, they found time for family prayer and worship. To me they have left a wonderful heritage."

The Davis and Spikes families have been long-time residents of Randolph county, and Mrs. Brown contributes this article to their memory.

THE HITE FAMILY

Harry Hite is a grandson of B. J. R. Hite, who came to Randolph county from Lee county, Arkansas, in 1859.

This being a new county and so near the Mason-Dixon Line the family returned to the old home when the War Between the States broke out in 1861. Being Southerners, they feared for their safety. After the close of the war the family came back to Randolph county in 1867.

The father of Harry Hite was Henry C. Hite, who married Laura McGuire. They became the parents of two children, Harry and Johnnie. The latter died at an early age.

Stephen C. McCrary, who married Harriet Susan Hite, came to this community at the same time the Hite family came back. The McCrary and Hite families were early residents of Lee county. Hugh McCrary, the father of Stephen, was a soldier of the War of 1812. His wife was Elizabeth Wilson. Hugh McCrary made the second cotton scraper ever used in Phillips county. Lee county was a part of Phillips county at this time.

After locating in Cherokee Bay the Hite and McCrary families, together with other settlers in that section, cleared the land and built homes. A log church was built at this time, which is still standing. It is located on the two-acre plot which is now the Hite cemetery. B. J. R. Hite gave the land for use as a cemetery and site for a church. He was a Methodist minister but other denominations were allowed free use of the building. This building was also used as a school for many years. It was here that Harry Hite received most of his education.

Some of the first neighbors of these families were the Luttrells, Reynolds, Shavers, Herrens, Bowdens, Duckworths, Fords, Watson, Winninghams, Slavens and Drew families.

Harry Hite married Miss Tommie Wells, November 7, 1894. Mrs. Hite is a great-granddaughter of Thomas H. and Barbra Mabrey Wells, who came to Randolph county from South Carolina and Virginia by way of Washington county, Missouri, in 1821. His son, the grandfather of Mrs. Hite, came with his parents to the county, as stated above, in 1821, the year he was born. His name was John Wells and he married Harriet Alcorn, July 13, 1848. A son of this union, William Wells, was the father of Mrs. Hite. He married Martha Ann Reynolds, a daughter of James M. Reynolds. She was a sister of Capt. Dennis W. Reynolds for whom the town of Reyno was named.

Both Mr. and Mrs. Hite have spent their entire lives in Randolph county, within a few miles of their present home.

In November, 1944, they celebrated their Golden wedding anniversary.

They are the parents of four children, as follows: Gordon Hite, Mrs. Tola Cox, Mrs. Etalka Tyler and Mrs. Mabel Wickersham. They have seven grandchildren. They are: Clement and Don Cox; Tommie Lee, Betty and Harold Tyler; Ben Hite and Charles Wickersham.

THE DR. MARTIN HOGAN FAMILY

Dr. Martin Hogan was born November 16, 1833, in Logan county, Kentucky. He was the son of William and Mary Wallace Hogan, who came to Kentucky from Virginia in 1808.

Dr. Martin Hogan married Mary S. White, in Lyon county, Kentucky, November 13, 1860. Mrs. Hogan was a daughter of George and Catherine Martin White, and was born July 17, 1840. She was a sister of Sol M. White of Pocahontas.

This couple were the parents of the following children: William, who was sheriff and collector of Randolph county four years and later a prominent merchant of Middlebrook, and later of Cotter and Norfork, Baxter county. "Bill," as he was always called, married Miss Mattie Lou Curd, daughter of Mrs. Rufe Roberts, March 15, 1891. He was also a timber dealer and was successful in this undertaking. Kate, who married John D. Webster, was a well known teacher of the county for a number of years. Lou, who first married D. F. Stewart in November, 1916. After his death she married Alec Shipman, March 20, 1927. She died the following September 17, 1927. Birdie, who taught school several years, dying at the age of 26, March 31, 1900. Lizzie, who became a nurse. Her last work was in Kansas City. Lina W., who was a carpenter by trade, married Elfleda Jones, March 8, 1924, at Reyno. He died at Pocahontas, January 24, 1945. Madison B., also a carpenter, married Fannie Bradley, January 2, 1924, at Maynard. She is a well known nurse. John, generally known as "Jack," the sponsor of this article, was born October 20, 1872. He married Miss Lawrence Cate, May 27, 1900. John Hogan is one of the best known public school teachers the county has produced. He is now retired. He is the first teacher from Randolph county who retired on the Teacher's Retirement Compensation, in 1938. He taught in Clay, Lawrence and Randolph counties. He began teaching in 1896 and taught until an accident disabled him in 1934. Mr. and Mrs. Hogan reared a large family and are good citizens of the town of Maynard, where they have resided most of their lives.

The father, Dr. Martin Hogan, was one of the pioneer physicians of the county. He also was a minister of the Church of Christ.

After attending medical school in Cincinnati, Ohio, he came south in January, 1871, and settled in Arkansas. He had a desire to learn the diseases affecting both the North and South. He became a successful practitioner. He later gave up preaching because the duties of both professions kept him away from home so much. At that time families lived so far distant apart that in performing his duties as a family physician, he was often gone from home a week at a time, going from house to house, administering to the sick. Such was the rugged life of the doctor at that time.

Dr. Hogan and wife were the parents of three children when they came to Randolph county in 1871. They were the three eldest, William, Kate and Lou. The other children were born in this county.

The family has long been prominent in the county. Three generations have been teachers in the schools. They have always been interested in all things for the bettermen of the community. The family for several generations have been members of the Church of Christ and they were among the leaders instrumental in the establishment of the Church of Christ at Maynard. Dr. Martin Hogan was a brother of Prof. John Hogan, Sr., and a brief article about him and his wife, "Miss Eliza", appears below.

PROF. JOHN HOGAN, SR., AND WIFE, "MISS ELIZA"

The above couple were among the most noted educators which have ever lived in Randolph county. John Hogan and wife came to Randolph county in 1872. He was a brother of Dr. Martin Hogan. They first taught school at Corning, soon after coming to this section. During the 70's they taught at their home which was a mile west of Maynard. They also taught at a house on their farm which was a mile and a half west of town and also at the "Cabin," another house on their farm. They also taught at Pocahontas during the early 80's. This school was held in the old Masonic Hall in Pocahontas. Soon after this, they taught the first term of school in the "new schoolhouse" at Middlebrook. Another place near Maynard which they tauch was at the Miller house on their farm. During the early 90's they taught at Warm Springs. This was their last work together. He retired from teaching at this time. After he retired, Miss Eliza taught at several places in the county, among which were Ainley, Pitman, Moore and Albritton.

Many fine young men and women who later became distinguished citizens of Randolph county, attended school which Prof. and Miss Eliza Hogan taught in the years between 1872 and 1900. Among these were, William Henry Johnston, Almus J. Witt, C. E. Witt, Lute Hurn, Tell Thompson, Ben A. Brown, D. C. and H. M. Bishop, John and Tom Albritton, Charles H. Carter, Misses Canda Ator, Ella Thompson, Lucy Hill, and many others. Lots of folks even to this day, when they think of leading educators of north Arkansas, think first of "Old Prof. and Miss Eliza Hogan." They were contemporaries with Prof. F. E. Tilford and wife, as teachers in Randolph county during this period and it is possible that this quartet is the four best known educators that the county has ever seen.

Dr. Martin died at Maynard, August 6, 1916. His wife, Mary White Hogan, died March 13, 1913. Prof. John Hogan died November 11, 1910. His wife, Eliza Jones Hogan, died July 27, 1912. The latter also died at Maynard.

The village of Maynard and surrounding communities are better communities by having had citizens like Dr. Martin and Prof. John Hogan and their wives live there.

THE INGRAM FAMILY

The Ingram family of Randolph county is descended from James P. and Rebecca Mansker Ingram.

James P. Ingram was born in Virginia in 1800, and his wife in 1811. He came to this county in 1824, settling on a farm near the present site of the Ingram cemetery, on the old Military road between Maynard and Supply. Here he lived until his death in 1874. James P. Ingram was an influential and prosperous citizen. He served in various official capacities for many years, being the county's fourth county judge.

James P. and Rebecca Mansker Ingram were the parents of 11 children. Among these were G. H. (Dock), Lurana, who married W. P. G. (Green) Johnston; Leddie B., who married Henderson H. Hatley; Hannah, who died at 20 years of age, and J. W. (Blind Bill). Mrs. Hatley was the mother of Mrs. Josie Lamb, mother of the author's wife.

The father of Rebecca Ingram was George Mansker, who came to Randolph county from Sumner county, Tennessee, in 1817, settling on the creek which bears the family name, just north of Pocahontas. Governor Thomas S. Drew was born in Wilson county, Tennessee, a few miles from the Mansker home and the families were intermarried before coming to this county.

The children of George and Elizabeth Mansker were Sarah, Margaret, Nancy, John, Casper, George, Coleman, Jackson, William, Catherine and Rebecca (Mrs. Ingram).

Sarah married John Fisher, Margaret married Matthias Mock, Nancy married King Fisher, Coleman married Martha Mitchell, Catherine married Carlton Lindsey and Rebecca married James P. Ingram. Who the other married is not known.

J. W. (known for many years as Uncle Blind Bill) Ingram, was born May 8, 1839. He married another Rebecca Mansker (same name as his mother), a relative of his mother's family, April 12, 1857. He was 18 years of age at the time. Among the children of this marriage were: Elizabeth, who married William Smith; Martha, who married William Jolly; Sarah, who married Robert Johnson; L. V., who married Benjamin Phipps, and William, who married Tennie Pond. William and Mrs. Johnson are still living in Texas, at this time. Mrs. Jolly was the mother of Joe Jolly of Supply; Claude of St. Louis; Mrs. E. Brown of Corning; Walter, Roy and the late Judge Rex E. Jolly, the last three deceased.

Uncle Bill Ingram's second wife was Josie Mock, a granddaughter of Matthias Mock referred to above. To this union was born the following who lived to maturity: Rufus G., who died in early manhood; Thomas F. and J. R. G. (Bob). Uncle Bill married Miss Mock October 9, 1870. She died December 28, 1883.

Mary P. Kerley Tilley became his third wife April 10, 1884. To this union several children were born, only one of which grew up. This was Lura Dean, who is the wife of Will Redwine of Maynard.

The third Mrs. Ingram had previously married William Tilley and was the mother of three children, one of which was Tom Tilley, now residing near Maynard. Tom Tilley is the father of Earle Tilley, present county tax assessor.

Thomas F. Ingram married Cina Brown, member of an early Little Black township family. To this union was born the following children now living: T. F., Jr., who married

Opal Sammons; Beulah, who married Clarence Fowler; and Ruth, who married Hite Hogan. T. F. and Beulah reside in the county and Ruth lives in St. Louis. Mr. Ingram died in 1943. Mrs. Ingram lives in the old family home.

J. R. G. (Bob) Ingram married Eliza Fowler, daughter of Rev. Alex and Belle Rapert Fowler. Uncle Alex was one of the pioneer preachers of the Supply community. The children of this union are: Gertrude, who married Less E. Allen, son of W. R. Allen, for many years a merchant and cotton buyer of Supply; Erman, who married Winnie Crawford, member of a prominent Missouri family. Erman is assistant manager of the Midwest branch of International Harvester Company, at Quincy, Illinois; Josie, wife of Roger Wills of Little Rock. Josie teaches in the Pulaski county schools; Fleeta, who married Troy Cockrum. Troy is the son of Henry and the late Ganie Taylor Cockrum of Supply. They live at Maynard. Oscar, married Dera Ford of Pocahontas. He is associated with Baltz Hardware Company. Eula, the youngest daughter, lives with her parents, and is a member of the Maynard school faculty, and Curtis O. of Pocahontas.

Curtis married Laura Morris, daughter of E. L. Morris. Mrs. Ingram's paternal ancestors, the Morris, Montgomery and Gill families, were pioneers of Adair county, Kentucky. They came into that section over the old Wilderness road with the first settlers. Her maternal ancestors were the Suttons, Wheelers and Camers, who have been residents of Pike county, Illinois, for over a century.

Mr. and Mrs. Ingram were married in 1918, just before Curt went overseas to serve in World War I. They are the parents of four children: Purcell, who served in the late war as M. P. with the Sixth Service Command; Eileen and Beverly, at home, and Yvonne, who married James Randell.

Other members of the family of Uncle Blind Bill Ingram who served in World War II are: Loren Jolly, who served as chaplain in the Pacific area; Burford Jolly, who was with General Patton, in a railway battalion; Raymond Brown, who participated in the African, Italian, French and German campaigns, being awarded the Silver Star; Beverly Ingram, who served through the New Guinea, Morotai and Philippine campaigns, taking part in four major battles. Beverly is a brother of Purcell named above.

The Ingram family has long been identified with the business and political history of the county. Uncle Bill and his brother G. H. (Dock), operated cotton gins for many years in the eastern part of Randolph county. Their brother-in-law, Green Johnston was also a cotton gin operator, and the same is true of another brother-in-law, Henderson Hatley and his brother Albert Hatley. The present generation still operate a gin.

Uncle Bill Ingram joined the Confederate Army and served first under Col. Robert G. Shaver. Later he was with General Price in his raid through Missouri.

In the floor of the old home near Supply was a trap door which opened into the basement which was used by Mr. Ingram when he was home on furlough, if the Yankees got too close. It is said that he escaped being captured several times in this manner. The old home stood until recently.

The first wife of Uncle Bill took her mother-in-law (the wife of James P. Ingram) and a Negro boy and drove an ox wagon from the old home to Cape Girardeau, Missouri, during the war, crossing Federal lines, to secure medical supplies for the community.

Uncle Bill lost his eyesight in January, 1873, on account of erysipelas, which was first contracted while attending the wounded on the battlefields, and throughout the remainder of his life carried on activities which many persons with good eyes did not venture to do. He was a large landholder and a benefactor to many people in the eastern part of the county. The story is told that any time misfortune and hardship overtook a family Uncle Bill was one of the first to ride over to "see what needed to be done." He possibly had as many friends at the time of his death as any man who ever lived in Randolph county.

He died in 1917 at the age of 77.

THE JARRETT FAMILY

The Jarrett family is one of the oldest of the county.

Dr. William Jarrett the "father" of the Jarretts of central Randolph county is said to have purchased land near the present-day Foster Ford on Fourche de Mas river from Richard Fletcher in 1801. Dr. Jarrett came to Randolph county from the state of Pennsylvania.

He later acquired other lands, some of it through his wife, Hannah Seavers, whom he married May 4, 1821. Her maiden name was Miller, she being the daughter of Martin Miller who made a will (recorded in the old Lawrence county records July 3, 1821) in which he bequeathed certain lands "On the waters of Fourche de Thomas" to this daughter.

Mrs. Jarrett had previously married Gabriel Seavers, who was a soldier of the War of 1812.

To Mr. and Mrs. Jarrett was born a son, December 3, 1827, named Henry Conway.

Dr. William Jarrett was one of the leading men of the county during his day. Dr. Englemann the noted German scientist who visited this section in 1837 states in his diary that Dr. Jarrett was a very learned man. He was justice of the peace for many years, was a leader in the move to locate the county seat at old Columbia when it was located at Pocahontas in 1836. Shinn's History lists him as one of the promoters of a Fourth of July celebration at that place in 1821.

His son, Henry Conway Jarrett, married Louisa Christiana Fleugge, November 4, 1847. Uncle Joe Jarrett tells us that at the time of the marriage of this couple, who were his parents, that his mother lived about three miles east of the present day village of Ponder, Ripley county, Missouri. Her parents were of German ancestry, who settled in Ripley county at an early day. Mr. Jarrett first met his wife when she attended church at the old "Salem" church which was located near the home of Dr. William Jarrett. He says she attended regularly, coming a distance of some 15 miles on horseback.

To the union of Henry C. Jarrett and Louisa C. Fleugge were born five sons, as follows: William H., who married Maggie Murray. He moved to Little Rock about 1870 where he became well known in that city. He was born May 10, 1849, and died in 1944; Lewis C., born March 4, 1851. He married Luella Adams (a relative of John Quincy Adams). Their children were William H., Jr., James C., Sular and Ida, who married Jake Roberts, a son of David Roberts and Susan Waddle Roberts. She has one son, Earl. The third son of Henry C. Jarrett was Charles Isham, who married Hessie Purdy. He was born February 10, 1853. Next was Joseph A., who is still living on the old home place and has never married. He was born February 3, 1864. The youngest son was James C., who married Alice Elizabeth Carroll. She was a daughter of Tone Carroll and Nancy Spikes Carroll. Nancy Spikes was a daughter of Jesse and Nancy Copeland Spikes. James C. Jarrett was born September 7, 1868 and was married January 21, 1892.

James C. Jarrett and Alice Elizabeth Carroll Jarrett were the parents of five children, the oldest dying in infancy; James Ervin, born January 6, 1894; Oscar McClure, born January 7, 1897; Joseph Albert born June 20, 1901, died

1908; Iva Christiana born April 26, 1908. Iva married Otis Kerley February 4, 1928, son of Richard and Tola Ingram Kerley. Their children are Wilbur, James, Katy Sue, Alfred, Betty Carroll and J. C.. James Ervin Jarrett married Alice Wooldridge, daughter of Lewis and Minerva Jarrett (no kin) Wooldridge, December 20, 1918. They are the parents of the following children: Bernardine, born in 1919; L. Conway, born in 1922; James Joe, born in 1926; Minerva Alice, born in 1932; Eldon, born in 1934; and Bennie, born in 1939.

Lewis Conway Jarrett, son of Ervin Jarrett, listed above, married Ervalene, daughter of Mr. and Mrs. John Shocklee of Ingram. Mrs. Shocklee was Pearl Condict before her marriage. Conway and Ervalene have one child, a daughter, Sharon Kay.

Oscar McClure Jarrett married Edna Lincoln, April 6, 1929. She is a daughter of William L. and Mattie Hurley Lincoln. They are the parents of Winnifred Lucile, born January 8, 1930, and Charles Isham, born June 9, 1933.

The Jarrett family has furnished men in all the wars in which this nation has been involved since the dawn of the nineteenth century.

Dr. William Jarrett was a major in the U. S. Army in the War with Mexico.

Henry Conway Jarrett was a Confederate soldier, entering service of the Southland and was one of the men who helped organize and train a company of soldiers in the bottom field near the present Fourche bridge in the Columbia community.

When World War I found our nation in the conflict, both Ervin and Oscar, sons of James C. Jarrett entered service and served many months in the regular army. Oscar served some time in France.

In World War II Conway Jarrett, and James Joe Jarrett, sons of Ervin Jarrett, served their country. Conway spent a period of three and one-half years in the Army Air Corps as staff sergeant, and James Joe is now in the Army Infantry, in the Pacific area. He is also a staff sergeant.

Ervin Jarrett has been a teacher in the schools of Randolph county several years. Both he and his brother Oscar and their sister Mrs. Kerley reside on the old home place and are successful farmers.

James C. Jarrett, Jr., son of Lewis C. Jarrett, is a successful business man of Colorado Springs, Colorado, and also a leader in the Democratic party of that state. He was a presidential elector from Colorado in the last presidential election, and has also held other political offices.

REV. SAMUEL LARKIN JOHNSTON

The subject of this sketch was born in Siloam township, two miles west of the present village of Middlebrook, April 6, 1866.

He was married to Sallie E. Carter, July 14, 1889. To this union was born 12 children: Otis, born April 27, 1890; Tula, born September 6, 1891; Roy W., born November 10, 1893; Lewis C., born November 10, 1895; Leland, born December 12, 1897; Lena B., born August 4, 1899; Lora B., born Auguest 5, 1901; Mary C., born September 11, 1903; Willie May, born May 11, 1905; Liston Lamar, born December 30, 1906; Ella V., born February 2, 1909, and Nona K., born July 14, 1911.

Mrs. Johnston was born the daughter of George W. and Elizabeth Jane Austin Carter. The father was born in August, 1834, and died in January, 1880. He was born in Dixon county, Tennessee. The mother was born June 25, 1842 in Graves county, Kentucky, and died in 1925.

FAMILY HISTORY

The family came to Randolph county in 1872. George and Elizabeth Carter were the parents of six children: Charles H., who is a former county judge of this county; Nannie Lou; James A.; George W.; Nora Idella, and Mrs. Johnston.

Our subject and wife have 35 grandchildren and nine great-grandchildren to date.

Samuel Larkin Johnston is a son of Lewis B. and Tennessee Spencer Johnston, who were married February 23, 1848, in Tennessee. Lewis B. Johnston was a son of George Gregory Johnston and Martha Burton Johnston, who came to Randolph county in 1849. Lewis B. did not come here until the next year. The Johnston family first settled two miles west of Middlebrook. From here the family spread over this and Ripley county, Missouri. The Johnston Chapel Methodist church, in Ripley county, about six miles north of the first home of this family was named for Lewis B. Johnston. It was located on his farm and the family was one of the founders. Lewis B. Johnston later moved back down into Randolph county where he and his son Charles G., opened up a store at Middlebrook.

The children of Gregory Johnston, grandfather of our subject, were: Arena, who married Rev. Jesse Robinson in 1844; Rev. Larkin F., who married Permelia Ann Lawson in 1864; Lewis B., who married Tennessee Spencer in 1848; W. P. G. (Green), who married Lurana Ingram in 1853; James F., who married Martha McDaniel in 1853; Sarah Jane, who married D. C. Moore in 1855; George Henry, who married Myra Reynolds in 1856, and Fletcher and Margie who died young.

Arena was the mother of "Jim Lewis" Robinson and other children. He was the father of Tom H. and Charlie of Biggers, Mrs. C. K. Black and Mrs. R. E. Salle of Pocahontas, Mrs. Jim Wisner and Mrs. John T. Robinson of

Reyno, Mrs. Sarah McCrary of Oklahoma, Mrs. Williams of Memphis and other children.

Larkin F. Johnston was the father of the late William Henry Johnston, father of Ben Johnston of Pocahontas. Green Johnston was the father of James Johnston for whom the old town of Johnstontown on Current river was named; also Gregory (Mrs. F. E. Belford and Reddin Johnston's father); Rufus M. of Reyno, W. S. of Maynard and other children. Lurana Ingram, first wife of Green Johnston was a sister of the wife of Henderson Hatley.

James F. was the father of Arena Kerley, Ganie and Ellen Mock, L. F. (Albertha Lewis), William "Billy," and other children. Sarah Jane Moore was the mother of Mary Ellen Taylor, wife of Ben F. Taylor, whose family history is also in this book. The other children of Greogry Johnston, Sr., left no heirs.

The children of Lewis B. and Tennessee Spencer Johnston were: Charles G.; Sarah, who married Jonathan Pulliam; Ellen, who married a Mr. Albritton; James; William; Jess M.; Cordie, who married Robert Cox; Permelia, who married Neely Moore; Arena, who married John Williams; Martha, who married Jack Keel; Peyton and Samuel Larkin, our subject.

Several members of the Johnston family have been public officials. Rev. L. F. was county clerk in 1850-52 and tax assessor three terms. William H. was tax assessor 1882-84. Charles G. was representative in 1887-88. Ben Johnston was county clerk twice by election and once by appointment. Green was coroner in 1866-68. Lewis B. was tax assessor and county judge in Ripley county, Missouri. At least a dozen have been constables, marshal and justice of the peace for many years.

There has been more ministers in the Johnston family than any other the county has produced. The first was

Larkin F., then Jesse Robinson, Jesse's son Don M.; S. L. (our subject); his son Liston; Chester and Sam Pulliam, (Sarah Johnston's grandsons); Walter (Lewis B.'s grandson); Kenneth, (Green's grandson). They were all Methodist ministers. Oscar, another grandson of Green, is a Baptist minister. A son-in-law of our subject, Rev. Wesley Henson, is a Baptist minister. Calvin Cox (Cordie's son), and Glendon Shaver (our subject's grandson), are ministers of the Church of Christ. There may be others not listed here. The Johnston family can be truly said to be one of the largest and best known families in Arkansas.

Our subject, Samuel Larkin Johnston, has lived a long useful life and now resides at Middlebrook with his invalid wife. He is one of the best known retired Methodist ministers in the county.

THE JOHN A. JOHNSON FAMILY

John A. Johnston was a son of William Torrence Johnson who came to eastern Randolph county in 1845. The mother of John A. Johnson was a daughter of Asa Taylor, who came here from Graves county, Kentucky, during the same period. The Taylor and Johnson families were instrumental in the establishing of the Glaze Creek Church of Christ the same year that the elder Johnson located in this section.

John A. Johnson married Susan F. Elkins, a daughter of William S. Elkins. The children of William F. Elkins and his first wife were: Sarah, who married John Riley Odom; Elizabeth, who married George Baker; Susan F. (Mrs. Johnson); Clemantine, who married Cord Parish and Alonzo and Nancy by a second marriage. Nancy married Tom Crawford and Alonzo married Ellen Hawk. Allie Baker, a niece of Mr. Elkins, was reared by him. She married Tom Luter.

John A. Johnson and Susan F. Elkins Johnson were the parents of the following children: A. S., who married Hattie Slayton. They are the parents of Ralph E., who married Mary Rogers; Susan Teresa, who married Frank Craft; Geneva Lynn, who married Oscar Spencer; Nell, who married Rev. A. B. Constantz, and Jehu A., who married Lucy Slaughter.

Another daughter of John A. Johnston, Cordelia, married W. E. Mathis. Their children were Elsie, who married Bill Martin; Mary Francis, Norvesta and Vera May.

Sarah Ella, daughter of John A. Johnston, married DeWitt Hagood. They were the parents of the following children: Orie, who married Mayme Chorice; Gilbert, who married Essie Taylor; Etta, who married Jess R. Pratt; Lena May, who married Orace Jones; John, who married Naomi Luter, and Edgar, who married Irene Pitman.

The twin sister of Mrs. Hagood is Mrs. Etta Johnston. Etta first married R. J. Stephens at Don (now Success) in 1891. They had one daughter, Christine, who married Garve Abbott. Mr. Stephens died 15 months after his marriage. Mrs. Stephens married John Talbott five years later.

They were the parents of the following children: Hassel, who married John T. Springer; Lois, who married Harold Britton; Lilly, who married Everett Bryant; Guy, who married Jane McCauley; Harry L., who married Dora Chappell, and Robert, who married Mary Evalyn Fowler. Mr. Talbott died in 1937.

In 1943 Mrs. Talbott married W. S. (Stedman) Johnston, son of Greene Johnston, early settler of Little Black township. Mr. and Mrs. Johnston now live at Maynard.

William Torrence Johnson, the father of John A. Johnson, was also the father of the following other children: Lavinah, who married Craven Wilson. Mr. and Mrs. Wilson were the parents of the following children: Mary Elizabeth, who married Dr. Val Seal; William Reuben to Lizzie Meeks, Johnnie Martin to Adna Jones, Chloe Hester to James Kidd, Veda Emily to Will Gillis, Fifa Myrtle to a Mr. Sadler and Pearl Denton, Moses Tolbert and Carl Craven, wives names unknown. The other daughter of William T. Johnson was Mary Elizabeth, who married John Calvin Cox. Mr. and Mrs. Cox were the parents of the following children: Susan Caroline, who married John Johnston and later Bob Robinson; Robert L., who married Cordia Johnston; William David, who married Mollie Carter; Joseph L., who married Leota Vester; Mary Bell, who married George Mansker, and Malissa Jane, who married Levi Helms.

For many years after the old Glaze creek church was established there had been no cemetery. Levi Helms, a grandson-in-law of William Torrence Johnson, one of the founders of the church, was the first person buried in the cemetery 90 years after it was established!

This family is closely related to some of the very first families of the county. Craven Wilson was a son of one Benjamin Wilson who located near the "Wilson Ford" on Fourche creek about 1840. Cordia Cox was the granddaughter of Gregory Johnston, who settled west of Middlebrook in 1848. James Kidd was a grandson of old "Parson Witt," early preacher of Siloam township. The Cox and Carter families were among the first to settle in what is now Richardson township and the same is true of many other of the relatives of the descendants of William Torrence Johnson.

LANDON CHRISTOPHER HAYNES

Landon Christopher Haynes was born at Nacogdoches, Texas, December 26, 1865. The son of M. H. and Mary King Haynes. The parents were Tennesseans who moved to the Lone Star State before the subject of our sketch was born. The father died soon after the latter was born and his mother married J. A. Douglas, who for many years was a familier figure around the courthouse and well known in Pocahontas, known as "Squire Douglas."

Mr. Haynes had three own brothers and two sisters, all now deceased. They were J. D., G. M. and R. L.; the sisters were Emmaline, who married W. W. Cooper, and Mattie who married Jesse L Lynch. Mr. Lynch is at present living with his daughter, Mrs. W. H. Phipps in Pocahontas. The half brothers, two in number, were Thomas D. Douglas, deceased, and Monroe Douglas of Newport, Arkansas.

Mr. Haynes married Miss Elmyra Virgin Knotts, January 9, 1895. Mrs. Haynes was the daughter of James R. Knotts and Elmyra Waldron Knotts. To this union was born one son, Thomas Dula, November 4, 1896. He lived only nine months and seven days, before the Lord called him home.

Our subject quit farming and moved to Pocahontas, April 1, 1906. He bought a grocery store from Harley Midkiff and operated this business several years. In 1922 the family moved to Success, Arkansas, where he again entered the mercantile business, in which he continued until January, 1944. Mr. and Mrs. Haynes still live at Success.

Mr. Haynes professed faith in Christ, August 9, 1899, and joined the Shiloh (Randolph county) Missionary Baptist church. After moving to Pocahontas he moved his membership to the church there and served as deacon and also church treasurer several years. After moving to Success Mr.

Haynes served as Sunday school superintendent and church treasurer in that church a number of years. He has always been a strong Baptist and a staunch Democrat.

They have two adopted daughters, Mrs. Belle Brown of Pocahontas, and Mrs. Dorcas Smith of Corning.

THE HOLT FAMILY

The Holt family of Randolph county is descended from one Tom Holt, who was born in Pennsylvania about 1790. His parents died when he was young and a neighbor family took the boy to their home. This family is said to have been so mean to the boy that a number of neighbors who were preparing to migrate west stole the boy and took him with them. They moved to Illinois to make their home. Here Tom Holt lived until he was grown. He then went to Madison county, Missouri, where he married and then later moved down into this county. He settled on the place which later became known as the Uncle Dee Mock farm. He was the father of three boys. Their names were John, William and David. Dave died a bachelor. John was the grandfather of John R. Holt of Pocahontas and W. A. Holt of Warm Springs. William was the great-grandfather of Tom and Edd Holt of Pocahontas.

John was the eldest of the three sons of Tom Holt. He was born about 1812. He married Mary Barrett and settled on what is now known as the old Isaac Whittenberg place. They were the parents of four boys and five girls. They were: George, who was killed in the Civil War William (Dock), Jim and Henry. The girls were Betty, Rebecca, Nancy, Eliza, and Martha.

John Holt, the father, died in 1861. William married Nancy Phillips and settled on a creek one mile east of Warm Springs. He was the father of John R. and W. A. He was always called "Dock." He was in the war with General Price. Jim died young; Henry married Sis Thorn. He died at Hoxie in 1886. He was a Baptist preacher. William (Dock), was born January 1, 1842, and died in 1926.

William A. Holt married Malissa Dalton. They reside at Warm Springs at present where they have lived almost three-quarters of a century. They have three sons and five daughters..

John R. Holt lives in Pocahontas at present. He was first married to Carrie Boas of Doniphan, Missouri. They were the parents of nine children, George W., Chester (deceased), Lilly (deceased), John Randolph, Freeman L., Perry Benton, Ena, Heber and Winnie. Chester married Laura Booger, Randolph married Mabel Mitchell, Freeman married Carrie Moore, Benton married Martha Yarbrough, Ena married Guy Chick, Heber married Judith Johnson and Winnie married Cleatus Price. George is not married.

After the death of Mr. Holt's first wife he married Estelle Tullis of Fairfield, Illinois, who became a very kind and thoughtful step-mother to the Holt children. The Holt family is well known in this section of the state.

FAMILY HISTORY

THE JOHN H. LAMB FAMILY

John H. Lamb married Josephine Hatley. He was a grandson of William Lamb, who was born and spent his life in central Kentucky. He was the father of a number of children, of these Wiley and William came to Randolph county in 1860. They settled in the community east of the present village of Maynard. Here they spent the balance of their lives and lie buried in the old Lamb cemetery near the present homes of Eugene Athy and William Evans.

William Lamb, Jr., married Lucy Ann Mills and they became the parents of two children, John H. and Amanda. After the death of William Lamb, his widow married D. Blackburn and they became the parents of three children, Delia, Bessie and Charles.

Amanda married James Reddin Hatley and they became the parents of six children who grew to adulthood, Zella, who married Floyd Flanders; Elvin, who married Della May McIlroy; Vera, who married Walter Strayhorn; Ila, who married Ayliffe Tipton; Crystal, who married Carl H. Brooks, and Rita, who married Jake Dunn.

Mrs. Hatley lost her life in a car wreck at Benton, Arkansas, in 1932. After the death of Mrs. Hatley he married Nora Riley. Mr. Hatley died at Biggers in 1938.

John H. Lamb married Josephine Hatley, a sister of James Reddin Hatley. This making Mr. and Mrs. Hatley and Mr. and Mrs. Lamb double "in-laws."

To the union of John and Josephine Hatley Lamb were born eight children, six of whom grew to adulthood. They were Marvin, who married Jewell Baker; Christine, who married Aubrey Carter (she died in Washington, D. C. in 1935); Irene, who married Lawrence Dalton, the author of this book; John, who married Fay Bundren; Sherrill, who married Jessie Parker, and Norma, who married Vince Manning.

John H. Lamb was born in Kentucky, November 29, 1855, and was brought to Randolph county by his parents when five years of age. He spent his boyhood near Maynard and removed to Reyno when a young man. Here he spent the remainder of his life. He died in 1920. Mrs. Lamb survives him. She lives near Biggers at the present time, with her youngest daughter.

Josephine Hatley Lamb is descended from George and Elizabeth Mansker who came to Randolph county from Sumner county, Tennessee, in 1817, settling on the creek which bears his name just north of the city of Pocahontas.

A daughter of George Mansker married James P. Ingram (the fourth county judge of the county). Her name was Rebecca. James P. Ingram and Rebecca Mansker Ingram became the parents of several children, among them were William (known as Uncle Blind Bill); George H. (known as Dock); Lurana, who married W. P. Green Johnston, and Leddie B., who married Henderson Hatley.

Henderson and Leddie Hatley were married January 14, 1866. To this union were born six children who grew to maturity. They were: James Reddin, George, Presley, Lou, Estis and Josephine.

As stated above, James married Amanda Lamb; George married Minnie Myers; Presley and Lou died before marriage; Estis married Ava Cherry, and Josephine married John H. Lamb. Estis and Ava Cherry Hatley had two children, Milford and Vivian. The children of Josephine have already been named above. The above are the maternal relations of Josephine Hatley Lamb.

The paternal grandparents of Josephine Hatley Lamb were Reddin and Delphia Kelley Hatley, who were born in North Carolina. Their parents came to America from the British Isles in 1770. Of the seven sons born to Reddin and Delphia Kelley Hatley we know of two of them. These were

Albert H. and Henderson, the father of Mrs. Lamb. The children of Henderson are named above. Albert H. first married Nancy Mitchell and they were the parents of two children. After her death Albert Hatley married Mahulda Abbott and they became the parents of several children, among these were Ellen (who first married Gus Reynolds and after his death, Isaac Ebberts); Atlas, who married Tura Phipps, and Eli. The latter two now living in Missouri and Oklahoma respectively. Naomi married Will Witt and Gussie, who married John McCrary.

The Hatley family came to Randolph county in 1851 and settled at Maynard. Among the first cotton gins established in the county were built by members of the Ingram and Hatley families. Both are large families and having intermarried with the other early families of the county, the result is that they are related to many of the leading families of this section of the state.

There are other branches of the Hatley family which we do not have the family data on. However, they are all of the same family origin.

ELDER JOHN M. LEMMONS
Early Randolph County Church of Christ minister, one of the founders of Hubble Creek Church.

FAMILY HISTORY

THE LEMMONS FAMILY

John M. Lemmons was born in Virginia in 1816. He moved with his parents to Warren county, Tennessee, in 1818. He married and lived in Warren county until 1851, when he moved to Arkansas, locating first in Independence county. After one year he moved to Randolph county.

In the same year, 1852, he and his older sons and two or three neighbors built a log church house on Hubble creek, one mile south of Birdell. In 1862, during the Civil War, this house was burned and in 1866 Mr. Lemmons with the help of others, built another house on Carter creek. However, the name "Hubble Creek" was retained.

John M. Lemmons was the father of seven sons, Thompson, Manson, Mannon, Josephus, Caleb, James and Peyton. He also had two daughters, Emmaline and Margaret. He died in 1898 at the age of 82.

Thomas Lemmons moved to Illinois in 1861. The other children all settled in Randolph county, and during the years have contributed much toward the development of the civic, religious and political interests of the county.

John M. Lemmons was a preacher of the Church of Christ and did much to help establish the church in north Arkansas. His son Josephus was licensed to preach July 18, 1868, upon the endorsement of the elders of the Hubble Creek church. He was called Amos (Josephus A). The elders of the church at that time were: His father, John M.; Cullen Pyland, L. D. Cartright, Samuel Donnell, and S. M. Hufstedler.

Peyton was also a preacher of ability. These two brothers were among the leading preachers of the Church of Christ of north Arkansas and south Missouri during this period.

The sons and daughters of John M. Lemmons have all passed on but their children, grandchildren, and great-grandchildren are among the leaders in the affairs of Randolph, Greene and other counties of the state today.

There has been a number of ministers in each generation and family of the descendants of John M. Lemmons. There has also been many successful farmers, teachers, in fact all professions are represented in this family.

A number of the grandchildren of John M. Lemmons are living in the county today, among them are George F., A. T., Mrs. Vessie Bates, children of Mannon Lemmons and the widow of Riley, another son; George H., a son of Caleb is also living in the county.

There are scores of later generations of Lemmons living in this and surrounding communities. This is a well known family and the old church which they established is one of the very first in this section of the state.

CHARLES WILEY McCARROLL

The subject of this sketch is descended from one James A. McCarroll, who came to old Lawrence county from Kentucky about 1808. His son, James A. McCarroll, being the grandfather of our subject.

James A. McCarroll married Rebecca Forrester. They were the parents of three children, Charles (known as Boob); Jane, who married James McGlothlin, and Andrew J.

Andrew J. McCarroll married Lucinda Milam, daughter of John B. Milam. They were the parents of three children who grew to adulthood. They were John H., Lucinda, who married J. A. Melton, and Charles Wiley, our subject.

Charles Wiley was born July 24, 1870, in Butler township, in Randolph county, Arkansas. His father and family moved to what is now the Engleberg community in 1874.

At the time the family moved to this section there were only about half a dozen families living in the community. Mail was carried from Pocahontas to Pitman's Ferry and the settlers in the Engleberg community were obliged to go to old Albertha on the Doniphan-Pocahontas road for their mail. Some of the settlers in this community in 1874 were Dock Davis, Jess Norman, the McAfees, Knotts, Fosters and Hanleys.

Our subject helped Isaac DeBow secure the DeBow postoffice in 1905 and was assistant postmaster for a period of 16 years, and served as postmaster for a period of 16 years. Serving a total of 32 years in the employ of the United States Postal Department. He retired in 1940, being the first man in the state of Arkansas to retire at the age of 70 years on postal employes retirement compensation.

When the postoffice was discontinued at DeBow and a new office established at Engleberg, Mr. McCarroll became the first postmaster. He has the honor of being the first postmaster, first merchant and first justice of the peace at Engleberg.

Mr. McCarroll relates that he and Mr. DeBow carried the mail from DeBow to Brockett, a distance of two miles, free of charge to the government the first six months after the former office was established, until the office was on a paying basis.

Our subject married Susanne Ulmer February 16, 1914. She was a daughter of John Ulmer, early settler of the Stokes community. She had previously married Jake Lowrey, and they were the parents of four children. Their names were Horace, Raymond, Mrs. Norman Harris and Van B. Mrs. McCarroll died December 4, 1941, and was buried "Pearl Harbor Day."

Mr. McCarroll and wife became the parents of two children which grew to adulthood. They are Eugene, who married Charlene Jackson, daughter of Mr. and Mrs. Gola

Jackson, and Catherine, who married Seigfried Yordt. The latter live in St. Louis, and the former lives with his father. Eugene and wife have one child and Catherine and husband have two children. Eugene's child, a son, is named Robert Eugene, born on V-J Day; and the daughter's children, a boy named Billy, and a daughter, named Margie.

Mr. McCarroll is a member of the Methodist church, becoming a member in 1915 at Oak Grove (Attica). He is a well known citizen of the county. Has served in a number of places of public trust and is a Democrat and always takes a great interest in the political campaigns.

It is a well known fact that when a man announces for office in Randolph county he does not wait long to approach Uncle Wiley, with the expressed intention of attempting to "get him on his side." But unless he can prove his worth, he is not always successful in the undertaking.

Mr. McCarroll is a good citizen, a good man and Randolph county is proud to claim him as one of her native sons.

THE W. L. (FAYETTE) MOCK FAMILY

W. L. Mock, always known as Fayette, married Miss Ganie Johnston January 19, 1888.

To this union the following children grew to maturity: Evaline, who married Lewis Wilson; Lehman, who married Gertie Mock; Grace, who married Lester Johnson; Isabella, who married Buell Loftis; Jessie, who married Crawford Hamm; Hite, who married Essie Pitman; Abe, who married Teula Lewis; Ouida, who married Robert Mattson, and Myra Lou, who married Arlo Tyer.

Mr. Mock passed away December 14, 1936, and Mrs. Mock makes here home at Maynard with her daughter, Myra Lou, who is a teacher in the Maynard school.

Mr. and Mrs. Mock reared their family on the old Mock homestead, on Mud creek just north of the old Ingram ford on the creek. The family resided here many years and for a long period of time Mr. Mock operated a large store and also a postoffice which was known as Mock.

The home has been known all through the years for its hospitality. All visitors were welcome and Sunday and special occasions usually found more "company" at Uncle Fayette and Aunt Ganie's home than any in the community. This family is descended from several of the very first families which came to this part of Arkansas during the days of early settlement.

W. L. Mock is a great-grandson of Matthias Mock, who settled on Mud creek in 1815, only a short distance up the creek from the old family home. The grandfather of W. L. Mock was Thomas J. Mock, who was a son of Matthias and Leah Shaver Mock. Leah Shaver was a daughter of John Shaver, who was also one of the first settlers on this creek. A sister of Matthias Mock, Matilda by name, married Minatree Carter about 1821. They were the parents of R. J. Carter, who was the father of the late Min Carter of Pocahontas. The wife of Thomas J. Mock is not known. Margaret Moore he married October 9, 1834. Thomas J. Mock was the father of Francis Marion Mock (who was known as General Mock).

Among the brothers of Thomas J. Mock were Griffin C., who was the father of the late Uncle Tom D. and other children and Isham J., who was the father of the late Elias C. and T. L. (Tive) Mock, and other children.

Francis Marion (General) Mock, married Jane Carter, who was descended from Minatree Carter, referred to above.

To the union of General and Jane Carter Mock a number of children were born, among these were A. T. (Gus), who married Ella Long and W. L. (Fayette), our subject.

After the death of General Mock's first wife he married America Shaver, daughter of Peter Shaver, who was descended from the first John Shaver named above. To this union two children were born. They are Otis M., now living in Pocahontas, and Mrs. Notra Price of Jonesboro.

Mrs. Mock (Ganie Johnston) is a granddaughter of George Gregory Johnston and Mary Burton Johnston, from whom all the Johnston's of this section of Arkansas descended. The father of Mrs. Mock was James F. Johnston, whose brothers were Rev. Larkin F., Lewis B., W. P. G. (Green), George H., and sisters Arena, who married Rev. Jesse Robinson and Sarah Jane who married D. C. Moore.

James F. Johnston married Martha McDaniel and they became the parents of the following children: Gregory, Dock, Jess, William, Sidney, Lewis F., Arena who married Tom Kerley; Ellen who married Tive Mock and Ganie, the wife of Fayette Mock.

The Mock family intermarried with several of the first families of the county. Among these are the Flecher, Stubblefield, Nettles, Morris, Johnston, Johnson, Dalton, Carter and Shaver families. The Shaver-Mock-Johnston family is the county's largest related family.

The children of Fayette and Ganie Mock have generally adhered to the tradition of the family by marrying members of the old families of the county. Evaline married Lewis Wilson whose parents, Johnny and Molly Murdock Wilson, were both early settlers' children. Lehman married Girtie Mock, whose parents, Thomas D. and Zilpha Dalton Mock represented two old families. Grace's husband, Lester Johnson, is a son of Tom and Minerva Carroll Johnson, whose families would be eligible to join a century club. Hite married Essie Pitman. Her family is one of the oldest in the county and related to Spencers, Smiths and other early Tennessee residents. Buel Loftis, the husband of Isabella, represents the early Jones, Crossen, Loftis and other early comers to Little Black township. Jessie's husband, Crawford Hamm, claims his ancestry to the Hamm, Brown, Wilson and other early "Columbia" settlers. Teula Lewis, the wife of Abe Mock, is descended from a family which came to old Lawrence county and settled at Davidsonville about 1812. Myra Lou's husband, Arlo Tyer is a member of the Tyer-Vermilye family. Ouida's husband, Robert Mattson, is the only member of the family not native to Randolph county.

Two outstanding characteristics of the Mock family is the inclination of different members of each generation toward the vocations of merchandising and school teaching. There has been merchants with Mock blood in their veins, in business in this section for a century and a long line of educators in this family signify their interest in education.

The family religious affiliation all down through the years has been almost 100 per cent with the Church of Christ, and early members of this family were instrumental in the establishment of some of the first congregations of this church in Randolph county.

THE MARLETTE FAMILY

The Marlette family is of Dutch descent. The ancestors of this family are reputed to have come to Pennsylvania from eastern Europe sometime near the close of the Revolution. From Pennsylvania the family came to the Wabash valley of southern Indiana about 1812. Epps Marlette was born in Pennsylvania about 1810. He married Nancy McDonald in Orange county, Indiana, about 1838.

To this union was born the following children: John, who married Anna Purcell in Gibson county, Indiana; David, who married, first, Sarah Spore in Gibson county, Indiana, and later married Molly Parker in Randolph county, Arkansas; Chessley, who married Martha Morris, sister of Jeff Morris of Randolph county; Isaac, who married Wilda Wallace, also of Randolph county; William, who married

Lula Lane; Alice and Perry, who never married. Alice died when a young woman and Perry lived about 60 years.

The Marlette family came to Randolph county from Gibson county, Indiana, in the fall of 1879, in a wagon train, crossing the Mississippi at Bird's Point and on down to this section over the old Military road.

The first night the family spent in this county was at the old Jarrett homestead. The next day they drove on down the road, through Pocahontas, to locate on the A. W. W. Brooks farm in Black river bottoms. After spending the winter there they decided to move back to the hills. Epps located near the Jarretts and Fosters and his son David lived his first year five miles north of Pocahontas on the old Biggers farm on Knotts creek. In December of 1880, a cyclone blew down the house they were living in, but no one was injured. The next year the family moved to near the village of Attica, locating on Fourche, east of the town. Here Epps Marlette spent the remainder of his life.

David moved up Fourche, and finally located across Fourche west of Middlebrook, where he lived many years, dying in 1930. Chessley, who married Martha Morris, lived several years in the vicinity of Ingram. They had two children who died when small. Here he and his wife died a few years after marriage. Isaac, who married Wilda Wallace of the same community, lived here a short time after his marriage but moved to Oklahoma, locating in the vicinity of Bristow. Here he died in 1942. His family resides in that section. The eldest son, John, never lived in this county. He spent his life in the vicinity of Carmi and Crossville, Illinois. William lived for many years in the Attica vicinity, but moved to near Light, in Greene county, about 25 years ago. After living there a few years his health failed and he came back to the vicinity of Middlebrook. Here he died in 1933.

Perry, who never married, living alone after the death of his parents. He spent the last known years of his life in Greene county, where he died about 1934.

Epps Marlette and wife are buried in the Gross cemetery. He died in 1905 and his wife died in 1907.

David Marlette and Sarah Spore were married in Indiana in 1870. Sarah Spore was a daughter of William Spore and a Miss Wade Spore.

They were the parents of the following children: Pinckney Monroe, who married Anna Grissom, daughter of John M. and Celia Poynor Grissom; Della (this author's mother), who married Elijah F. Dalton, son of David and Christiana Everett Dalton; Dolphus S., who married Laura Davidson, daughter of William and Amanda Davidson; Isaac Elvin, who married Josie Davidson, sister of Dolphus' wife; W. C. (Chessley), who married Lois Stuart (of Illinois), and Pearl, who died young.

After the death of Sarah Spore, the first wife of David Marlette, he married Molly Parker, daughter of James Parker, native of eastern Randolph county. To this union was born three children, Arvil, who married Mina Davidson of Monette; Luther, who married Lola Dalton, daughter of Joseph and Dilla Grissom Dalton; and Lucy, who lives with her mother west of Middlebrook.

David died in 1930. His first wife died in 1886. Both are buried in the Siloam cemetery near Middlebrook. Luther lives at Biggers. Arvil lived at Monette until 1943, when he moved to California where he died a short time after arriving in that state.

P. M. (Monroe) died in 1939. His family lives in the county. The other children of David Marlette live in Randolph county, except W. C., who lives part time in Michigan and at Success, Clay county.

The family of Epps Marlette is the only family of this name which has ever lived in this section of the state.

THE MAYNARD FAMILY

One of the pioneer families of Randolph county was the Maynards. The first Maynards to come here were three brothers, John, Stith and Thomas, and their families who came here from Tennessee, settling in the then, undeveloped part of the county where the thriving little town of Maynard is now located. The family is of French-English ancestry.

John came in 1872 and Stith and Thomas in 1884. The town of Maynard derived its name from this enterprising family. John and Stith both served their county in the Civil War, John acquiring the office of captain.

John was a pioneer in the mercantile business, having established the first store in Maynard, which he named "New Prospect." It was located on the hill where the old Maynard home now stands. He later moved it to a place nearer where the present business section is located. He also owned and operated an old-time treadwheel cotton gin, which served the surrounding country at that early date. Stith and Thomas were engaged in farming and stockraising.

John married Sally Adams of Missouri, and to this union was born three children: Fayette, now of Mobile, Alabama; Eugenia, deceased wife of the late Dr. H. L. Throgmorton, and John of Colera, Oklahoma.

Stith married Elizabeth Tuck of Tennessee and to this union three children were born: Ed R. of Tucson, Arizona; S. L. of Albuquerque, New Mexico, and Vera, wife of Clifford Price of Pocahontas, Arkansas.

Thomas was married twice, first to Mat Glasco of Tennessee, and to this union six children were born: Thornton, deceased; Ethel, deceased, she was the wife of Robert Anderson; Toby, deceased; Mrs. C. E. Witt of Little Rock; Elvis of Maynard, and Eugene of Pine Bluff.

His first wife died in Tennessee before the family came here. His second wife was Lizzie Beemis of Kentucky. To the last marriage three children were born; Almus, deceased; Ella, wife of Earle Richardson, now living in Texas, and Paul of Little Rock.

These brothers were together in many things, but politically were different, John being a Democrat and Stith and Thomas, Republicans.

These three brothers and their families were progressive, energetic Christian citizens, ever ready to help in any worthwhile project which would make their community better or help their fellow man.

They were all Missionary Baptists. John, Stith and their wives helping in the organiaztion of the Baptist church at Maynard, being charter members. Thomas and his wife joined later. They were also members of the Masonic Lodge and Mrs. Stith Maynard was a members of Easter Star.

These families were also interested in the educational and political growth of their community and county. Mrs. Thomas Maynard taught music for many years at Maynard.

The Maynards are truly one of the best known families of Randolph county.

THE MARTIN FAMILY

James Martin was born in Richmond, Virginia, in 1808, and died in Randolph county in 1863. The family came to the vicinity of St. Genevieve, Missouri, and lived a short time, coming on to Randolph county in 1833.

The home of James Martin was in Columbia township and the place is still called Martin's Spring. The Martin family purchased this farm from Thomas Foster, who had settled here about 1820. Mr. Martin built a fine Southern style home and developed the farm into a typical Southern plantation. Here the family lived many years. They were living here when the Civil War broke out. Two of the sons of the family died in service of the Confederacy. It was at the home of James Martin that Henry Wythe, brother of Mrs. Martin, was killed by jayhawkers.

The eldest daughter of James Martin married Capt. Wibb Conner. Her name was V. Ellen. She lived to a ripe old age, dying at Reyno a few years ago at the home of her daughter, Mrs. L. W. Hogan.

James Martin was appointed postmaster at Pocahontas in August, 1838. In 1842 he was elected to the office of county judge and served four years. Judge Martin was a man of means and a leading citizen of the county. He was identified with the affairs of the county for many years.

Four of the sons of Judge Martin, Andrew, Joseph, John F. and James, are remembered by many persons today as composing the firm of Martin Brothers, pioneer business men of the old town of Reyno, before the coming of the Fisco railroad, which spelled death to the old town. It was here that one of the sons, Joseph, married Anne E. Reynolds, daughter of Capt. D. W. Reynolds, founder of the town, February 9, 1888. The mother of Mrs. Martin was Mary Ellis, who had married Captain Alvah G. Kelsey, the officer under whom Capt. Reynolds served in the Confederate Army.

After the death of Captain Kelsey she married D. W. Reynolds.

Joseph and Annie Reynolds Martin were the parents of Lancelot R. (Lantie) Martin of Pocahontas. Other children of this union were Lila, Edith, Thelma and Joseph. Lantie Martin married Ona Sallee, daughter of the late Joseph Sallee, well known farmer and manufacturer of Pocahontas. To this union was born two children, Joseph and Jean. Jean married C. E. Olvey, Jr. They are the parents of one child. Joe married Jo Ann Belford.

C. E. is a son of Mr. and Mrs. C. E. Olvey, Sr., of Harrison. The Olveys are leading people of Boone county. Mrs. Joe Martin is a daughter of J. B. and Grace Creason Belford of Corning. J. B. is a leading business man of that city and Mrs. Belford is a member of an early Randolph county family.

C. E. and Joe are both associated with Lantie in the Martin Insurance Agency of Pocahontas. Lantie Martin has long been one of the leading business men of Pocahontas. He is also known as one of the most civic-minded men that has ever lived in Pocahontas. Anytime there is a movement on foot for the advancement and betterment of the city you will find Lantie Martin, if not at the head of it, one of the major boosters.

He is the head of the Martin Agency which was established in 1908, and is one of the largest and most successful agencies in north Arkansas. He is also associated with the Pocahontas Federal Savings and Loan Association, and the Guaranty Investment Company, which are located in the same building with the Martin Agency.

The Martin and Reynolds families have been identified with the business and political history of Randolph county for over a century.

Mrs. Anne Martin, widow of Joseph Martin, Sr., is living in Pocahontas at the present time, in the old family home on Thomasville Avenue.

JUDGE OSCAR PRINCE

Oscar Prince, Sr., is the grandson of Peter Prince and Miss Davis Prince, early settlers on Janes creek, in western Randolph county. The parents of Oscar Prince were Thomas J. Prince and Malissa Bloodworth Prince. Thomas Prince was born in Janes Creek township and Mrs. Prince was born in Oregon county, Missouri.

The parents of Mrs. Prince were Mr. and Mrs. Alfred Bloodworth, who came to the Ravenden Springs community from Tennessee. Mrs. Thomas Prince was married to James Higginbotham before her marriage to Mr. Prince. To this union were born R. L., Henry and Rosa (Henley) Higginbotham. After Mr. Higginbotham's death she married the father of our subject and they became the parents of four children, Oscar, Alfred, Ed and Birdie.

Oscar Prince was born December 13, 1890. He was married to Lockie Campbell, daughter of the late John D. and Beulah Brady Campbell. The Campbell family is one of the oldest in Lawrence county. Oscar and Lockie Prince are the parents of one child Oscar, Jr., who has recently been discharged from three years service in the U. S. Army Air Corps, serving in the European theater.

Oscar, Sr., is the present county judge of Randolph county, having entered the office January 1, 1945, and recently received the Democratic nomination for a second term without opposition. This is the first time on record in the county where a county judge of Randolph county had the honor of being unopposed for his second term. Besides being county judge he is associated with the son in the mercantile, farming and livestock business. Judge Prince has spent several years of his life as road contractor, besides dealing extensively in cotton farming and livestock raising.

He is a member of the Arkansas Livestock Sanitary Commission, this being his sixth year on this board. He has been justice of the peace several years, is a member of the Surridge School Board, and takes an active interest in all things of a civic nature.

Judge Prince is well known over the state and the Prince family is one of the leading families of the county.

THE A. F. RICKMAN FAMILY

A. F. Rickman, known during the past few years as "Uncle Frank," was born on Janes creek in Randolph county, the son of John and Dicy Bellah Rickman. His parents both died before he can remember. He had two brothers, James, who lived near Ravenden Springs, and Levi, who moved to Texas many years ago.

For many years Frank Rickman has been known as one of the best farmers in the county. He received very little schooling when young, but this did not keep him from being a success in life.

Mr. Rickman married Maud G. Wells, August 2, 1883. To this union were born eight children. Seven are living now. They are, Daley, who lives in Craighead county; Tom and Leo, who reside in this county; O. B. of Ravenden Springs, also of this county; and three daughters, Disa Cochran, Lovis Peevyhouse and Johnnie Cochran, all of Craighead county. They have 24 grandchildren living; of these, five grandsons served in World War II.

The Rickman family are of the Church of Christ belief and affiliation, and are all good Democrats.

One son, Leo, made the race for county treasurer in 1934, and carried more townships than the winner, however, losing two large townships to the latter. He entered this race again in 1938, but withdrew on account of the condition of the health of his aging parents.

Mrs. Frank Rickman is the daughter of John Wells, who was born in Washington county, Missouri, January 4, 1821, and was brought to Randolph county by his parents the same year. John Wells married Harriet Alcorn, July 13, 1848. She was the daughter of Isham Alcorn, one of the early settlers of this section, and was born on the farm where the Rickmans now reside, February 5, 1828. The children of John and Harriet Alcorn Wells were: Margaret, who married Shelton White; Susan, who married James McLain; Thomas H., who married Nettie Tweedy, who died young. He later married Lively Dalton; Lola, who married Robert Stubblefield; Mollie, who married Rufus C. Dalton; James P., William and Mrs. Rickman.

The father of John Wells was Thomas Wells, who married Barbra Mabrey. He was born in North Carolina in 1796 and she in Virginia in 1798, and died in Randolph county, Arkansas, in 1866 and 1869, respectively.

Mr. and Mrs. Rickman celebrated their 63rd wedding anniversary recently.

THE RUFF FAMILY

Dr. Redman Ren Ruff moved to Pocahontas from Hollow Rock, Tennessee, in 1866. In 1870 he moved to Pitman Ferry. He was born at Hollow Rock, Tennessee, April 25, 1831. His father, Major John Ruff, was born in North Carolina in 1770. The family originally came to Virginia from Scotland, in 1700, and then moved to North Carolina later.

Dr. R. R. Ruff's mother was Chloe Eason. The Easons were natives of Virginia. They moved to Tennessee about 1775. Dr. Ruff's first wife was also an Eason. Four children were born to this union. Mrs. Leota Ruff Shemwell of Batesville, Arkansas, is the only one now living. She was born in June, 1860, at Hollow Rock, Tennessee. Dr. Ruff's second wife was Amanda Wilson Legate, whom he married at Pitman in 1873. Her father was Rev. John Tarpley Legate, a Methodist preacher, born in Tennessee, October 15, 1818, died at Pitman, March 15, 1871. Amanda Legate's mother was Isabella Jennings Reeves, born January 17, 1822, died March 21, 1860. Mrs. Ruff was born October 21, 1848, in Tennessee, and died at Pitman, May 28, 1920. Dr. Ruff died at Pitman, September 21, 1898.

Horace Ewing Ruff, son of Dr. R. R. and Mrs. Amanda Ruff, was born at Pitman, July 15, 1873. Attended common schools and Southern Illinois Normal University, Carbondale, Ill. Graduated from the Missouri Medical College, now the Medical Department of Washington University, St. Louis, Missouri, March 26, 1894, with the degree of M. D.

Dr. Horace E. Ruff first married Charity Brown, daughter of Frank and Amanda Brown, October 6, 1895. She died at Pitman, December 11, 1905. To this union were born two children, Horace Ewing, Jr., July 2, 1899, and Flavia, July 16, 1897. Dr. Ruff was married a second time to Effie Agnes Lehman, daughter of John Milton Clayton and Tommie Harris Lehman, at Maynard, December 23, 1906. To this union were born two sons, Lehman Len Ruff, November 3, 1907 at Pitman. He died at Heber Springs, Arkansas, November 13, 1913. John Legate Ruff, born at Heber Springs, June 15, 1913.

Dr. Horace Ewing Ruff was elected representative of Randolph county in the lower house of the General Assembly and served the terms of 1905 and 1907. He was elected senator from the 26th district, composed of the counties of Cleburne, Conway, Van Buren, and Searcy, and served in the sessions of 1915 and 1917. In 1900 he was chairman of the Randolph County Democratic Committee; a member of the Arkansas State Democratic Central Committee and a delegate to, and attended every Democratic convention from Little Black township to the National

Democratic Convention in Kansas City. The Ruff family are good Democrats and Methodists.

Dr. Ruff was commissioned first lieutenant in the Medical Corps of the Arkansas National Guard, October 30, 1915; promoted to captain, June 19, 1916; major, January 8, 1917; on the Mexican border at Deming, New Mexico, with the first Arkansas Infantry, 1916 and 1917. Later served with the National Guard Division at Camp Beraregard, La., from November, 1917, to March, 1918. Major Ruff was sent overseas in May, 1918, where he joined the Third Division of the U. S. Army as surgeon of the 7th Infantry. He was in practically all the engagements fought by this U. S. Army. His outfit was in the Meuse-Argonne over 30 days. He was wounded and gassed at Cunel, France, October 21, 1918. After two month's hospitalization he rejoined his outfit at Andernach-on-the-Rhine and arrived at Camp Pike, Arkansas, September 1, 1919. He was later commissioner in the Medical Corps, January 9, 1926.

Colonel Ruff was recommended for the Distinguished Service Cross, received the Purple Heart, Order of the Silver Star. These medals were publicly presented to Colonel Ruff by Colonel (now President) Harry Truman at Camp Pike, Arkansas. He also was given a Mexican border medal and French Medal of Honor. After discharge from the Army, he was appointed general medical examiner for the U. S. Veterans Bureau and served in the Little Rock regional office as examiner and chairman of the rating board for 10 years. He now resides at Thirteenth and McAlmost Sts., in Little Rock.

Dr. Horace E. Ruff, Jr., the eldest son of Dr. Ruff, Sr., married Neecy Wood of Strong, Arkansas. Was in the Navy during World War I. Has his A. B. degree from Hendrix College; his Masters degree from Louisiana State University and Doctor of Philosophy from Ames, Iowa. He is now a professor of science at Louisiana Polytechnic Instiution, Ruston, Louisiana.

Flavia Ruff married Capt. William L. Thompson, Jr., at Camp Beruregard, Louisiana, Christmas Day, 1917. They have three children, William, III, Julia and Rosemary. Captain Thompson and family live at Magnolia, Arkansas. His son William served in World War II, is married and has one child, Patricia Ann. He is still in the Army Air Corps.

Dr. John Legate Ruff married Ruby Allen, January 11, 1943. They have one child, Marilyn, born in Little Rock, July 24, 1944. Dr. J. L. Ruff is a graduate of Little Rock High, Little Rock Junior College, Hendrix College, Conway, Arkansas, and the Medical Department of the University of Arkansas. He interned at Iowa Hospital, Iowa City, and was resident physician at Midway Hospital, St. Paul, Minn. He entered the service May 4, 1942, as first lieutenant, Medical Corps; promoted to captain, May 15, 1943. Wounded by Jap sniper on Leyte, December 16, 1944. Received special citation and Bronze Star. Honorably discharged January 29, 1946, and returned to private practice.

SHRIDE FAMILY AND ANCESTRY

Arthur Monroe Shirde is the oldest son of D. H. Shride. He was born December 23, 1900, at Wirth, Sharp county, Arkansas. He is the grandson of the late J. M. and Sarah Francis Shride of Ravenden Springs, Arkansas. His mother was Zilla Belle White, daughter of the late Howell and Susan White, early residents of Randolph county.

The brothers of Arthur M. Shride are Clifton of St. Louis, Missouri; Floyd of Manila, Arkansas, and Orville of Rector, Arkansas. His sister, Mrs. Monnie Bryan, lives near Dalton.

The Shride family are descendants of European immigrants who first settled in Pennsylvania. Howell White was a native of North Carolina.

Ruby Blanche, wife of Arthur M. Shride is a daughter of B. E. and Zilpha Chester Brown, and a granddaughter of the late George W. and Martha Brown. George W. Brown was born in Georgia, moving to Texas in an ox wagon, and later came to Randolph county, where he spent the remainder of his life.

B. E. Brown was born in Texas, August 5, 1872. He came with his parents to Randolph county, where he met his wife, Zilpha, daughter of James and Caroline Chester. Mrs. Shride has four sisters, Mrs. Henry King, Mrs. W. T. Foster, Mrs. Hershel Hackworth, all of Dalton, and Mrs. L. C. McIlroy of Little Rock.

A. M. Shride and Blanche Brown, teachers in the public schools of Randolph county, were married September 18, 1925. They have two daughters, Peggy and Janell. Peggy was born November 7, 1931. She likes music, books and outdoor sports. She is now a junior in high school. Janell was born February 5, 1938. She is in the fourth grade and likes books, bicycling, boatriding and both indoor and outdoor games.

Arthur has served the public in various capacities. In addition to his regular profession as a teacher, he has served as school director, justice of the peace, chairman of the Randolph County Teacher's Association, a member of the County Equalization Board, assistant tax assessor and barber.

The family has made Randolph county its home, with the exception of two years spent in Detroit, Michigan, during the recent war.

This family is related to many of the first families who settled on Elevenpoint river.

THE WILLIAM TIPTON STUBBLEFIELD-NANCY DALTON STUBBLEFIELD FAMILY

William Tipton Stubblefield and Nancy J. Dalton were married February 25, 1880. The former is descended from one of the very first families which settled on Elevenpoint river. He is a grandson of Fielding Stubblefield, who settled on this stream at an early date, probably coming here with his father and other members of this family before 1820.

When the first courthouse was built at Pocahontas, Fielding Stubblefield was one of the public building commissioners. Another member of this family, Coleman Stubblefield, was a member of the Territorial Legislature from old Lawrence county in 1829.

The parents of our subjects were Tipton Stubblefield and Sarah Garrett Stubblefield, who were married September 8, 1858. Our subject was the only child of this union. After the death of Tipton Stubblefield, his wife married Felix Mock and they became the parents of two sons, Tom and Jack Mock.

A sister of Tipton Stubblefield married Lewis Dalton, January 4, 1860. Her name was Sarah Anne, but was known as Aunt Sally. A cousin of William Stubblefield, Jeff D. Stubblefield, married Zilla Dalton, daughter of William Dalton.

The Garrett family was French. They came to America as refugees of the French Revolution.

William Tipton Stubblefield was born August 3, 1860, and died in August, 1941. He and Nancy J. Dalton were the parents of seven children. They are Rufe, who married Katie Cohn; Sarah, who married Thomas Carroll; Lawrence, who married Elvie Magruder; Myrtle, who married Myrt Bennett; Mara, who married Leonard Crews; Orlean, who married Major Christian, and Thomas and Pearl, who are not married. There are 20 grandchildren now living.

Mr. Stubblefield was a learned man. He was known to have been one of the best authorities on county government in the state. He served the county as tax assessor in 1892-3, and was auditor for the county many years. For many years this family had more public school teachers than any family in the county. It was a common saying in Randolph county for many years, "If you want to know anything about the records of the county, see Bill Stubblefield."

The family lived at Warm Springs many years, moving to Pocahontas about 1905. Uncle Bill and Aunt Nancy kept open house and hundreds of people enjoyed the hospitality of this home. She was a good cook and was always courteous and cheerful toward their guests.

Nancy J. Dalton Stubblefield is a descendant of one John Dalton, who was born in Ireland and came to the United States about 1760. the family moved to North Carolina, Virginia, and later to Kentucky. John Dalton served in the Revolutionary War. After the close of the Revolution he moved with his family to Madison county, Missouri. From here he came on down into Ripley county, where he spent the remainder of his life. This was about 1812.

He setled on Fourche Dumas creek at what is still known as the Dalton Mill ford, where the old Warm Springs-Doniphan road crosses this creek. He and other members of the family lie buried out in the bottom field near the present ford.

John Dalton was the father of Elijah, Jack, David, Maria and other children. Elijah was the father of Lewis Dalton and other children. Jack was the father of "Forg" Dalton, who was the father of Dr. J. W. Dalton late of this county. Maria married James Keel. David married Priscilla Dennis of Greenville, Missouri, in 1826. They were the parents of another Elijah, another David, Sarah who married George Matney, Susanna who married William Cross, John who died in the Civil War, Nancy who married Harrison Davis, Ruth who married James Parker, Priscilla who married John Bond and David who first married Christiana Everett.

Elijah, son of David Dalton and Priscilla Dennis Dalton, was the father of Nancy Dalton Stubblefield, one of the subjects of this sketch. This Elijah Dalton was born in southern Ripley county, Missouri, October 28, 1829. He married Grace Jane Head in 1857. They were the parents of the following children besides Nancy Stubblefield, our subject. They were John C., who first married Susan Poynor and later Sally Spencer; James, who married Nora McIlroy (who married Joseph Dalton after James died); Mary, who married William McIlroy; Sarah M., who married W. A. Holt; Elijah A., who married Ida Bell Mock, and Rufus, who married Daisy Downey.

The mother of our subject was, as stated above, Grace Jane Head, who was a daughter of Alexander and Elizabeth Head of Wayne county, Missouri. Mrs. Head's maiden name was Clubb. Elijah Dalton died in 1906 and his wife died some 10 years previous.

Nancy Dalton Stubblefield, our subject, died June 14, 1936.

The sponsor of this article, Mrs. Myrt Bennett, is a daughter of William T. and Nancy Dalton Stubbefield. Mrs. Bennett was born February, 17, 1893, her husband, Myrt Bennett, was born November 3, 1891. They are the parents of one son, William Myrt, Jr., who was born January 12, 1920. The son has recently been discharged from the U. S. Navy, where he served from August, 1942, to February 3, 1946. He was a lieutenant junior grade, and served as air traffic controller on the aircraft carrier *"Intrepid,"* and was also an officer on an LST.

Myrt Bennett is the son of Henry S. Bennett and Sadie Pratt Bennett, who were married July 20, 1878, and lived south of Warm Springs.

Both Mr. and Mrs. Bennett are former Randolph county school teachers, but for several years Mr. Bennett has been engaged in the mercantile business at Biggers. He also owns considerable real estate. His business is located at present in the three-story Biggers building, which he purchased from the Biggers family in 1945. He does a general furnishing business and has one of the best locations in the county.

The Bennett family are early residents of the central part of the county.

THE EUGENE GARDINER SCHOONOVER FAMILY

Miss Estelle Waddle and Eugene Gardiner Schoonover were married June 10, 1896, both of them being members of old and leading families of Randolph county.

Eugene G. Schoonover was a grandson of Daniel and Elizabeth Jacks Schoonover, natives of Pennsylvania. Jacob Schoonover was the son of Daniel and the father of Eugene.

Jacob Schoonover came to Arkansas in 1858, first settling in the town of Marion, but at the outbreak of the Civil War he was living in Randolph county and joined the Confederate Army under Col. Robert G. Shaver, at Pocahontas. He was married to Martha J. Wear of Pittstown, Pennsylvania, in 1870.

To this union five children were born, Eugene, Herbert W., Adelaide Virginia, and Parke and Vista, twins, the latter dying in infancy. Herbert was never married; Adelaide married Rev. W. R. Bennett and had two children, Katherine and William R., Jr. Martha Wear Schoonover died December 22, 1878, and her children were taken by Jacob Schoonover's various sisters in New Jersey and Pennsylvania, where they were reared to maturity and only Eugene and Herbert ever returend to Arkansas to make their homes. On January 5, 1882, Jacob Schoonover married Miss Ella Bolen, daughter of Capt. J. N. Bolen, a former newspaperman and postmaster of Pocahontas, and Mary Caroline Bolen, later affectionately known as "Granny," who died in the year 1941 at the age of 104 years. Jacob and Ella Schoonover had three children, Robert N., Jacob and Mary, Jacob dying at the age of 15 years and Mary becoming the wife of Ulric H. Reynolds. Jacob Schoonover was engaged in the mercantile business in Pocahontas for several years, but was elected to the office of circuit and county clerk in 1876 and served six years in this capacity. He was a Mason. Ulric Reynolds died in 1923, leaving two children Ulric, Jr., and Curtis Dennis. Both served in World War II and are now living in California.

Eugene Gardiner Schoonover was born in Pocahontas September 30, 1871, and died February 5, 1944. Shortly before his death it was said that he was the oldest man living in Pocahontas who was born there. For more than 50 years he was a member of the Randolph County Bar, was considered the most eminent attorney ever produced in Randolph county and had a statewide reputation for legal learning. He was graduated from the Law School of the University of Michigan in 1893. He was a member of the Methodist church and a Royal Arch Mason. He was a Past Master of Randolph Lodge No. 71.

Estelle Waddle Schoonover, on her paternal side, is a granddaughter of Dr. Jacob Waddle and Sarah Elizabeth Crepps Waddle, who were natives of Virginia and Kentucky. Her maternal grandparents were Adolphus H. and Mary A. McElrath Kibler, both of whom came to Randolph county in 1856 from North Carolina. Adolphus Kibler was county treasurer from 1878 to 1886. He was a Methodist and a Mason. His parents were Michael and Catherine Lorance Kibler.

Dr. Jacob and Sarah Elizabeth Waddle had two children, William H. Waddle (father of Mrs. Schoonover), and Isabella, who was the first wife of John P. Black. After the death of Dr. Waddle, his widow married William A. Hamil and they became the parents of Robert N. Hamil and Kate Hamil Henderson.

Adolphus Kibler and wife were the parents of seven children, Hattie, who married Dr. Crosby; Alice, who married Dr. Wise of Greene county; Ada, who died when 17 years of age; George, who married Louisa Bollinger; an infant named Willie; Bettie Ida, who died in infancy, and Augusta L., who married William H. Waddle to become the mother of Estelle Schoonover.

William H. Waddle and Augusta Kibler were married April 4, 1867, and were the parents of six children, as follows: John A., who died in infancy; Jacob Adolphus, William Walter, who died July 14, 1904 at age 26; Gordon Kibler, who died when four years of age; Mary Ives and Estelle. William H. Waddle died December 29, 1919, and his wife, Augusta, died in 1930, each at age of 82.

Mr. Waddle was a leading merchant of Pocahontas in the late 60's and early 70's. After this time he was prominent in insurance and real estate business. He was an Odd Fellow and member of the Methodist church.

Mrs. Waddle was also a Methodist and was active in church work as long as she was able. She fell, breaking her hip in 1912, and was never strong afterwards.

Jacob A. Waddle resides in Pocahontas at the present time, with his wife, the former Mayme Clopton, whom he married in 1920. Mary Ives married Harvey Midkiff in 1903. Mr. Midkiff died in 1941. The widow lives in Brinkley, Arkansas. They were the parents of the following: William Gordon, Mary Afton, Samuel Waddle, Richard H., James P., Thomas Woodrow and John Harvey.

Four children were born to the union of Eugene Gardiner Schoonover and Estelle Waddle. Martha Sylvesta and Eugene McDowell died in infancy in 1897 and 1899. William Jacob was born August 27, 1903, and Wear Kibler on

March 18, 1910. Jacob is a practicing attorney in Pocahontas, where he has been so engaged for 21 years. He was graduated from the University of Arkansas in 1923 and also from his father's alma mater, the University of Michigan at Ann Arbor, in 1926. He married Miss Verma Decker, in June, 1932. She is the daughter of Judge Joe S. and Oma Pickett Decker. They have one daughter, Adelaide Virginia, born May 17, 1933. Jacob Schoonover is a Mason; a Past Master, and also has been secretary of the local lodge for years.

Wear Kibler Schoonover, unmarried. With the exception of three and one-half years in the U. S. Navy, has been an attorney in the solicitor's office, U. S. Department of Agriculture, Washington, D. C., for more than 10 years. He attended the University of Arkansas for seven years and was graduated with honors from both the Literary and Law School. He attained national prominence in athletics, having been selected on the All-America football team in 1929, and was an all-conference performer in basketball, and also a member of the University baseball and track teams. In 1930 he accompanied a group of noted football players to Hollywood, where they made the picture "Maybe It's Love," which was shown in all leading theaters in the nation. He was a lieutenant commander when discharged from the Navy.

Eugene Schoonover died in February, 1944. Mrs. Schoonover still lives in the old home in Pocahontas. She is a member of the Methodist church and is active in religious and civic activities.

S. A. (DORE) SMITH

S. A. (Dore) Smith was born April 18, 1882, in Terre Haute, Indiana. Maud L. Murdock was born June 25, 1884, at Oxford, Arkansas. This couple were married March 4, 1904.

The father and mother of S. A. Smith were James Madison Smith, born in 1856, at Frankfort, Kentucky, and died July 4, 1918, at Datto, Arkansas, and Maria E. Herrington, born January 20, 1859, died February 15, 1905 at Datto, Arkansas.

The family of S. A. Smith moved from Terre Haute, Indiana, to Greenville, Illinois, in 1884. The family lived there 17 years, moving to Greenville, Missouri, in 1901. The next year, in 1902, they moved to Datto, Arkansas. In 1905, the year after their marriage, Mr. and Mrs. Smith moved to St. Louis, where S. A. took up an apprenticeship in the monument trade. They moved to Pocahontas in 1907 and have resided here ever since.

Politically, Mr. Smith has always been a Democrat. Religiously he first joined the Methodist Church in childhood. After his marriage he became a member of the Church of Christ. This is the church affiliation of the family, both Mr. and Mrs. Smith being consistent members.

Before becoming interested in the monument business Mr. Smith served 12 years as a baker.

Maud L. Murdock is a daughter of James Murdock and Martha Wallace Murdock. James Murdock was born in the state of Georgia and came first to Missouri with the Hamilton family, who adopted him after the death of his parents. He lived a short time in Eastland county, Texas, but died in Weber Falls, Oklahoma, in 1897. Mrs. Murdock is still living at the present time, in the home of her daughter, Mrs. Smith, in Pocahontas, at the age of 86. Her father was

FAMILY HISTORY

Silas Wallace, who lived in Siloam township, this county, about 40 years ago. There were 10 children in the Murdock family, four boys and six girls. There were seven children in the James Madison Smith family, four girls and three boys.

S. A. Smith and Maud L. Murdock are the parents of the following children: Cordia, born March 12, 1905; Henley, born March 21, 1909; Burrus, born May 30, 1912; and Lucille, born May 11, 1914. Lucille died May 6, 1946.

Cordia married Abe Hepner, April 16, 1944. She has two children by a former marriage, Jeanne and Patsy. Patsy married B. E. Foster in 1946. Henley married Mary Lou Stricklin, June 30, 1938. Burrus married Earlene Weir, October 13, 1939. They have one child, Dianne. Lucille married Elmer Bowen, February 1, 1932. They were the parents of one son, Joe. Lucille and family lived at Jonesboro at the time of her death.

Henley and Burrus are the owners of the Imperial Theater in Pocahontas, and have made an outstanding success in this business.

Cordia now lives in Indiana.

Mr. and Mrs. Smith recently moved into their new home, on the Dalton road near the Baptist College. Until this year Mr. Smith was engaged in the monument business, which he had followed several years.

The Smith family is well known and a highly respected family of Pocahontas, where they have lived 39 years.

THE SHAVER FAMILY

The Shaver family is one of the largest which has lived in Randolph county. Being one of the first in the county, they have intermarried with many of the other first families, the result of which is that many persons in this section of the state today have Shaver blood in their veins who have varied family names.

There are three "families" of the Shavers in this section of the state who trace their ancestry to a common source. One of these is the family now represented in Sharp and Fulton counties. Another is the Shaver family which settled in the extreme lower end of Cherokee Bay, soon after 1800. Col. Robert G. Shaver of Civil War fame was a member of the Sharp county Shavers. Shaver's Eddy on Black river about 10 miles above Pocahontas is near the first home of the Cherokee Bay Shavers. This is just south of the lower end of Cherokee Bay. Here Michael, Daniel, Jacob W. and other Shavers lived around 1820 or before. This branch of the family is closely related to the Shavers of which this article will deal.

John Shaver came to Randolph county from Georgia about 1828, after other members of his family had already settled here. He settled in what is now possibly Ingram township, where he lived the rest of his life, dying in 1850. He was married in 1823 to Nancy Cook, before coming to this county. To this union was born 11 children, eight reaching maturity. They were William, Robert, James F., Alexander, Martha who married C. Johnson; Caroline, who married John Johnson; Nancy, who married Jesse Johnson; John, who was killed at the Battle of Shiloh in 1862, and Peter. William was a minister of the Church of Christ, as was Peter. The two brothers organized and preached to some of the first congregations of this church in north Arkansas.

There is in this section of the state today descendants of all the children of John and Nancy Cook Shaver, named above, especially that of James F. and Peter.

The children of James F., who married Elizabeth Waddle, were: Alexander, Jacob, J. H., Louis, James, Matilda, who married Jeff Morris; Sarah, who married Eli Morris; Rufus L., Peter M., W. M., Joseph A., and Daisy, who married Lee Bolen. Peter Shaver married Lucinda Waddle, a sister of James F. Shaver's wife.

The parents of Elizabeth and Lucinda Waddle were Henry Waddle and Sarah Biggers Waddle. They were married in 1836. Mr. Waddle came to this county from Tennessee in 1832. Besides the wives of the Shaver brothers, they were the parents of the following children: Sarah, who married (Muxy) Jim Johnson; Susan, who married David Roberts; Caroline, who married Vincent Segraves; Marietta (Aunt Queen), who married Frank Hawk and T. J. Tiner; Matilda, Jefferson, James and George.

Peter Shaver married Lucinda Waddle in 1853. To this union was born the following children: Louvenia, who married Alexander Davis; Jane, who married J. B. Long; America, who married General Mock; Susan, who married James Edwards; Nancy, who married Alfred Payne; Robert D., William (twins), G. R., Joseph and A. B. (Robert, William and Joseph died young).

The only living members of this family at this time are Mrs. Edwards, G. R. and A. B. Mrs. Edwards lives in Clay county; G. R. (Ran) lives on the site of old Ingram (Gooberhull), the old Shaver homestead, and A. B. lives in Pocahontas. A. B. is a minister of the Church of Christ and has spent many years in faithful service of the cause of Christ.

A. B. Shaver and Martha Fowler were married in July, 1897. To this union were born eight children, six sons and two daughters. They are, Horace, who married Glen Kerr;

Hardy, who married Amy Ford; Willie, who marred Lilly Rice; Carl (deceased); Curtis and Arlo, who have recently been discharged from service in World War II, they are not married; Florence, married Walter Mays and Hassel married Delbert Johnson.

A. B. Shaver entered the ministry when he was 25 years of age. During these long years of service for his Master, he has baptised over 4,000, held over 3,000 funeral services and performed over 2,500 marriage ceremonies. He has the honor of performing the first marriage ceremony in the new Randolph county courthouse.

There are about 35 active congreagtions of the Church of Christ in the county and Eld. A. B. Shaver has the distinction of being instrumental in the establishment of as many as 20 of them. He has also met in public discussion 10 times.

Louvena, daughter of Peter and Lucinda Waddle Shaver, a sister of Eld. Shaver named above, married Alxender Davis, a native of Illinois, in 1876. She was born December 23, 1854. Mr. Davis died April 22, 1916. Mrs. Davis died April 28, 1942. To this union was born three sons and one daughter. They were G. G., A. B., J. B., and Essie May.

J. B. (Baxter) married Emma Wright, daughter of George W. Wright. They were the parents of two children, Charles E., a barber of Corning, and Lessie Mae, who married George Guyns. She also lives at Corning.

A. B. (Amos) married Ganie Mock, daughter of Isham and Elizabeth Morris Mock. They live in Pocahontas. They are the parents of four children, Arvil C., who recently returned from overseas service in the German area; Marie, who married Fred Cousins. Her husband also is a veteran of World War II; Lowell R., who married Jessie Long, daughter of Rayburn and Vada Long. Lowell also served in the late war, in the Japan area; Athlene, unmarried at home.

Essie Davis married Press Ramsey, both are deceased, as is one of the four children. The living children are, Gladys, who married Martin Fowler; Charlie, who married Laura Hayes; Jessie, who married Burley J. Sutherland, and Beulah, who is deceased.

G. G. (Green) married Nettie J. Starling, August 12, 1900. Mrs. Davis was a daughter of George W. and Fronia Howard Starling.

They were the parents of four children. Three died in infancy. One, Rector L., lives in Pocahontas, and is a barber by trade. Rector married Ada Spikes, daughter of Jack W. and Ina Johnson Spikes. Rector and wife have one son, Henley Leland. Nettie Davis died October 12, 1944. G. G. survives her. He lives with his son in Pocahontas at the present time.

Green Davis is a native of the Ingram-Palestine community where his maternal ancestors (the Shaver family) have lived for a century and a quarter. He served for many years as justice of the peace of Ingram township, and other official capacities. Since the death of his wife he has resided in Pocahontas, where he is now serving his second year as deputy tax assessor of Randolph county. G. G. is noted for his penmanship, being possibly the best Spencerian penman in the county.

During his younger days he also built up quite a reputation as a "southpaw" pitcher on the Ingram ball team, which for many years was one of the best in the county. This family history article was sponsored by Eld. A. B. Shaver and G. G. Davis.

MR. AND MRS. WILLIAM HENRY JOHNSTON

UNCLE WILLIAM AUNT MARTHA

Top: September 8, 1878
Bottom: September 8, 1928

FAMILY HISTORY

THE SPIKES FAMILY

(Contributed by Ben Johnston)

William (Pappy Billy) Spikes, born in 1784, and died in 1855. The family is of English descent. Part of William Spikes' family was born in or near Raleigh, North Carolina. In 1815 they moved to Graves county, Tennessee, remaining here only five years, landing in 1820 in the foothills of the Ozarks, on a beautiful creek which he named "Tennessee," at a point near where the Ingram postoffice is now located. He built his log residence near an everflowing spring, and in 1828 homsteaded the land. In 1830 he built his first church on this land and named it "Mount Pisgah." This house soon proved to be too small, on account of the increase of new settlers, and a larger one was built in 1840.

William Spikes died in 1857 but the settlers continued to fill this area and a third church was built between 1880 and 1885 by his family and friends. All these buildings were built by donation labor. Just who did the work on the first two is not known. Of the last building, we have the names of William Deaver, James Hurn, James Barnett, Isaac and Thomas Hopkins, Frank Tiner and Nathaniel and Jackson Cox, in addition to the Spikes family. Of course, there are other names who assisted as it was a large well-built frame building ,a credit to any rural community.

Possibly Rev. Larkin F. Johnston, my paternal grandfather, a young minister from Tennessee, was the first resident preacher for this church.

William Spikes first married Elizabeth Biddle, of Scotch descent, and to this union were born Jesse, Joseph, William, Nancy and Martha. His second wife was Malinda Masterson, and to this union was born Flin, Samuel, Elizabeth and Mary.

Due to the time involved and the fact that the family is so badly scattered, I will confine this article from here on, to my own branch of the family tree.

Jesse Spikes was born April 2, 1808 and died, January 7, 1887. He was my grandfather. The information included herein is taken principally from an article prepared by my mother, about the family, for her children, kinsmen and friends.

Jesse Spikes first married Nancy Copeland and to this union were born, William Anthony, Nancy, Joseph Washington, David Lafayette, James Monroe, Jesse Hezekiah and Elizabeth. His second wife, my grandmother, was Eliza Stone, maiden name Kersey. She had two little girls, Mary and Octava, daughters of her first husband, Rufus Stone, another Tennessean. To the union of Eliza Stone and Jesse Spikes were born Ben F., John W., Martha and Malissa.

James, William and David were Confederate soldiers. James died in Bowling Green, Kentucky; William in Little Rock, Arkansas, and David soon after he returned home from the war, from exposure during service. Nancy married Tone Carroll; Joseph W. married Judy Nelson; Jesse H. married Nancy J. Early; Elizabeth married John R. Davis; Ben F. married Sarah P. Dalton; John W. married Tuda Foster; Malissa married Rufus C. Dalton and Martha, my mother, married William Henry Johnston.

My father and mother were married September 8, 1878, to which union were born Ben E. (the writer); Anna E., Magdeline, and Martha Ella. Father was born January 5, 1852 and died December 20, 1929. Mother was born August 2, 1859 and died February 10, 1938. Anna E. was born March 1, 1886 and died July 14, 1908.

The Spikes family, generally have been tillers of the soil, however several have been public officials of Randolph county and elsewhere. Some are teachers, doctors, preachers, lawyers, merchants, etc.

In the deed records of Randolph county will be found proper deeds for the four-acre church lot and the four-acre cemetery lot which was deeded to the Methodist Episcopal Church, South, and for use as a cemetery, by Jesse and Samuel Spikes. Soula M. Spikes lives on a little farm nearby and takes great interest in the property.

Some day, who knows, when the cycle is turned, but what this now almost abandoned section may again become the pride of the county, and some far-seeing future "Pappy Billy" lead the way to the erection of a shrine in the form of a church, school or hospital, on this beautiful little four acres of gently rolling primitive land. Then this courageous pioneer can look back with pride to this, once wilderness spot, which he and his neighbors dedicated as a pioneer community, a better place to live and enjoy God's blessings. —Ben Johnston.

THE BENJAMIN FRANKLIN TAYLOR FAMILY

Benjamin Franklin Taylor was born September 9, 1860, the son of Alexander Taylor and Martha Dismang Taylor, near Supply, Randolph county, Arkansas. He married Martha Ellen Moore in September, 1880. She was a daughter of D. C. and Sarah Johnston Moore. Mrs. Taylor was born January 12, 1859, and died July 26, 1929, in St. Louis and was buried at Poynor, Missouri. Elders W. A. Goodwin and T. E. Sherrill of the Church of Christ conducted services.

To this union was born five children, three girls, Francis Evaline, born November 3, 1882; Alice, born March 31, 1884; Jessie May, born March 3, 1886; two boys, Robert Lee, born April 13, 1888, and Benjamin Palmer, born October 19, 1892. Mr. and Mrs. Taylor moved over the line into Ripley county, Missouri, in September, 1892, where they cleared a large farm and reared their family.

The father of Benjamin Taylor was born November 19, 1823, and died in 1880. His mother died in 1859. To this union was born five children. They were, Sarah Francis, born in 1850; General Marion, born in 1852; Albert Anderson, born in 1856, our subject, and an infant named Ollie. After the death of his first wife, the father of our subject married Miss Candy Pearce and to this union was born three boys, Columbus, Andrew and Henry, all deceased.

The grandfather of Benjamin Taylor was one Asa Taylor, who moved from Graves county, Kentucky to settle near Supply, Ark. Asa Taylor was born February 5, 1801, and died in 1865. His wife was born November 29, 1803, and died about 1856. Asa Taylor was married a second time July 3, 1858, to Miss Nancy Ainley. William Torrence Johnson, who was the father of the late Uncle John A. Johnson, was a son-in-law of Asa Taylor. The elder Johnson settled near Asa Taylor in 1885.

The Taylor family is of Scotch descent and a majority of this family are members of the Church of Christ. This family, together with the Cox, Johnson and other families established the old Glaze Creek Church of Christ, which is still in existence and one of the very first churches in this county. Our subject, Benjamin Taylor, states that "while none of the family have been known to turn the world upside down they have been honest and I never knew of one of them going to jail." He remembers when almost everything used in the home and otherwise, was home-made. He states that he can remember, as a boy, watching his father grind the tanbark for use in making his own leather, with which he made shoes for the family and neighbors. When the doctor was called in that period, Mr. Taylor states that he brought a "saddle bag full of roots and herbs which he brewed up his remedies of, and after treating the patient, charged a dollar and went home." In giving us this family history article of his family, Mr. Taylor dedicates it to the pioneers who, as he states it, "I hold a warm spot in my heart for all those old pioneers, including my ancestors, who fought through thick and thin, so we might have a Christian nation to live in."

As a parting admonition to his children and grandchildren he states, "I am writing this, in order that you and your children may know more about your foreparents than we at present do. Also, in closing, I admonish you, girls when you start out in life and choose a companion, resolve never to allow lips which touch liquor to touch yours, and to the boys, remember that boys who go to Sunday school regularly seldom ever go to prison for committing crimes."

WILLIAM JEFFERSON McCOLGAN

(Contributed to his memory, by the Author)

The subject of this sketch was born in south-central Illinois about 1856. The writer knows very little about his family, except that he had a sister, Mrs. Tom J. Buck, who lived at Reyno several years and a brother, Wesley, who was a prominent citizen of Dexter, Missouri, 25 years ago. "Uncle Jeff," as he was familiarly known, married a cousin of the late Judge J. W. Meeks, long a resident of Pocahontas, and was the father of one daughter, who married Rolla Irvin. Uncle Jeff was an early educator of Wayne county, Illinois. Judge Meeks was a pupil of his. He was also a schoolmate of the late Senator William Borah of Idaho, who was reared at Fairfield, Illinois. Uncle Jeff was one of the commissioners who designed and built the present courthouse at Fairfield, Wayne county, Illinois.

Uncle Jeff McColgan came to Reyno about 1910 and stayed a while and then came back in 1924, to spend the rest of his life there, where he died in March, 1935. He was mayor at Morehouse, Missouri, when that town was a much larger town than Sikeston. After coming to Reyno, he served as mayor for about six years and was one of the best officials which this town ever had. It was the privilege of the writer to serve as recorder of the town at the time Uncle Jeff was mayor. He dealt justice to all who came into his court "without fear or favor" in the fullest sense of the word. We served during the hectic days of the bootlegging heyday. While other folks would have made a lot of enemies, Uncle Jeff had a way that kept most of the folks as his friends. One fellow who often found himself in the mayor's court, said: "We cuss Uncle Jeff all winter and then vote for him in the spring."

In memory of one of the greatest characters I ever met, I dedicate this brief article to the memory of William Jefferson McColgan, pioneer educator, public official, and my departed friend.

EUGENE THOMPSON

Louis Thompson, great-grandfather of the subject of this sketch, was born in Ireland in 1776. His father had lived in the Colony of Virginia many years, but, being a loyal supporter of the English Crown, he returned with his family to Ireland about 1775 when the war clouds began to gather over the American colonies. As a youth he was imbued with the spirit of American freedom, and the fireside stories of his parents augmented his desire to cast his lot with the peoples of the New World. So, on reaching his majority, he came to Virginia, and a few years later migrated to Tennessee, the youngest and perhaps the wildest state in the Union. Here on December 15, 1805, he married Nancy Biddle, a daughter of a Scotch landholder, who was a well-to-do planter of that time.

He fought with Jackson in the War of 1812. After the Battle of New Orleans, January 8, 1815, he returned home on the Biddle plantation in Hawkins county, Tennessee, where he died a short time later from the ravages and exposures of war. So far as is known he was the only member of his family to make a permanent home in America.

The family records show that he and Nancy Biddle were the parents of five children, all born in Hawkins county, and that the mother died in 1817. The children, John Biddle, 1806; Nancy, 1808; Elizabeth, 1809; Mary, 1811, and William, 1813—were placed with Biddle relatives, inasmuch as there were no Thompson relatives in America to share them. An uncle, William Spikes, received our subject's grandfather, William Thompson. In 1820 he came with this Spikes family, who settled on Tennessee creek in Randolph county. He lived the rest of his life here.

He was a farmer and wagon maker and served as judge of the county (1860-2). January 2, 1836 he married Mary McLain, a lady of Irish descent, who was the mother of John Biddle, William Washington, Nancy, Elizabeth, Samuel Wilson and David Dixon. By a later marriage to Sarah Jane McCoy he was the father of Gideon, Olin, Stephen Tell (Pocahontas postmaster Cleveland first administration), and Willis (McIlroy), who have descendants in Randolph county. John Biddle and William Washington fought with the Confederacy in the War Between the States, and, as his father often said: "They fought all day on Sunday hard; the latter one was slain at sundown of the second day on Shiloh's bloody plain."

Sam Wilson Thompson, born December 9, 1845, was married to Maria Elizabeth Adams, born April 20, 1849, in Bedford county, Tennessee, on December 20, 1866. To this marriage two daughters and two sons, living in Randolph county, were born—Beatrice Hufstedler, Birdell community, who has three sons and four daughters living there and two daughters in Oklahoma: H. Ella White, whose son Tell Thompson lives in Philadelphia; Edward, whose sons, Earl of Kansas, Ralph and Joed, in Memphis, and a daughter,

Jessie Lee Davis, Pocahontas; and Eugene, subject of this sketch. He served the last two years in the War Between the States with Capt. Wibb Conner's Cavalry Company and was elected first county tax assessor under our present State Constitution. He farmed practically all his life on Massingale (Thompson-Baker) creek and died there April 20, 1921. Mrs. Thompson's father came from Tennessee in 1856 and settled on Elevenpoints, the farm later being known as Pratt place and is now owned by Judge Bledsoe. She died November 15, 1914.

Eugene Thompson was born on a creek farm in what is now Shiloh township January 14, 1882, did farm work and attended rural schools. Later he attended high school in Pocahontas and Walnut Ridge under the tutorship of Professor Watkins and went to business school in Little Rock. From 1901 to 1915 inclusive he taught in grade and high schools of Randolph, and played first base for Water Valley, Shiloh and Ouachita-Maynard Academy teams. He was county school examiner (1910-14) and in 1931 was elected to a six-year term on the County Board of Education, of which he was chairman. He was elected county coroner in 1942 and is incumbent.

In 1916 he went into the general mercantile business on Bettis Street with his brother-in-law. On account of age Mr. White retired in 1931, and in 1934 Thompson changed to groceries exclusively and was in that business until 1942, when he retired to retain his health.

November 8, 1918, he married Ethel Miller, daughter of Martha and the late William F. Miller of Ravenden Springs. Born to this union were one daughter and two sons—Mrs. Eileen Moore of Park Avenue; Samuel William, instructor in University of Minnesota working for doctor's degree in chemistry, and Everett Eugene, GI student in Arkansas University since being discharged from Air Corps as lieutenant. She died April 27, 1925. Two years and two months later he married Mae Galbraith, daughter of the late George and Belle Galbraith, granddaughter of John Janes, reputed to be the first white settler of Randolph county about 1805 on Janes' creek.

(Author's note: A few days after the article above was submitted to us for publication in this history, Samuel William, son of the subject of this sketch was accidentally drowned. This occurred June 16, 1946, in Minnetonka Lake, in Minneapolis, Minnesota. Young Thompson was with a Sunday school party when it happened.)

THE WYATT FAMILY

The Wyatt family is descended from a long and honorable line of Norman, French and English stock. Adam Guiot (the Norman spelling of the name), came over with William the Conqueror, and took part in the Battle of Hastings, and settled in south England, where his descendants took a prominent part in English history.

Sir Henry Wiat (a later spelling which still later became Wyat), was a favorite of King Henry VII and King Henry VIII. He was the father of the famous poet, Sir Thomas Wiat.

Sir Hawthe Wiat was a minister at the Coloney of Jamestown, under the governorship of his brother Sir Francis, and became the head of the Wyatts of Virginia. A descendant, Daniel Wyatt took part in many engagements of the Revolutionary War, and was also an early settler in Tennessee. Daniel Wyatt, the head of the Randolph county clan, came to this county in 1837, accompanied by his wife, Janesy Nichols Wyatt and three children, Daniel, Evaline and Albert P. Seven others stayed at their old home in Stewart county, Tennessee. The writer has not been able to secure much information regarding this part of the family.

Daniel was educated in the schools of this county. On Elevenpoint river still stands an old rock chimney which he helped to build when 11 years of age. He was married three times. His first wife was Nancy C. Burrow, widow of Jesse Burrow. They had five children, Letha C., Ella, Marion and two that died in infancy. Letha married J. T. Bennett. They moved to Oklahoma and reared a large family. Ella married J. W. Knoy and they moved to Texas and also reared a large family. Marion married Ella Jane Bryan. He became a teacher for many years in the schools of Randolph county. His last home was at Maynard where he died in 1914. They had 10 children, four of whom are living, in 1946. Oscar E., postmaster at Bono, Arkansas; Katie Clarice Wilkinson, Baton Rouge, Louisiana; Vera Mabel Watkins, Monette, Arkansas, and Daniel Bryan, Richmond Heights, Missouri.

Daniel's second wife was Bethany J. Flannery and they had three children, Marvin (his children are a son Daly who lives at Kennett, Missouri, and a daughter, Mrs. Tola Johnson who lives at Pocahontas); John, who has a large family living at Havana, Arkansas, and Nancy Jane, who with her husband, C. H. Tyler, lives on the old homestead built near Elevenpoint by her father. The Tylers have a son, Arthur of St. Louis; a son Hubert, assistant postmaster at Newport, and a daughter Elsie Magruder, living in Chicago.

Daniel's third marriage was to Mrs. Ellen A. Chesser, maiden name Ellis. They had one son, Jethro, who married Florence Lemmons and had three children. Dora, Dorothy and Eugene. He died at Egypt, Arkansas, in 1938.

(Contributed by Oscar E. Wyatt.)

SOLOMON M. WHITE

The subject of this sketch is one o fthe best known citizens of the county. He was born April 22, 1859 in Lyons county, Kentucky, and came to Randolph county in September, 1880. For several years he was one of the county's leading teachers. Mr. White was county treasurer four years and county judge four years. "Uncle Sol," as he is affectionately known, is a member of the Church of Christ and is a very devout member, seldom missing Sunday services. He is an active justice of the peace and keeps regular hours at the courthouse each day.

Mr. White has the following to say about his family:

"My grandparents on my father's side were Ezekiel and Elizabeth White. They lived in Beverly, Massachusetts. I only know of three children of this union: my father George, an Uncle William and Aunt Edna. My father was a sailor on the high seas from a boy until about 40 years of age. At that time he came to Kentucky where he met and married my mother, about 1838. To this union nine children were born. Their names are as follows: Mary Susan, who married Dr. Martin Hogan; Samuel, Eliza, Matthew, Elizabeth, John E, Sarah, Edna and myself. I am the only one living of the family at this time. I never knew my uncle William or Aunt Edna. They settled somewhere in Tennessee. Aunt Edna married a Mr. Fraizer and they moved to Texas. I made some effort to locate the families in recent years but failed to find them.

"My mother's people came from Vermont to Kentucky about the close of the seventeenth century, and settled on the east side of the Cumberland river, in what was then called Caldwell county, now Lyons county. The settlement was called 'Yankeetown.' My great-grandparents were named Hill. I do not know their given names. My grandparents were Jonas and Mary Martin. They were the parents of six sons, as follows: Solomon, for whom I was named; George, Henry, William, Truman and Isaac. Five daughters, Mariah, Sarah, Lucy, Susan, and Catherine, my mother. I only remember seeing Uncles Solomon and George, Aunt Sarah and mother.

"My father died when I was a small child and I remember very little about him. My mother also died when I was small. I was reared by other folks who told me very little about my people. My mother's relatives, who came to Kentucky from Vermont, were the Hills, Martins, Hawleys, Walkers, and Lyons. This Lyon family was the same as General Matthew Lyons.

"Since I came to Arkansas in September, 1880, I have taught school, worked in stores, in fact did almost all kinds of work except make ties.

"In 1881 while making my home with Prof. John Hogan and wife, I met Miss Katie E. Jones, a sister of Mrs. Hogan. She and two sisters, Miss Annie Jones and Mrs. Lillie Curd, a small son and daughter, came here from Murray, Kentucky.

"On December 7, 1884, I married Katie Jones, at the home of the late W. H. Tipton, just east of Maynard. To this union three children were born. They were, Annie Maye (now Mrs. Annie Maye Cherry), born February 21, 1886; Jimmie, born September 11, 188, died in infancy; Thomas, born September 9, 1889, died September 10, 1903.

"After the death of my first wife I married my present wife, Miss H. Ella Thompson, September 29, 1895. To this union one son was born January 15, 1897, named Tell Thompson White. Tell is a civil engineer and works for the Federal government. He is stationed at present in Philadelphia, Pennsylvania. He graduated as civil engineer at the University of Arkansas at 18 1-2 years of age. He is also a geologist and petroleum engineer.

FAMILY HISTORY

"I was elected to the office of county treasurer in September, 1902, and served four years. In 1906 I was elected county judge and served four years in this office."

Such is the family story of Judge Solomon M. White, aged 87 years in the year 1946.

PIONEER MERCHANDISING IN RANDOLPH COUNTY

The modern historian and writers have written volumes about the early educator. Politicians have recorded the activities of their predecessors in office. Statues have been carved from stone and set up to honor the deeds of valor of the man who went to war. Songs have been sung in memory of the early men of God who went forth in a new land to proclaim the gospel of our Savior. But who has honored the early "storekeeper"?

As little as we may think about it, the man who set up the early trading post in the wilderness community was a very necessary part of what we now class as the "economic structure" of the community. He lived no hero's life and died to no martyr's death, yet he contributed much to the endless chain of transformation of the land from its primitive setting to the picture we see spread before us today.

Just who the first merchant in what is now Randolph county was will never be known. Who ever he was, he was undoubtedly located at Davidsonville on Black river, 10 miles below the present site of Pocahontas, at the Fourche de Thomas village, which was located where the old Southwest Trail crossed the stream of the same name or at Pitman's Ferry, first called Hix's Ferry on Current river, where the stream runs into Arkansas from Missouri.

William Hix opened a ferry here between 1800 and 1803 and it is likely that he operated a trading post in connection, as we find a flourishing frontier village here only a few years later. Seven miles on down the old road to the southwest, at Fourche de Thomas, Dr. William Jarrett, John Gould Fletcher, Resin Davis, Jasper Blackburn, Matthias Mock, John Shaver and a number of other pioneers had already hewed out a settlement and at least one trading post was open soon after the first days of 1800. Dr. Jarrett was the neighborhood doctor and there is some evidence that Dr. Peyton R. Pitman was also here this early and was the first merchant also. He became owner of Hix's Ferry about 1810 or 1812, and the place has been known as Pitman's Ferry ever since. So Dr. Pitman has the distinction of being one of the first settlers at both Pitman's Ferry and Fourche de Thomas. The name of Fourche de Thomas was changed to Columbia and the community and township is still known by that name. When Dr. George Englemann, the noted German scientist, came down the old Southwest Trail, which later became known as the old Military Road, in 1837, David Plott was the village merchant here. He states in an account of his journey that Mr. Plott was an industrious "Pennsylvania Dutchman," who had been living here several years at the time. He states that Plott operated the store, a nice farm which had a very fine orchard and a distillery in another village. Merchandise for the stores was hauled in ox wagons from Greenville, Mo., a distance of 100 miles north. The first wholesaler in Southern Missouri was located at Greenville and he bought his goods in St. Louis and New Orleans and they were shipped by steamboat and other watercraft on the Mississippi to the old French river town, St. Genevieve, and hauled over the hills of Southern Missouri to the first named village. Merchandise for the stores at Pitman evidently came the same way. Possibly some light boats ran up Current river as far as the state line but we have no proof of this.

The Hanover brothers, three Jews, opened a store at Pitman around 1825 and later at Columbia. They became wealthy and owned much real estate. After Pocahontas became the county seat they opened a business in the town and for half a century their names were identified with the business of the town.

Another of the first merchants of Randolph county was John Miller, who opened a store at Davidsonville about 1814. He was the father of Gov. William R. Miller. Lewis de Mun, a Frenchman and the first clerk of old Lawrence county, was also one of the first men in business at this place, as was John Davidson, a jeweler who is given credit for the establishment of this town which became the first postoffice site in the state, besides having the first courthouse also. Descendants of Davidson now reside in Nashville, Tenn., which is located in Davidson county, named for the family. Other descendants of the family, a member of which the first postoffice in the state was named, also live in Ripley county, Missouri.

An interesting story is told of an incident that happened while John Miller was in business at Davidsonville. Miller sold whiskey, in addition to many other items. A fellow came to his store one day and purchased a barrel of liquor and a week later was back for another one. When questioned by Mr. Miller about disposing of so much in such a short time replied, "Waal, I don't think this is so bad since there is 10 of us in the family, and we don't have any cow."

There was a French trading post where Pocahontas is now located as early as 1790, but we know no names connected with the old village. We do know that whoever was here traded with the Indians in the vicinity and Fourche de Mas (now called and written "Dumas") creek which runs into Black river just north of the present city limits is supposed to have gotten its name from an early French trader by that name (de Mas). No one seems to know just how Pocahontas came to be named for the Indian princess who saved the life of Capt. John Smith. The first settler on the site of Pocahontas is reputed to have been Ransom S. Bettis. He operated a trading post here, dating from 1815. Tradition has it that there was a place called Pocahontas located a short distance down the river below the present town, but the actual site of Pocahontas was known as Bettis Bluff from 1815 until 1835, when it was made the county seat of Randolph county. In view of this, Mr. Bettis, a North Carolina native, is given credit for being the first merchant of Pocahontas.

It is a well-known story that Thomas S. Drew, who

married the only daughter of Mr. Bettis, met her on one of his visits to the store of Bettis, while on a trip through the county as an itinerant peddler, several years before he became governor of Arkansas.

Merchants of Pocahontas who came soon after Bettis were Hunter and Rayburn, Oaks and Truly and other names famous in the county history, including Hubbell, a saddle and harness maker, and B. M. Simpson, who was the county's first treasurer. A Mr. McCleary was the first tanner, a very necessary occupation at that time, and John L. Glasscock, who was licensed by the first County Court to "sell all kinds of liquor and groceries for a period of one year for a license of $10." On down the line of Pocahontas merchants came John and William McDowell, R. Nicholas, John P. Black, Isaac Hurst, Jacob Schoonover, Levi Hecht, R. N. Hamil and many other men who made good in this field and were valuable citizens in the county and town.

Getting away from the county seat again, we find D. W. Reynolds as the first merchant at the town of Old Reyno, where he was one of the founders and for whom the town was named. Here Mr. Reynolds and other men supplied the settlers of Cherokee Bay before the days of the Civil war. At Peru with a steamboat landing on Current river near by, called Sims Landing, was another early trading post in that section. Thomas S. Drew and his wife Cinderella Bettis Drew, lived on a plantation which was given the latter by her father, Ransom Bettis, in the early 1830s, on what is now the site of Biggers. There was evidently a trading point on the river here at that time, but we have no evidence to that end. In 1889 B. F. Bigger established a ferry, store and distillery on this site and a village named for him sprang up, which received a boost when the Frisco railroad came this way in 1902. Daniel McIlroy was the postmaster and merchant at Peru, mentioned above, in 1883. The store and office was at the present site of the Nick's store and service station near Current river beach. McIlroy also operated a cotton gin in partnership with Albert Hatley, here.

Merchandise for the first stores in Cherokee Bay came up Current river in boats which originally started either from St. Louis or New Orleans. Possibly the actual boats that were used on the Mississippi were not used on the smaller streams, although some were. This was true of the first shipments to come to Davidsonville, Powhatan, Pocahontas and on up the rivers to the head of navigation.

The inland towns like Maynard, Ravenden Springs, Warm Springs, Middlebrook, Dalton and other places, received their merchandise from the same sources, but this necessitated an overland haul of several miles at the final end of the journey.

Other early merchants not listed above, in the county, were Pitman and Looney at Pitman, Thad Ator at Cedarville, an early trading post on Fourche creek near the state line, above Middlebrook. Middlebrook came into existence soon after the close of the Civil war, with Reuben Wilson and Lewis B. Johnston as merchants, and Dr. William Carrens as first postmaster and physician. The office was first called Siloam, after the old church nearby which was built about 1840. John Maynard at Maynard and Wm. Fowler at Supply were other inland pioneer storekeepers. The writer's uncle, Elijah Dalton, opened a Store on Dry creek, about four miles northwest of Middlebrook, during this same period. He first hauled his merchandise from Cape Girardeau, Mo., on the Mississippi. This was a long rough road 150 miles long. Later when the first railroad was built south out of St. Louis, he drove his ox team to Ironton, the end of the road. Later when the road was built through to Little Rock, he moved his receiving point to Harviell, on the main line, south of Poplar Bluff.

The first merchants of Warm Springs followed

PIONEER MERCHANDISING

about the same route to market. Mose Bailey was the first merchant at this inland health resort town. He operated a store here in 1850. Wm. L. Rice already had a tavern and other accommodations for the traveling public here at that time. My uncle later moved to Warm Springs from his first place of business on Dry creek. The story goes that one time about 1880, he made a trip to St. Louis for merchandise and a neighbor went with him. This being the neighbor's first trip to the big city, he came back with a lot of almost incredible stories of what he saw. One of these was that of finding ice water in many places in the city. When he told one of the citizens of the town about this, the man said, "Now look here, John, we've been believing you right along, but this is too much — ice water in July—."

The merchandise carried in the old time store was confined to a lot fewer numbers than the present day merchandise mart. Early stores sold few packaged goods. No paper bag had come into use 75 years ago. Drugs, gunpowder, salt, sugar (brown and rich), sulphur, etc., were all sold in bulk. No canned goods were as yet offered in pretty colored containers. No soap or washing powder was for sale. Nails were made in the local blacksmith shop. Dry goods, which consisted of a few pieces of silk, later some "factory" (which we now call domestic or sheeting) and a piece or two of "suitings," just about made up the list until after the War Between the States. Hats, "jeans" cloth, hosiery, soap, etc., was all made in the homes of the settlers. Wild honey took the place of sugar, dried fruits, or that which was canned in stone jars, made up the fruit menu, when not in season.

The modern store with the beautiful front, the electrical equipment, fancy colored jars of fruits and meats, beautiful ready-made clothing, all the packaged and ready-to-use articles, sanitary methods of handling, etc., are far better than the ancient store, in some ways, but the old fashioned trading place with the traditional open cracker barrel and pot-bellied stove had something that the modern store doesn't. It was an institution. Here the widely scattered neighbors met to swap horses, get their grinding done (there usually was a watermill near by), get their horses shod at the local shop, and during election year, voting and speech making were usually held at the neighborhood trading point.

Good times or bad, hot or cold, wet or dry, the old time merchant held forth in his respective community, a sort of benefactor of mankind. When lean years and misfortune hit his customers he seldom failed them. When approached for credit on these occasions he usually answered them, "Well, Bill, all I can say is, so long as I have, you have." The methods of business operation were often crude, but they usually prospered anyway. A story is told of an old fellow who operated a store many years in the central portion of Randolph county, that one of his customers came in one fall day to pay off. The merchant could not write very well and often drew pictures of the items charged. After paying his account, the customer saw a circle drawn opposite a charged amount. Asking the merchant what this was, was told it was a hoop of cheese. When the customer told him that he had never bought a hoop of cheese, the old fellow studied a minute and then replied "Oh, yes, I remember now. That was a grindstone and I forgot to put in the hole." So on and on goes the story of the first merchants. They have gone the way of the gourd at the spring, the stagecoach, the herb doctor and homemade vinegar with "mother" in it, but the story is ever new — in this age of atomic energy, penicillin, political purges and television.

LAWRENCE DALTON'S COLUMN

As we pass through this life we meet many kinds of problems and propositions. Sometimes we are prone to think that we have just experienced a special kind of happening. We sometimes think that destiny has fixed up for us — just us — an especial kind of plateau to perform from. We do not think that down through the avenues of time the millions who have gone on, experienced similar conditions. Next time you get to thinking that eternity has hewed out some special niche for just you, stop and think. When you get to thinking you are a chosen product of the God of Nature just go to your library and read that immortal poem, "Oh, Why Should the Spirit of Mortal be Proud?" Throughout the fourteen verses of the poem the author admonishes us to remember that we are just another one of God's common mortals who are now passing through our allotted space of time. Here is the first verse and we are solemnly brought to the sobering thought which comes out so vividly throughout the poem. It says, "O, why should the spirit of mortal be proud? Like a swift fleeting meteor, a fast flying cloud, A flash of the lightning, a break of the wave, Man passes from life to his rest in the grave." High or low, rich or poor, we all make the same journey. Ponder on this.

*****

We were made happy one day this week when answering a knock on the door we met the face of our old friend, Henry De Clerk. We were very glad to see him. We really did appreciate his thinking of us and paying us a visit. Needless to say, we talked about a lot of subjects. Both of us having had considerable selling experience in the past, we were made to think about the days of long ago, when the "Drummers", of which he was one, would ride the "local" Frisco freight up to Biggers, Reyno and several of the other towns up that way and make their calls on the merchants, sometimes while the train was doing its switching. Mr. DeClerk mentioned selling "Youkon's Best" flour. We will remember selling it and this was the first time we had thought of it in years. Retailing flour back in those days was quite different than what it is now. Back in those days our customers would come in about the first of November and purchase two or three barrels "to tide them through the winter," wherein now we make a weekly purchase of a five-pound sack, sometimes it is ten. A lot of his early travelling was in Oklahoma and the country out there was rough and wild. He was telling us about the fine facilities that they had in Oklahoma City, where he now resides, for the elderly folks. He said there was something for everybody's taste, and helped the retired. We talked about the changes which have come about here in Pocahontas. We remember the picture of the train "turning over" down by the depot. We believe it was about 1914. Henry was on that engine when it happened and he said that after the engineer jumped from the falling train, he jumped right after him and landed right on the engineer. There were a lot of other things we talked about. We do not know when we have passed a more enjoyable period of time than we did that morning. Come again, Mr. DeClerk!

*****

We note the passing of the periodical, Look, from the list of magazines which have survived the rough going of such magazines over the past few years of competition and the fierce added expenses of the period. This brings back to our mind the names of several other magazines we used to read when we were young which are no longer in existence. We are sure many of you elders remember the old "Comfort," which came to us monthly from Augusta, Me. A big feature in it was the letters from children from all over the nation. It was always a welcome visitor at our house. Then there was

LAWRENCE DALTON'S COLUMN

the old "Delineator" which, as well as we can remember, was a sort of fashions magazine which was devoted principally to the problems of the mother in the home. Then, for many years the old "Successful Farming", published in Des Moines, Iowa, was almost the farmer's bible. It dealt with most all the farmer's problems back before the days of crop control and government interference. Then, among the last, during the past decade which have passed into oblivion was the staid old "Saturday Evening Post," first published by the pioneer Benjamin Franklin. During the last days of this publication it was generally known simply as the "Post" but the latter never was the great product which the first one was. Our national magazines of today devote too much of their time to Fifth Avenue, scandals, more or less degraded public figures and other materials which we, personally, would class as trash.

November, 1948

Speaking of elections, I have thought a lot of times about what Tip Potter said to John Moore the morning after Roosevelt was elected the third time. John J. said, "Well Tip, we done it again, didn't we?" Thereupon Tip remarked, "Heck yes, John, don't you know children ain't never gon'na kill Santa Claus."
—0—
Three more good citizens of Pocahontas passed on during the past few days. They were Clifford Price, Ran Shaver and Joe Tom Spikes. All three were members of early and well-known families of this section. The maternal ancestors of Mr. Price and Mr. Shaver, the Johnsons, came to this section from Tennessee during the first days of settlement. By intermarriage with other early families, the families are related to many folks in north Arkansas. The Spikes family landed in Randolph county in 1820 coming from Tennessee also and settled

on the creek in central Randolph county which they named for their old home state. A lot of good citizens have come from these three families. The Shavers came to the same community about 1815.

—0—

Someone made the remark the other night that the fellows of the Kiwanis Club were pretty good politicians, because of their success in putting over the hospital project which they sponsored (with the help of many other good citizens of the county). I think the reverse is true. I think, aside from the general knowledge of how badly we needed the institution, that the success of their efforts was because they kept it out of politics. There are some things which are a lot bigger than politics anyway. This was one of them.

—0—

I like to meet friendly people — for instance, J. B. Weaver just stopped in to greet me and tell me that he was still improving physically, for which I am glad. And Burley French dropped in for a cheery word, and then Uncle Dave Crawford visited with me awhile and told me how much I would be missed when I leave the courthouse in about six weeks now (possibly everyone won't look at it like Uncle Dave does ha!) All this made the day a lot brighter for me.

—0—

Speaking of visitors, Miss Katheryn Smith, attractive daughter of Dr. and Mrs. R. O. Smith stopped in the office this morning in search of material for a theme, with stories of Randolph county as the subject. Glad to be of assistance to the young lady. But after she left (here I go talking about people's kinfolks again) I got to thinking about all the well-known names in her family before her. There are the Smiths, Walkers, Pearsons and Crooms of Izard and Fulton counties on her father's side and the Bigger, Lewis, Russell and Simingtons of Randolph county in her mother's family. Eight noted pioneer families of north Arkansas.

LAWRENCE DALTON'S COLUMN

Some great and good man said a long time ago that "Nothing is politically right that is morally wrong." Isn't this true today, the same as it was over a century ago? Abraham Lincoln once said "Let us have faith that right makes might, and in that faith let us to the end dare to do our duty as we understand it". Grover Cleveland said "A government for the people must depend for its success on morality, justice and the interest of the people themselves." With this in mind, I desire to here write the final chapter in the matter which I commented on recently on the subject of clean elections. First I want to ask, do you think it wrong for a dissatisfied people to rise up and protest when they are convinced that wrong has been done? If you think they shouldn't object, then forget about what happens when corrupt elections take away your liberties. There is general opinion over the county that in some instances our recent election was not conducted as it should have been. This was true in only a few places but that many was just that many too much. Aside from such practices being illegal, it is beyond me and many others just why folks who occupy trusted positions will violate their oath and everything which stands for decency and honor in their attempts to put over things they advocate. It is pretty disheartening at the time to see such things done and their instigators profit by it, but we still believe that the old adage of "Every man's chickens finally come home to roost" will in the end take care of this situation. The day of reckoning comes to all. It is nothing but the duty of all good citizens to rise up and fight anything which even shows a trend towards taking away the great rights which our founding fathers gave us when our nation was founded. Just so long as I believe in the kind of government which our nation is supposed to operate under, I will always object to unfair tactics being employed in elections and I really do not believe I owe anybody an apology for saying so.

—0—

HISTORY OF RANDOLPH COUNTY

December 9, 1948

We see a lot in the state papers about our tax problems. This is a subject which vitally concerns all who have made a study of our public financial problems. It is natural for us personally to avoid any extra payments possible. Yet we clamor for a lot of things which must be paid for out of public funds. The money must be obtained from some source. I have contended for a long time that we do not need just a tax raise. We need an equitable assessment. If all the property in Arkansas was assessed at twenty five percent of actual value and then this amount, collected and a sound business like administration of the affairs was followed we would have all the money we needed for the satisfactory construction, maintenance and operation of all public items. I know we need to reform our assessing system, no one will deny that, but if the money that is already being paid in, all the way from the smallest hamlet to Washington was applied in the way it should be, a lot of our problems would already be solved. But let me add here that this is true all over the state and no one man is guilty.

One of O. K. Baker's boys dropped in to see me the other day. He had grown up since I had seen him last when the family lived at Reyno several years ago. I enjoyed talking to him. He is a smart chap and has a lot of ideas in his head that not everyone has, especially of that age.

Things sometimes turn out funny don't they? Not so many months ago we were almost daily reminded that there were a number of fellows down at Hot Springs who would soon be looking out through spaces between cold gray steel bars, because of grave and revolting crimes they had committed against society. Much high praise and credit was given certain individuals for starting a movement to "put these fellows where they belong." What happened? But is this funny?

LAWRENCE DALTON'S COLUMN

January, 1960

Pocahontas merchants who sell seeds received their package garden seed display racks January 3. Anyone now desiring to plant an early garden need not hold back for want of seeds. A recent New Year greeting received stated, "The year 1960 may go down in history as the year when golf carts got bigger than automobiles — when Americans spent more than 36 billion dollars on leisure goods — when there was a lot of unemployment, even among people who had jobs. Scientists started work on a toothpaste containing food particles for folks who can't eat between brushings — TV was drenched with adult westerns where the hero wears a 45 Colt and the heroine a 38 sweater, and medicine advanced to the point where an ounce of prevention was worth about eighteen dollars and seventy-five cents." At any rate last year went like sixty.

Sorry to hear of the passing of Dr. J. S. Carrens of Pitman. I remember Dr. Carrens a long, long time. I well remember his father, the late Dr. William Carrens and his mother, Aunt Lucy. I have somewhere in my possession a postmaster's commission issued to the elder Dr. Carrens for the first postoffice at what is now Middlebrook, in the year before the son, Dr. J. S., was born. This is now more than eighty years ago. The name of the office at that time was Siloam. I well remember the elder Dr. Carrens riding his horse across the hills from Warm Springs, five miles away to visit the sick in our home when we were growing up. One trip I remember he came when there was snow and ice falling and his clothing was covered with the frozen sleet and ice. Along about this time we remember other old time doctors. Among them were the late Dr. Clarence Finney, Dr. Moses Wilson, Dr. Tom Swindle and Dr. Hughes. The latter was the father of Drs. Jack and Ed Hughes. Along with these was Dr. John Riley Loftis. There were others contemporary with these great old men in the county, but these were the ones who we remember as coming to our home in that long ago period between the time the Spanish or somebody else blew up the battleship Maine in Havana harbor and Kaiser Bill decided to move to Holland and cut wood, at the end of 1918.

Another death here this week which made us think of other days was that of Mrs. Ben A. Brown. I remember her and Uncle Ben A. as far back as I remember almost anyone. I also knew her father, Uncle John Lehman. I remember him back when he was at Maynard. I especially remember that, as a small child, I wondered why he had a lock of almost white hair in his head of much darker hair. Mrs. Lehman, as a small girl, whose name was Tommie Harris is credited with saving the life of Dr. John W. Bryan, at his home near where his grandson, Willard now lives up near Bakerden, during the Civil War, when a bunch of jay-howkers attempted to rob Dr. Bryan. I remember Uncle Bill and Aunt Beth, the parents of Ben A. Brown, too. One time a long time ago I remember being at a "dinner on the ground" at the Middlebrook school building and in the afternoon Aunt Beth was walking down the path which led to the well at the Uncle Randolph Johnson home and in someway stumbled and almost fell. In doing so she grabbed me just as I was passing her, as I walked up the hill. I still remember how embarrassed I was as a bashful boy in those days sometimes was, when she said, "Oh please excuse me honey, I almost hugged you." She was a sister to Dr. Moses Wilson and his brothers, Uncle Johnny and Uncle Craven, and other children — all fine old citizens.

Fifteen year ago this week I entered the county treasurer's office. Times sure have changed in fifteen years. There was snow on the ground that New Year's Day, too. Guy Amos fell and injured his shoulder on it. Carl Brown was in Europe and Lora Mae was operating the circuit clerk's office in his absence. Oscar Prince

LAWRENCE DALTON'S COLUMN

went in as county judge. Rex Jolly had been dead only three weeks. Wesley Nibert was county clerk. We lived out where Mrs. Nema Hughes now lives. Uncle Newt Horsman lived as our neighbor where Burke Camp now lives. Uncle Sol White was justice of the peace and visited us each day, in our office in the court house. Dr. F. W. Cox looked into the door of our office one day that week and asked me, "Do you suppose the finances of Randolph county will be safe now"? The same week Uncle John A. Allison walked in and said, "Lawrence, I suppose it is in order for me to congratulate you, but I don't know whether I am happy to see you in here or not". When I asked him why, he remarked, "Well, I think you are a good man now and I would like to see you stay that way". I humbly appreciated what he said but it is regrettable that even though the number may be few, but there have been enough men who have sacrificed honor and conviction while in office that the word "politics" carries with it a subdued meaning which should never have been allowed to happen.

That same year fifteen years ago I set out a cottonwood sprout in my yard when it was not over six inches high. At this time the same sprout if cut down would make a saw log twelve feet long and fifteen inches in diameter.

Recently ate my first hominy grits, even though I am a Southerner, I had never even tasted any before. To me they were just about the same as the old fashioned corn meal mush we used to eat a long time ago.

If we close this column this week with a wish to all of you for a very happy and prosperous New Year, we will be doing just what millions of others are doing, but we still like to say it so here goes, "Happy New Year!"

Lawrence Dalton

I'd give a lot to possess the kind of personal disposition I see in George McCarroll, Ervin Jarrett, Frank Pettyjohn, Frank James, Johnny Jones (Middlebrook), Perry Baker, Frank Massey, and a lot of other even tempered folks. You know me — occasionally "blowing my top" in "righteous indignation" over something. But I get some consolation from this by thinking of such characters as Andrew Jackson, Alfalfa Bill Murray, Carrie Nation and reading about the Saviour overturning the tables of the moneychangers in the temple.

At this time of year we always receive a lot of pretty Christmas greetings. We highly appreciate each one of them. It always gives us a thrill to know that there are those who are scattered around over the land who always remember us. We especially appreciate those we receive from folks who knew us long ago. The first one we received this year was from Mrs. Alice Kidd Galemore. Aunt Alice was our neighbor away back yonder when we used to live in western Siloam township. Many times we have stopped by her home, on hot summer days and drank from the old well, as we were returning from some big day at Brakebill, Siloam or when we had been down to Middlebrook or Tom Phipps' mill to get our "grinding done."

The government spy hunt which we read about intermittently in the papers reminds us of our games we used to play in school. When we used to play "King's Base" we would yell out something to attract the off-player's attention so that we could gain the desired spot. It looks like we sometimes point in one direction to keep folks from looking in another direction and discovering something we don't want them to.

Quotations with no offense intended. Uncle Dan Bates told me one day last summer that he could tell me a recipe which would cause all the golf courses in the nation to grow up in just one year. I asked him what it was. He remarked "If the player will just plant and cultivate a good garden." Another one — last spring early one morning Herman and I were walking across the part of town just east of our home, into the Lakeview Addition and we came across our good friend George Steimel out there with his shirt off digging up some bushes. He was very busy and sweating freely. After we passed on Herman remarked that not many lawyers would be out there working that way. I told him that here was one man who could be a good attorney and still do work like this — all to a credit to himself.

Randolph county has the distinction of being the home of a number of people who are identified with well-known businesses and institutions outside of the county. I can't think of all of them but here are some. Hadie Beal lives near Dalton but is the editor of the Doniphan Prospect-News, a county seat paper clear out of Arkansas. Then there is Ben Lincoln, dean of Lawrence County's Southern Baptist College, a resident of Pocahontas. And Clyde McIlroy lives in Pocahontas but works "far and wide" for the Brown Shoe Co. and flies a plane to and from his work in other states, each week.

I'd like to be a real estate agent in a town in which J. B. Weaver, Joe S. Decker and Hamilton Moses all three lived. Speaking about towns, if I were the traffic cop of a town like Pocahontas I'd look a lot closer for violations by cars with Pocahontas tags, than those from out in the country. I believe our business folks would back me up in this. We all know what would happen to Pocahontas if it were not for the folks coming to town.

October 13, 1960

During the next two or three weeks residents of this section and those who travel through this area will be treated to the overwhelming beauty of our hills and dales. Nature really stages a colorful showing in the days just before and just after the first frost. A lot of roads which lead out of Pocahontas are beautiful driveways at this time of year. To name just a few we will begin with the highway from here to Grandin, by way of Doniphan and then west by Van Buren, Big Spring and on by Mountain View down by West Plains, Thayer, Mammoth Spring, Hardy and back home. This drive can be made in an easy day's drive with plenty of stopovers. Another which can be made in a day but requires more time and driving but which pays up for the difference is the highway from Pocahontas to the top of the hill just this side of Harrison where the highway turns south to run through one of the most scenic routes in the nation. A number of routes can be taken in your return trip home. We prefer going down by Marshall, Gilbert, Shirley, Leslie and cut through to highway 67 by way of Pangburn and Searcy. But you can turn east at Harriett and come through by Mountain View and Batesville. Either route is absolutely beautiful at this time of year. In fact this route is very scenic anytime. If you want to make a short run, drive up to Doniphan and go west to Thayer and either go on around by way of Salem and back to Hardy or drive down U.S. 63 from Hardy to Imboden and then home that way.

  This week marks a lot of anniversaries. Forty two years ago yesterday Sgt. Alvin York captured a whole drove of German soldiers in Europe to cause him to momentarily become one of the world's greatest military heroes. And now, broken in health, finances and almost blind and in a wheel chair he is under indictment for income tax non-payment. Such are the glories of war.

  Today (Oct. 11), is the birthday of our old friend Jeff Hufstedler. It is also the birthdate of Jess Seawel and the editor of the Star Herald. All are not of the same age but were born on the 11th. Our brother Roscoe, who lives in Memphis and our niece, Mrs.

LAWRENCE DALTON'S COLUMN

Charlotte Sullivan of St. Louis were born October 16. We are sure there are others we do not remember. Oh yes, the same week that Sgt. York captured the Germans our father Elijah F. Dalton, became postmaster at Old Burr, Mo., and remained so until the office was discontinued to make way for the eastern rural route out of Warm Springs. Jerry Burrow Sr., was the first postmaster at Burr.

Speaking of birthdays and persons, we have long admired our fellow townsman E. L. Dickson. Mr. Dickson was our banker when we operated a store at Reyno. Mr. Dickson comes from a noted Indiana family and is one of the most thorough bookkeepers we know. I like to talk to Mr. Dickson.

The coming election is one of the most important this country ever had. After eight years of no war and the best times we have ever had in history when we were at peace is worth considering very carefully. Locally, in the state we mean, we find state officials clamoring for higher salaries, just at the end of a huge tax raise. Also just after a fight in which those now in the offices seemed to be very anxious for the jobs at the present prices. Then there are all the amendments, etc., most every one of which calls for more tax dollars. It would be very good time spent for all of us to take a little time off and acquaint ourselves with the issues coming up for us to vote on November 8. This is true of our local issues, too.

Recent interest in the job of marking Civil War sites in Randolph county merits our attention. This is a period in which much revenue comes from out of state people. The more places of interest we have, the more visitors we have and every mile they drive and every hour they spend here means dollars in our pockets. While not all are, many folks are interested in visiting historical sites. With the coming of the Civil War Centennial celebration over the nation in the next four years more interest will be focused on these sites. Here in Randolph county we have at least five definite places which should be marked. The Camp Shaver site on Mill Creek southwest of town, the skirmish in Cherokee Bay near Old Reyno, the site of the first training ground for Confederates in the nation, just below the Jarrett bridge on Fourche and the battle grounds at Pitman Ferry. The first recruiting point in Arkansas was at Pocahontas (Camp Shaver). The most important battle in eastern Arkansas at Pitman (two battles) are especially important. Much Civil War history is linked with these places. The noted African explorer who found Dr. Livingston, joined the confederacy here at Pocahontas. These places should all be marked on the sites and a large directive marker should be erected on U.S. Highways 67-62 telling the travelling public how to reach these places. A lot of this kind of marker can be found along the highways in the eastern states. I will never forget the thrill I felt the first time I passed the marker on one of Virginia's highways which contained the inscription which read: "Three-fourths of a mile southeast of this spot Cyrus Hall McCormick cut the first grain with a mechanical reaper in the the world".

Oh yes, in listing all the anniversaries occurring this week, we forgot that Oct. 12 was Columbus Day. It was on that date in 1492 that Christopher Columbus came over to this hemisphere, looking for something to take back to Europe and most of the time since a lot of Europeans kept looking for something from over here—and getting it most of the time.

February 7, 1963

Our thanks to Mrs. Ann Carroll who is carrying on for Mrs. O'Baugh in her "Here and There" Column, for the nice things she said about us last week concerning our knowledge of Randolph county history. My wish is that I knew a lot more and a lot of other folks knew a lot more than I do. The job of acquiring knowledge of my homeland just sort of "happened" for me. I can't remember when I did not have an almost acute hunger for all kinds of human history. About the time I first learned to read in a very limited way, I remember seeing George Washington's picture in a seed catalog and when my mother told me briefly the story of the Father of Our Country, I dreamed about him that night and the homely face of Abe Lincoln had a sort of fascination for me akin to that of the photos of my grandfather's. My father and I used to pass along through the old homestead where his grandfather settled about 1826 which was the same place where his father (my grandfather) was born in 1844 and he would tell me about the pioneer days as he remembered them and as he had also been told by his father and I would silently wish I could have lived during the days when the first trails were cut through this wild and wooded land.

February 7, 1963

Again speaking of history two interesting facts concerning Randolph county, but not generally known, is that less than a year after the founding of the Arkansas Gazette a newspaper was launched at Davidsonville by a Mr. Watkins and an "academy" was established in Pocahontas on Christmas Day, 1840. And another thing, the first mill in Arkansas was built on Mill Creek near the site of the old steel bridge, in southwest Pocahontas in 1822.

When I spoke of Lincoln above, made me think about the times I have been kidded about being a "northerner" during my life. Of course this is not true because I am the fifth generation of my father's family which has spent their lives within 25 miles of

Pocahontas. But I will admit that I think I have as fair a viewpoint of both the north and south as anyone living. My reason for saying this is that my mother was born on the banks of the Wabash in Indiana. Her father had a brother, who was a Northern soldier, died in the terrible Andersonville, Georgia Confederate prison and three members of my paternal grandfather's family served in the army of the South. One member was killed in service and my grandfather carried a bullet to his grave which he received in the battle of Prairie Grove. I have heard the Civil War fought a thousand times and the subject of slavery was a well-known subject to me when I was old enough to go to school. Whether you call me a "Fed" or a "Rebel" I feel proud. Not because of the terrible war of the 1860's but because my ancestors on both sides of the family were willing to fight for what they thought was right — something a lot of folks will not do today. Entirely too many good folks shrug their shoulders today and say, "What's the use" or something else in a mood of resignation, when enemies of our freedom are working day and night right here in our own land to undermine and destroy the very things which have made our nation great.

The extreme cold weather of the past month has made its mark in this section. Most years at this time of the winter you could drive out across the country and see some real green fields where small grain had been sown the fall before. But this year all the color has been taken out by the cold. About all the natural greenery you can see now is cedar and pine trees. This (Tues.) afternoon my smallest grandson, John Elijah and I went out to the farm and walked around in the nice warm sunshine, but we found ice almost four inches thick covering the ponds out there.

October 24, 1963

We have a lot of things in mind to write about this

week, but since it is Industrial Appreciation Week here we will begin by mentioning that possibly the first industry in our area was the old Janes water mill on Janes creek or the old Dalton Mill on the south fork of Fourche river.

John Janes is reputed to have come to Janes Creek valley about 1809, but we do not know just how soon the old mill was built. John Elijah Dalton settled at what is still known as the Dalton Mill Ford on Fourche in 1812 and is said to have begun immediately to build a water mill and trading post. There are undoubtedly others whose founding date was around this same period. The Demun brothers were operating a water mill just above the old steel bridge on Mill Creek in southwest Pocahontas, just below Cypress Springs in 1822. Some of these were converted to steam in later years. This must have been our first form of industry here.

Our pioneers loaded up his "turn" of corn and carried it to one of these mills and had the grain ground into meal. Some of the mills also had a small sawmill in connection.

Then came the tanneries. Folks needed shoes, saddles, harnesses and other items best made from leather. The tanner built vats, etc., and processed the hides of various animals, mostly cattle and horses. He often had this work done by the tanner and then took the hide home and made the various things he needed by hand. In the town of Pocahontas we find among the first industries mentioned were a man named McCleary who was a tanner and one named William Hubble who was a harness maker.

A man by the name of David Jones was one of the first sawmillers in the area. His mill was located on the bank of Black river, near the present site of the handle mill. James P. Ingram and his son-in-law, Greene Johnston, built one of the first cotton gins in Randolph county, on what is still known as the Old Greene

Johnston farm on the Old Military road between Maynard and Supply, just this side of the old Ingram place. Industry has grown a lot and has seen a lot of changes in the time since the first mills were built here. Anyway, we salute all our industries and appreciate all they have done for our section.

Many of you are familiar with the fact that about this time of the year we always do a certain amount of raving about the beauty of our hills and valleys when the leaves are all red, yellow, green and present a wonderful scene. As we all know this will not happen to the degree it usually does in this section this year, due to the prolonged drouth. But I had not realized the seriousness of the case until I went out into my yard Sunday afternoon and saw all the thousands of berries which usually are such a beautiful red, covering the pretty dogwood tree, had turned black for want of moisture. This is the case most everywhere around.

Was very interested in what our editor said last week about the class record plates imbedded in the walks at the recently abandoned old school building here in Pocahontas. With the records of all the years and years of graduates from our local high school inscribed upon them, they should be preserved! As just a suggestion from yours truly, let us suggest that a walk be laid out, out at the new high school building and these plates be removed from the old building to the new walk. A walk running down towards the highway out there at the high school building could grow into a copy of the walk in front of Old Main at the University of Arkansas, over at Fayetteville. History is preserved in the thousands of names inscribed over there in that walk which, to us, and thousands more, is the most interesting walk in the world. Let's make a copy of it here. I have an interest in one of these plates and will do my part in getting this job done. How about it, graduates and school board?

I suppose that I am reaching the age where the rest

LAWRENCE DALTON'S COLUMN

of the population good naturedly condones a certain amount of palaver from folks like us concerning our grandchildren. Most of us never really realize how important being a grandchild is until we become a grandparent. Not only are they our flesh and blood, they are our pride, joy and future. We love them and enjoy them and it is a pity that every grandchild in the world does not realize this. Some of the happiest moments of our life comes when Sandra comes school hopping down the street to show us her pretty new dress or hairdo; when David, in his sober way, comes in to tell us all about what was in his Sunday school lesson today — he especially enjoys this, or when frisky, jolly little John Elijah runs to meet us to tell us something about how he is getting along in his first year in school or what is new in his rock or bug collection "Oases in the desert of life" — these little incidents.

I know there are not a lot of folks in the world who want and crave world peace more than we. We think this is true of most of our people. But we are saddened, to say nothing about how disgusted we get, when we view all the many times and ways we as a nation, have been "taken for a ride" by those who sooner or later will cause us grave trouble. The ratification of the test ban treaty and all the buttery speeches which were made about what it would mean, not only disgusted us, but put fear in our hearts also. Made us think of what our father once told us about dealing with dishonest people. He said, "Don't you know that anytime you give a crook your solemn promise in exchange for his that you are at a very great disadvantge. You will do what you promised. He will not" The agreement between us and Russia isn't worth a red cent. We should know by now, from past experiences that the Reds do not honor their word. We are just being sung to sleep by the soft sweet siren of Khruschchev and his gang. Don't we remember Yalta? Potsdam? Geneva and Camp David?

Oh yes, the fellows in "higher places" told us we

were safe. They were negotiating for peace on Dec. 7, 1941. You don't need to be told what happened anyway. We do not want to be a crepe hanger or an extremist, but we are in grave danger. Another little sweet song about how we "Ran Russia out of Cuba" might win another national election but it will never bring us world peace.

All the little sweet pills of promises of more and more "crises" without conflict which have been handed us the past few days by politicians may result in getting them what they want, but if our nation does not wake up and take a firm stand, stop being Santa Claus to the world and start teaching honestly, firmness, honor, thrift and integrity here at home, we as a nation are doomed. A noted speaker recently stated in a talk over at Memphis, "Civilizations do not collapse from pressures from without, but from moral decay within." Inner moral decay results in treaties, appeasements, weak agreements and other dangerous hookups with those without, who see our weakness. In his last speech before retirement, George Washington warned our nation from engaging in dangerous foreign alliances. The present national administration has just placed our nation on a diplomatic banana peeling with its "good relations" policy with the Russian empire. When you operate a bank you can't form a peace pact with a bunch of outlaws.

Changing the subject abruptly — A long time ago the late Will Luter who used to live out at Old Albertha and who incidentally was known as the "sweet potato king" in his day, once told me about having an ancestor who weighed over 800 pounds. The man lived over a century ago over in east Tennessee and I believe Uncle Will said he was his mother's uncle. His name was Miles Darden. I had not thought of the story for years until, recently a story appeared in one of the Memphis dailies telling about one Miles Darden, dying over near Darden, Tenn., in 1897 at the age of 98 years. He is buried near Life, Tenn., and is reputed to have been 8 feet and 5 inches tall and weighed over the 800 pounds alright. Mr. Darden would never allow anyone to weigh him. One day some boys noted how far down he mashed the wagon seat when he sat down. They marked the line and after his departure they piled enough stones in the seat to mash it down that far and weighed them! This is how they found out how much the big man weighed.

February, 1966

Had quite a chat this week with Roger Wills of Walnut Ridge. Roger and his wife, the former Josie Ingram, have been living in California several years but have come back home at retirement. Mrs. Wills and my wife are both descended from George Mansker and Judge James P. Ingram, well-known Randolph countians in the years of long ago. Mansker Creek here at Pocahontas was named for Mansker, and Ingram Cemetery and Ingram township are named for the Ingram family.

Roger is a descendant of A. W. Brooks, well known Black river bottoms resident a century ago. My mother's grandfather, together with her father and family migrated from southern Indiana in 1879 to Arkansas — first locating on the Brooks plantation near the present Fay Sallee farm. My mother was 2 years of age then. They came down by way of the lower Wabash Valley across to Cairo where they crossed the Mississippi on a flatboat. I remember her stating that the boat was propelled by logs paddled in the hands of several men and that there were no banisters to the boat. After locating on the Brooks farm in the winter of 1879, so the story comes to us, some of the folks over that way told grandfather that since they were "Northerners", they had better "head for the hills" as the malaria which was so prevalent in the lowlands at that time, would be too much for them. During the late winter they moved out to Knotts creek, near where Clifton Haulcroft now lives. The Biggers family lived there then.

In December a cyclone came through the country and blew grandfather's home away. Luckily no one was killed. They salvaged most of their belongings and then moved on up Fourche, to near the Grosses, Fosters and Carrolls, where great grandfather Epps Marlette lived the rest of his life. Later my own grandfather moved further up the river to the Middlebrook community where he spent his remaining years.

Thanks to everyone for the written and spoken words of congratulations concerning recent articles we have been responsible for appearing in the Star Herald. A lot of folks appreciated our "two bits worth" concerning the recent bond issues. Thanks folks, a whole lot.

There are at least two sections of terrain in Randolph County which intrigues me when I think of them. These are that section of road from Mrs. Arthur Cooper's south to the intersection of U.S. Highway 62, near the Sutton church. In this several mile stretch of road I do not think of but one small depression where the water actually crosses the road. The land is that level for that many miles. The other is when I think that all the water which falls around adjacent to Supply, although in the actual Current river watershed, runs into Fourche river near Pocahontas. After it gets into Winningham Creek at Supply it flows southeast to the "old Clay county corner" where it is then intercepted by the big dredge ditch which flows from there to almost Pocahontas, along the foothills.

During the days before man invaded this country, Winningham creek flowed across the country, east, and entered Current River not far below the old Downey Ferry, or Box House landing place.

The Lemmons creek which flows down from Maynard to the C. E. Smith farm east of Maynard,

LAWRENCE DALTON'S COLUMN

where it intersects another fork of the stream, at one time finally entered Current river across what was known as the "scatters", out northwest of Biggers. Now unless there is a big overflow the water never mixes with Current river water until it gets to the mouth of Fourche, just above Pocahontas. This is true of all the streams mentioned above.

Our thanks this week for a birthday greeting and one of the nicest letters I ever received, from Mr. and Mrs. Leonard Maple, here on Waddle Street in Pocahontas. And of course thanks to all the others who remembered my natal day this week. And speaking of greetings, our kinsman, Roy L. Dalton, who is a church missionary in Europe, mailed us a Christmas greeting which just reached us this week. He is now located in Ronda, Malaga, Spain . . . stopped by to see Aunt Lizzie Blankenship the other day. She came around to talking with me about the long ago — which is easy to do with me — and told me about her sister, Mrs. Taylor who lives here in Pocahontas and my aunt Ida Dalton setting a barn afire while they were playing in a barn at Middlebrook when they were little girls. Aunt Ida (Irvine) passed away in Florida in December, over eighty years of age. So this must have been a long time ago.

Not much over a year ago I wrote an article in which I stated that the day was coming when we would appreciate more our good productive lands not only in this area but all around the world. Last week huge headlines appeared in various big newspapers around the country proclaiming "Curbs on Farming May Be Relaxed for Hungry World." In the articles they stated almost exactly the same things I have been doing for several years, in that good, productive land is being taken out of use for many unneeded uses when we would see the day it would be greatly needed to produce foodstuff. I heartily agree with the slogan of a certain publication whose slogan is "Civilization begins and ends with the plow". Shortage of food and possibly actual starvation is predicted by many well-informed men, for even our own United States within five to ten years, if the waste of this good land is not halted drastically.

July, 1966

A miniature "gold rush" took place one day last week when Junior Wooldridge unearthed a large bunch of soft drink bottles as he was bulldozing at the back of the old Skinner property near the courthouse. A lot of the bottles contained the original stopper which, if you desired to open it you stuck it under the counter or table and shoved upward, sending the stopper and metal loop down into the bottle and the contents flowed out around the obstruction. How many remember this kind of bottle being used? I do. It is supposed that the bottles were left there during the days when the former owner, the late W. H. Skinner owned a bottling plant here in Pocahontas. It has been around fifty years since any bottles of this kind have been used.

I believe if I had the time and space that I could record some interesting happenings and some fond remembrances of our older citizens living, or have lived in each community in Randolph county. For instance just today I have been thinking of Little Black township (Supply and Pitman). In the days of long ago we used to go with our father from our old home in western Siloam township, across the country to the cotton gin of Uncle "Blind Bill" Ingram. The old gin was located a short distance south of the present day New Home church. It took all day and part of the night to make the trip. Some of the older citizens of that community in that day were the Redwines, Duffs, Fowlers, Allens, Prides, Cockrums, Jacksons, Ruffs, Legates, Shemwells, Jollys, Johnsons and dozens of other family names which stand out to me are: Uncle Bill Ingram, Will Allen, Uncle Oscar Cunningham, Uncle Ben Legate, Riley Fowler, John Redwine, Uncle Lindorf

LAWRENCE DALTON'S COLUMN

Parrish, Don Ruff and his brothers, Charlie Ennis, Uncle Pete Sammons, Tom Fowler and others we wish we could think of now.

At that period of time there were two or three large stores, and two cotton gins at Supply. Uncle Henry Cockrum was the blacksmith. Riley Fowler operated a store upon the Warm Springs Brideport road, just east of the Old Military Road crossing.

Most everyone in this part of the nation who writes a column writes about this time of year being "hog killing time". In the old days hog killing time meant a day when water was heated in large outside kettles. A scaffold was built — usually against a tree and a large pole to hang the butchered hogs upon, was placed on top. After the hogs were scalded in the boiling water from the kettles which had been transferred to a large barrel. From the carcass of the lowly swine came some of the most delicious food ever found by the human family. Head cheese, homemade sausage, fresh liver, pork ribs and ham from this manner of production was far more delicious than that which we cut up in pieces and freeze for six months or a year. Each clear crisp frosty morning brings all this to our minds. We don't see much of old time hog-killing these days.

1966

Phil Sloan brought us an old St. Louis Globe Democrat which was printed June 13, 1896, the other day. The seventy year old paper was very interesting. The whole city was agog with excitement over the coming Republican National convention which was to be held in St. Louis that year. One of the ads in the ancient paper was for a blacksmith to shoe horses in a shop at 4964 Delmar Ave. Some of you Boys now living in St. Louis write and tell us what is located on that site now. We would like to know. Good middling cotton was sightly above 6 cents in the lint for spot sales. The day before the paper was printed 313 bales were sold on the St. Louis market, while only 98 were sold at Memphis the same day. Spring wheat was 55 cents per bushel. Lard was $4.50 per hundred. Butter was priced from 9 to 12 cents a pound and eggs were steady at 9 cents per dozen.

The June issue of the Reader's Digest has an interesting article in it about flood control on Sandstone Creek in Oklahoma. The story relates how that creek and a similar one not far away had for a number of years been a veritable trough for the eroded hillsides which made up its watershed, to spill its rain water into with destructive results. A movement was started and some 400 large stock ponds or small lakes were built at the headwaters of that many branch tributaries of the big creek, terracing and contour ditches were built, lands were sodded and as a result during a recent damaging flood on the other big creek nearby, the Sandstone did not even get out of its banks. This is the logical plan for flood control on any stream. Hold the rainfall where if falls or plan for slow release and there will be no floods down stream.

Dr. J. S. Carrens of Pitman was in to see us the other day. We are always glad to see him and it brings back memories of the days of long ago when his father, Dr. Wm. Carrens and his good wife Aunt Lucy lived near us and the good doctor spent a portion of his time and drugs in the job of "breaking" the malaria chills for us. He was a contemporary along with Dr. W. T. Swindle, Dr. Hughes (Dr. Ed. and Dr. Jack's father) Dr. C. Finney and other old timers in the medical field fifty years ago. And speaking of doctors and Phil Sloan's old paper again. An ad in the old paper signed by Dr. F. L. Sweaney, Corner Market and Broadway, St. Louis, advertised among other things that any poor folks unable to call on him at his office, Friday afternoons of each week, for to pay for services were invited free professional services.

LAWRENCE DALTON'S COLUMN

We welcome Mr. and Mrs. Callison of near Ravenden Springs, to our county. They have recently moved here from South Dakota. Mrs. Callison will teach in the Ravenden Springs school next term. We think it would be a mighty nice thing if we had some kind of setup wherein each time new folks located in our county we would extend to them some kind of "salute" or recognition. This would help us all get acquainted with them and make them feel more at home. Some of the best citizens we have in Randolph county today were once newcomers to our community. Most new folks become valuable assets to our locality. They often bring new ideas, new occupations and new methods to us. Just this week we were talking to a man who has only been in Randolph county two years and he tells us he is doing right good growing veal calves. He buys them when young. Puts them on soft feed a few days and then onto a shelled corn diet and in six weeks to a couple of months he has a fifty to sixty dollar calf for the market. The baby calves cost him from eight to twelve dollars. For a man to do this to make the principal part of his "living" is something new in these parts.

Tourist season has arrived once more. The sections of the nation which have attractions for these folks will reap a rich harvest during the next four months. Our natural fishing grounds in the rivers we have nearby bring us some notice in this respect, but otherwise we have done little to cause the traveller to stop in our community. When you see a car loaded with folks, camping parphernalia and an out of state license you never know what they are interested in. Some want to fish. Some want to hunt. Some just want a nice quiet place to lounge around. Some are looking for places of historical interest. Some like to visit cotton or livestock farms. Why, oh why, don't we make some concerted effort here in Randolph county to fill the wants of these folks. Lots of strangers drive down Highway 67, 62 and 63 daily during the summer who would eagerly drive down to Old Davidsonville to the see the site of the first postoffice in Arkansas, if there was anything there to make them recognize the place when they arrived. Right there our folks are laying down on the biggest tourist asset in the county, to say nothing of the historical and sentimental value to homefolks. Lots of folks do visit and more would, if Ravenden Springs was developed into a truly tourist town and the same is true of Warm Springs. Edward Everett Dale, Professor of History at the University of Oklahoma made the remark to a bunch of us in Little Rock some time ago that if Arkansas had capitalized on the names of our noted men and places in Arkansas in the way Tennessee had John Sevier and Oklahoma had Will Rogers, and California had her rugged scenery, we would be taking in several million dollars a year from folks who never come to Arkansas now.

Lawrence Dalton

www.ingramcontent.com/pod-product-compliance
Lightning Source LLC
Chambersburg PA
CBHW060348080526
44583CB00012B/223